THE OLD ALCALDE

THE OLD ALCALDE

LIFE AND TIMES OF A TEXAS FIRE-EATER, ORAN MILO ROBERTS

JOHN A. ADAMS, JR.

Published by

Stoney Creek Publishing Group

StoneyCreekPublishing.com

ISBN: 978-1-965766-30-9
ISBN (ebook): 978-1-965766-31-6
Library of Congress Control Number: 2025918539

Cover design by Market Your Industry.

Printed in the United States

In memory of
Ronald Sims Adams
1953–2023

CONTENTS

INTRODUCTION

The life and times of Oran Milo Roberts have long been a neglected topic in Texas history. His experiences reflect the state's development in the latter half of the nineteenth century, yet no comprehensive biography exists. Unpublished works about him barely skim the surface, offering only brief introductions to his dynamic, controversial, and often tumultuous life. One notable exception is Leila Bailey's 1932 dissertation at the University of Texas, in which she had the rare opportunity to interview two of Roberts's children, Margaret and Oran Jr., residing in Austin.

The reasons behind the lack of a comprehensive biography of Roberts remain unclear. It may stem from biographers' reluctance to tackle his vehemently pro-secessionist and racist views. Alternatively, they may believe that existing studies have covered his life sufficiently. The lack is all the more perplexing if we consider equally controversial southern fire-eaters of the period, such as John C. Calhoun and Barnwell Rhett of South Carolina, John Milton of Florida, Louis Wigfall of Texas, Edmund Ruffin and Beverley Tucker of Virginia, William L. Harris and John Quitman of Mississippi, Georgians Robert Toombs and brothers Thomas and Howell Cobb, and William L. Yancey of Alabama—each of whom has long ago been studied in depth and given a published assessment.

Previously I have written a biography of the Civil War governor of Florida, *Warrior at Heart: Governor John Milton, King Cotton and Rebel Florida 1860–1865,* and a book on Lawrence Sullivan Ross, the frontier Texas Ranger, Confederate general, state senator, governor, and Texas A&M University president, not as precursors but more as an opening for the background of the dynamics facing the South and the postwar era in the late 1800s.

Oran Roberts left behind a substantial body of work and a memoir filled with rich primary content, offering a remarkable glimpse into his life and times. He was unquestionably shaped by the politics and the social and agrarian dynamics of the deep South's cotton culture. What stands out is his early ability to piece together an education, which was rare for his time, and eventually to obtain a law license. Like many restless youths from the deep South, he was drawn westward to Texas. The lessons and political philosophy he acquired in Alabama from family, teachers, and mentors profoundly influenced his life.

In the lives of major public figures there are chapters, events, and political leanings that are controversial and sometimes offensive.

Roberts is no exception. Starting in the early 1840s, Roberts served as a district attorney and a district judge, held three separate tenures on the Texas Supreme Court, and was a colonel in the Confederate army. After the war he was elected as a U.S. senator but was denied seating in Congress. He later served two terms as Texas governor. The present book is set against the context and dynamics of the period in which Roberts lived. In addressing him, scholars have generally focused on his advocacy to protect and perpetuate the institution of slavery and his active role in orchestrating the secession of Texas from the Union in 1861. These are significant aspects of his public career; yet there is more to the story. He was one of the first governors to champion public higher education for both whites and Blacks. During his tenure as governor he was an avid supporter of institutions such as the Texas "Deaf and Dumb" asylum. In his final years of service he played a pivotal role in the establishment of the University of Texas and served as the first dean of the Texas Law School. Roberts's life and activities parallel the transition of Texas from a frontier setting and economy at mid-century to an emerging economically diversified and dynamic state by the dawn of the twentieth century. Understanding how a "fire-eater" came to these roles is both informative and interesting.

Roberts had a lasting impact on the formative years of jurisprudence in Texas—a legal system in transition, addressing the dynamics of laws and precedence bridging colonial-Spanish Mexican influences and the emergence of the law in the new Republic of Texas. He was instrumental in the organization and procedural crafting of legal and court protocols. Yet this biography of Roberts, while highlighting many of the legal milestones in Texas and his pivotal court decisions as a judge, is not a legal history.

In many ways Roberts was a most unlikely fire-eater. His speaking ability can only be described as uninspired and lackluster, to put it charitably. He never took an active part in organized religion. He was a member of the Masonic Lodge but not noteworthy in its leadership. His financial affairs were comfortable, but he did not belong to the financial elite. Prior to his nomination as governor, a position he did not actively seek, he was among the leading Texas jurists of the late 1800s. Roberts enjoyed success due to his knowledge of issues important to Texas voters and his mastery of legal arguments to address his clear passion for governance.

A full assessment of Oran Roberts's life and times is made possible by the wealth of rich material he left about each stage of his active career. The several books he authored, his recollections of his college days at the University of Alabama, and the dozens of court cases he was involved in as lawyer and judge add depth to his story. Furthermore, his contribution to Dudley Wooten's *History of Texas* (1898), major coverage by Texas newspapers of the period, and documents in the state archives provide rich windows into his life. Newspaper articles about social events rarely mention him or his family. During the last years of his life as a professor at the University of Texas Law School, a number of his lectures were published. He was also a founding member of the Texas State Historical Association. Many thanks are extended to Bill Page at the Texas A&M Evans Library for his insightful observations and timely location of documents.

Roberts's publication of *A Description of Texas: Its Advantages and Resources, With Some Account of Past, Present and Future* (1881), centered on his experiences in East Texas and is rarely cited, yet in many ways it rivals the descriptions of Texas by Frederick Law Olmsted some two decades earlier. In his preface Roberts noted: "I am a small farmer, a lawyer, and a judge."

CHAPTER 1

FROM ALABAMA TO TEXAS 1815–1849

As usual then, as it is in some schools still, every youth that entered the school must have his metal tried, I was peculiarly a fit person for this trial, being a raw-boy from an obscure mountain region, although I was not then aware of the custom. . . . The trial was for those entered in the last [freshman] class. I passed and then prevailed amongst the students.

— ORAN MILO ROBERTS REFLECTIONS ON THE UNIVERSITY OF ALABAMA MARCH 30, 1892

Oran Milo Roberts is one of the major jurists, political strategist-power brokers, and southern social barometers of the second half of the nineteenth century in Texas. The full scope of his multifaceted career has yet to be explored. The roots of these dynamics can be traced to his early family upbringing and education in Alabama. As a "son-of-the-South" he was raised in an era when the philosophical underpinnings and formative years of states' rights—a cumulative set of values and perceptions that intertwined the dominant cotton culture with slavery, with defined property privilege, and an inherent local independence—were developed and fostered by political leaders across the South.

The deep South's economic and social structure of his youth were driven by cotton and slave labor. From an early age it was made clear to him that the protection of southern traditions, independence, slavery, and self-determination would be his guideposts. Roberts, among the southern fire-eaters, would thus be driven by a distaste for northern interference with slaveholding and by any attack on the economic underpinnings of slavery. As a result, he was very suspicious of the federal government and thus prone, if necessary, to contemplating "redress" and secession. It was from this backdrop that Oran Roberts had a significant impact on the people, politics, and social well-being of whites—as one historian noted: "to preserve the old order as much as possible."[1]

Early Life

It is hard to know how aware Oran Roberts was of the image he projected and how it contributed to his career. He was born in Laurens District, South Carolina (not far from the home of John C. Calhoun), on July 9, 1815, to Oba and Margaret Ewing Roberts. The youngest of six children, Oran, aged three years, moved with his family to northern Alabama in 1818, along with his three brothers and two sisters. It is possible that the move westward was triggered by a dramatic climatic event following the massive eruption of Mount Tambora in Indonesia that sent dense ash airborne worldwide and caused freakishly cold weather in the eastern part of the United States, which destroyed southern crops during the summer of 1816 through much of 1817.[2] The Robertses were of Welsh ancestry and the Ewings of his mother's family were Scotch-Irish. Oran's family had a strong military heritage, with his grandfathers Obadiah Roberts and Samuel Ewing being veterans of the Continental Army during the Revolutionary War. The family settled in St. Clair County, carved out of the northeast Alabama Territory near Fort Strother on the northern bluff of the Coosa River, a fort that a decade earlier had been a supply center established by General Andrew Jackson's Tennessee Militia in 1813. Local lore noted that both scout David Crockett and young Lieutenant Sam Houston spent time at the fort during the Red Sticks Creek Wars. This was where the young newly commissioned lieutenant first met his lifelong mentor, General Jackson, who commended Houston for his coolness and courage, though severely wounded, at the Battle of Horseshoe Bend in March 1814.[3]

The small Roberts farm was a mile east of the county seat, Ashville, originally known as St. Clairsville. Oba served first as a county constable in 1819, followed by a term as justice of the peace in Ashville. He owned seven enslaved people: four men, George, Prince, Nick, and Alick, along with Isabel and her young children Jack and Lewis. The enslaved men worked the fields with the Roberts sons. A biographer in 1885 noted that their "early life was attended with many difficulties and trammeling circumstances . . . while never absolutely poor they were in moderate circumstances." Perhaps their situation was "moderate" compared to the elite classes, but they were wealthier than most of the yeoman farmers and tenant class. The newly incorporated county was the home of a large influx of settlers from Georgia, Tennessee, Virginia, and South Carolina. Newly arriving immigrants were looking for fresh fertile land for upland cotton. To encourage new settlement, federal land was made available at $1.25 per acre. The upland hilly county of St. Clair was a well-watered mix of heavy wooded areas and promising farm land. Cotton quickly dominated agricultural production as a cash crop, followed by some limited production of corn, livestock, and lumber. This extensive opening of new land and settlements helped in the gradual push westward toward Texas over the next few decades. Alabama at the time of statehood in December 1819 boasted a population of some 120,000, a third of whom were enslaved people.[4]

The remote rural location in St. Clair did not preclude a lasting interest in education by Roberts, encouraged by his parents and older brother Dr. Jesse Carter Roberts, who had studied medicine prior to arriving in Alabama. Oran having attended only the local St. Clair school, the extent of his early education is unknown. However, he was further encouraged and impressed by visiting circuit lawyers and judges whom the family occasionally entertained. Tragedy struck shortly after Oran's twelfth birthday, with the sudden death of his father. At the probate of the estate it was learned that there was a considerable amount of debt, not unusual in the demanding frontier economy, which often rested on the success of each year's crop and heavy reliance on barter. It was easy for farmers to slide into debt. For example, merchants in nearby Ashville ran "factorage" businesses that consisted of advancing supplies to farmers and taking payment when the crop was sold, with any year-end negative account balance carried forward to the following year. This was well known to planters, merchants, and the courts. Joshua Hooper and son-in-law Robert Bourland, as the court-appointed administrators of Oba's will, addressed the liquidation of the debts through sale of equipment, household items, and livestock. Once the estate was settled, Oran's mother retained the farm and the slaves valued at $2,900. Oran and his seventeen-year-old brother Ford remained on the farm for the next few years to help their mother. Oran continued his home education with his mother, who was an avid reader and a religious follower of the fundamental Universalists. His teenage experience of working and living the uncertain life of a southern cotton farmer, who depended on slave labor, left a marked lifelong impression on his opinions and worldview. He was always proud to be associated with farming.[5]

Reflecting on the formative years of social structure of cotton farmers in the early 1800s antebellum South, historian Thomas P.

Abernethy noted: "The early history of Alabama appears to have been deeply influenced by the relatively close contact between the planters and farmers. The frontier conditions which threw men upon their own resources and promoted rapid changes in 'station,' the relatively narrow extent of the cotton-producing areas and the consequent proximity of numbers of planters [defined by the ownership of twenty of more slaves] and small farmers [most of whom owned no slaves]; the moderate estates of the planters and the lack of extensive society outside the largest towns—all these conditions made Alabama a state where democracy among white men was the rule in spite of slavery."[6] Roberts would face these same dynamics in years to come, both in his early years in East Texas and in later years as he crafted the strategy to unite slave owners and non-slave owners to support Texas' secession.

In addition to the raw clout of material wealth and prestige gained from being a successful cotton farmer, another means of advancing one's "station" was through educational attainment. Roberts's dream to break away from the farm was fully encouraged by his family. His much older brother Dr. Jesse Roberts, prior to Jesse's departure for the Arkansas Territory, offered the advice that Oran should pursue the study of law, noting, "It is the high road to fame and fortune in this country and is more pleasant in every way than the profession of medicine . . . a drudgery for which I was not fitted . . . don't you commit the same error." The advice left a deep and lasting impression on Oran and confirmed his long held interest in the law. Jesse opened a medical practice in Arkansas and was elected to a term in the territorial legislature, and then he tragically died "attending upon patients" during the cholera epidemic of April 1834.[7]

In 1831 Oran attended the first private academy opened in Ashville by a young attorney, Joshua W. Hooper. Offering classes in the classical languages of Latin and Greek, it closed after six months. For a few months he then attended a new private academy opened by James Lewis. It also closed, when Lewis was elected county circuit clerk. Learning of the demand for instruction, Ralph Lowe, a local lawyer, offered to tutor Roberts and three other students from the old academy in his law office until the end of 1832. Lowe's mentoring confirmed Oran's intent to study law. A lifelong friend, Lowe moved to Iowa, where he became a supreme court judge and governor (1858–1860). The usual course to being admitted to the bar was to study law under a licensed lawyer, receive that mentor's endorsement, and then sit for an examination before a judge and panel of local lawyers. Roberts determined that a university education, following the course taken by his brother Jesse and mentor Lowe, would enhance his path to becoming a lawyer as well as providing an added dimension to his career. Not all his family encouraged his education. His brother-in-law Robert Bourland had a different opinion, urging him to stay at home, and if he did not like farming, to get a respectable job as a store clerk in Ashville in order to make money immediately. After discussing the situation with his mother, Oran decided to remain a student in Lowe's office for another eighteen months to study Latin and Greek and to improve his writing skills.[8]

University

Lowe intervened with both Robert Bourland and Oran's mother to assure them that the university was the correct course of action. Once they agreed, the next critical step was to pay the large annual tuition of forty dollars plus living expenses. Oran's mother made sure he received his share of the inheritance, which included two enslaved people from his father's estate. To cover his expenses the family agreed to send one of Oran's slaves, Prince, with him to Tuscaloosa. Franklin Ford, Prince, and Oran loaded the family hack for the 100-mile drive to Tuscaloosa. Once Oran was at the University of Alabama to enroll in February 1833, Prince would be "hired out" under a contract payable to the seventeen-year-old Oran to cover his expenses. "The most common source of bondsmen for hire was estates undergoing probate," as historian Randolph Campbell noted, "providing a source of needed cash and income to support widows and children." Thus, Prince, a product of Oran father's probate, was that source of cash. While there is no record of who hired Prince, family legend stated he was a steamboat cook on the Black Warrior

River at forty dollars a month. Twenty years later, in 1856–57, then Texas Supreme Court Justice Oran Roberts would rule on cases involving the slave-hire system that had helped pay for his university education.[9]

Upon arrival Roberts, accompanied by his brother Franklin Ford, called on university president Alva Woods. He enrolled four months after the balance of the freshman class had started in October 1832. No reason for the delayed enrollment was given. During Oran's entry exams conducted by Professor Henry Tutwiler it was noted that he was proficient in Greek, Latin, and math but fell short in a number of subjects he had never studied. After a careful review of Oran's potential he was admitted by the faculty but assigned to Professor Henry Hilliard, along with Professors Brumely and Bonfils, for the balance of the spring semester, to be tutored on subjects in which he was deficient. Sixty years later, in a May 1892 presentation to the Eurosophic Society at the University of Alabama, Roberts recalled that "as my brother said good-bye and drove away in the hack, I went off to myself north of the buildings and had a good cry. I had never been five days separated from my relatives before, and felt alone in a new world." By May the personal attention from Professor Hilliard had accomplished the preparation of Roberts, who quickly adjusted to college life. After a year of diligent studies he stood sixth in the class. He confidently adjusted to campus life and fit in with the other freshman, noting: "Having been raised partly on a farm and accustomed to labor, I had, though tall and slender, grown up healthy and strong, which enabled me to do any amount of study without injury. . . . My raising and mode of life up in the mountains fitted me well. . . . I soon had more reputation in that field of effort than I had in the school room." The "raw boy from an obscure mountain region" had the traits, individual confidence, and drive portending his future activities.[10]

After the first year of adjusting to the university, its students and campus pranks, faculty class demands, and the new world of activity in the state capital, Roberts settled into school. More important, the university enhanced his social contacts and provided interactions he had not found back in St. Clair. One activity that opened up new opportunities and a means to improve his debating and speaking skills was joining the university chapter of the Eurosophic Society. The debates brought into better focus the issues of the day as well as interactions that challenged the student presenters' views and conclusions. Debaters had to be keen to formulate and defend their positions. Both as an observer and then as an active participant, he found that the society and its forum helped to improve his presentation style. He would refer to this experience through the years as a major preparation for his future. Tuscaloosa provided a wealth of activities to observe as well as a distraction from his studies. The society encouraged members to be active in the local events, and especially to observe local civic activities and learn from the many speakers of the day—preachers, politicians, traveling road shows, and memorial services, for example, such as the public observance and speakers' presentations held by the university on the death of the American revolutionary hero the Marquis de Lafayette. Students became well aware of the not so distant history and the impact of the colonial revolution and the formative years of the new "Republic"—all useful lessons and dynamics; Roberts would come face to face with many of the same issues in Texas.[11]

When he returned for his second year at Alabama, the Eurosophic Society increased their membership and activities to include routine visits to sessions of the state legislature and supreme court. In later years, he recalled, "It was to me as if I had dropped down in a new world . . . it fastened on me a lasting impression." After his sophomore year Roberts returned home and contemplated transferring to Miami University in Ohio, the alma mater of his mentor Ralph Lowe. However, Oran became sick at home due to an epidemic of "chills and fever" that engulfed farmers across St. Clair County. Planning to return to Alabama, Oran learned that his share of the inheritance was exhausted. He considered teaching in one of the new Ashville academies to earn enough to return to his studies. Impressed with the progress of his brother-in-law, Robert Bourland agreed to lend Oran the money needed to finish his degree. Upon returning to Tuscaloosa, Oran noted that the class had dropped in size, yet his close friends were back: Franklin Bowdon, Washington D. Miller, and Walter Coleman—all members of the debating society.

Visits continued across the capital to events and legislative hearings. During his senior year it was customary to have a member of the class serve as university librarian. Roberts was selected to this first post, which gave him full access to the library as well as daily contact with faculty and students requesting books—also affording him the opportunity to delve into any book he wished. Furthermore, he was elected president of the Eurosophic Society for the 1835–36 school year. Working together, he and Bowdon selected the debate subjects and format. Roberts and Bowdon often opposed each other in campus debates, with Roberts considering Bowdon the better debater. Little did they know this was just a precursor of later days as lawyers facing off in Texas courts.[12]

As the senior year drew to a close, the 1836 presidential campaign gave Roberts and his friends in the society added opportunities to face off. The society took sides, with Roberts and a student known only as Mr. Fox "standing alone" for Democrat Martin Van Buren, the incumbent vice president and designated successor to follow retiring President Andrew Jackson. "All the rest" debated on behalf of Hugh White of Tennessee with the Whig party. In Roberts's 1892 manuscript Reminiscences of the History of the University of Alabama he does not mention the third candidate, a fusion of defectors from the Whigs and the Anti-Masonic Party, William Henry Harrison. The spirited debates were the highlight of the semester. Recalling the moment years later, Roberts concluded: "Van Buren was elected, and I came out in the majority at last. You must not understand from that fact, that I was controlled by political wisdom. The truth is, that it was then understood that General Jackson was for Van Buren, and I for him against any odds. *Such was my raising in the mountains.*"[13]

The years at the University of Alabama were pivotal in shaping Roberts's outlook on life and his future. He never forgot his humble upbringing, remembering years later, "Having been brought up in and near a very small village, the county seat in a mountain region, where there [were] few educated people, and but little wealth, my going to the University at Tuscaloosa, a considerable town and capitol of the state, where the legislature convened once every year, it was almost like I had been transported to another world. It gave me an enlarged idea of everything, and a state of society that I had previously but little conception of."[14]

Young Lawyer

The class of 1836 at the University of Alabama finished with twelve graduates. Franklin Bowdon, the leading orator in the class, delivered the valedictory address and Roberts made a short presentation at the graduation ceremony. Roberts's plans were to return to Ashville and read law in the office of Samuel Hinton. However, during commencement, university President Woods introduced Oran to Judge Ptolemy Harris of Washington County. The judge was looking for a tutor for his three children, and for room and board and a monthly stipend, Oran could study law in the judge's office in preparation for the bar exam. The job was in the small town of St. Stephens on the Tombigbee River, about one hundred miles from Mobile. In June 1837, eager to locate in a larger city, he moved to Talladega to work in the office of William P. Clinton and George P. Brown. After a few months, he applied to Judge Eli Shortage to sit for the bar exam. Meeting at Chilton's office, Chilton and Brown indicated that Roberts was "proficient," whereupon, on September 22, 1837, the judge hand-wrote a license to practice law. For the next year Roberts remained as an associate in the Clinton-Brown firm in Talladega, learning the trade and continuing his legal studies. Restless about his future, Roberts wrote to classmate Washington D. Miller, who had secured his law license and immediately moved to Texas to set up a law practice in Gonzalez, that "times are not interesting at all" in Alabama. Only time would tell.[15] Few documents survive Roberts's earliest years in Alabama. However, one letter found in 1904 and presented to then president of the University of Texas, Prather, was written by the judge shortly after the death of Roberts's wife Frances:

Austin, Texas, March 13, 1894
Mrs. Thomas M. Owen
Alabama State Archives

I came to the University [of Alabama] a rude boy from the mountains in St. Clair County, and was there during four sessions, from 13th of February, 1833, to about the middle of December, 1836. College boys then usually boarded at the Steward's hall, and had but little social intercourse with the families that resided in Tuscaloosa.

True, I went to dancing school, and parties occasionally, and was mainly in that way acquainted with many of the girls in the city, and to tell you the truth, liked some of them very much; but I can not say that I loved them very much, as I probably would have done, if it had not been that I had left my sweetheart back in the Mountains, the prettiest girl in all that mountain country, and I thought the best, as she was up there waiting for me two years until I could get my education and a profession. We lived together forty-six years, less fifteen days, and I never regretted that she waited for me.

I will tell you why she waited for me. I spent Christmas week at home, and the time came that I had to go back to school, and on Monday morning the horse was saddled and my clothes were packed, and my spurs were on my boots, but something was lacking, and I could not start. I had long wanted to do it but never had told her what I wanted. I walked, spurs, leggins, overcoat and all right to her father's house, and upon entering it, found her and her mother and two sisters sitting around the fireplace doing some sowing. Without stopping except to say "Good morning," I said, "Frances, please walk with me in the garden." We took seats on the little framework for vines to run on. I told her that I could not go away without telling her that I wanted to marry her when I get through my schooling—that was all. I did not want her to answer me then. She said not a word, and I carried her back to the room she left; and walked through it, not one of the girls or the mother looking up at me as I walked through the room and out of the house. You may say that was a very rude thing for a youth of twenty to do, and so it was. But the earnestness of it, and the resolve that could make me do such a thing, they knowing me well to have been [a] rather modest, studious boy, impressed her, who knew that I loved her, and her alone, for years back, and it impressed the whole family, and I never heard that she or they thought it was something that I ought not to have done. So she waited for me, and we had many pleasures together through life, and I never quit loving her.[16]

Respectfully,
O. M. Roberts

In December 1837 Roberts married Frances Edwards in Ashville, a neighbor in St. Clair County he had courted for a few years. In August 1838 Oran and Frances moved back to Ashville to open his first legal office and to help care for his mother. Known to many in the community, his practice steadily grew with clients in the adjoining counties. As an active public figure, he was elected a colonel, more ceremonial than functional, in the St. Clair County Militia Regiment. And on October 20, 1839, the Robertses welcomed their first child, Sarah Jane Roberts.

Eager to test the political waters in Tuscaloosa, Roberts entered the fall 1840 election for representative from St. Clair County in the state legislature. His opponent was a fourteen-year incumbent, John Massie. After a short and hectic campaign Oran won by an easy margin. Notwithstanding his many visits to the state capital and his observance of legislative activities while a student at the University of Alabama, his arrival as a freshman legislator provided a humbling experience. Political factions from the Black Belt region of the state and seniority within the elected body controlled all procedures and offered no room for unseasoned newcomers. Roberts, surely disappointed, was unable to introduce any bills, and there is no record of him speaking from the floor of the chamber. Because the term of office was only one year, he returned home and did not stand for a second year. It was not a total waste, given that he was appointed as a delegate to the Alabama Democratic Convention in 1841 and helped campaign for the winning candidate for governor, Benjamin Fitzpatrick. These activities gave him his first insight into party politics as well as an introduction to one of the state's leading power brokers and fire-eaters, William Yancey.

The year-long experience caused him to refocus his priorities on his law practice and future. Letters and news from Washington Miller, who had left for Texas in late 1836, proved to be major motivator in Roberts's decision to go west—to Texas. The decision was made even easier given that Robert Bourland held title to the family farm where his mother lived, thus relieving any ties or obligations Oran had to St. Clair. Brother Ford had already abandoned the farm to go and join the Texas army. On October 8, 1841, Oran Roberts at the age of twenty-six loaded his wife, child, mother, and two slaves, one of them Prince, in a wagon with all their worldly possessions and headed west. Fond memories of his early life in northeast Alabama would be ever present, with Roberts often reminding flat-land Texas friends over the years, that as a "raw boy," his grit came from his having been raised in the rugged "'Bama mountains."

Gone to Texas

After about a six-week trip westward across the Mississippi River and through Louisiana, Roberts and his family arrived in the Republic of Texas in mid-November 1841—leaving the United States for the infant sovereign nation. In 1841, in what was known as "deep East Texas," the zone along the Sabine River and Louisiana border represented the largest regional concentration of population in the young republic. Margaret Roberts's older sister Jane Elizabeth Ewing, married to Nathan J. Davis, had immigrated to Texas in 1822. Oran Roberts and family settled in Shelby County near the bustling city of San Augustine, with Nathan and Jane there to greet their Alabama relatives. San Augustine, along with nearby Nacogdoches, situated near the old Spanish *Camino Real* (King's Highway), made up the gateway to the region as well as its commercial, political, and social hub. It was settled by Father Antonio Margil de Jesus in 1716 to build a mission to assist the Ais Indians. "Mexican officials always claimed the area," as D. W. Meinig noted, "and the settlers [by the late 1830s] were well aware of the ambiguity. . . . East Texas, therefore, was Mexican in soil but Anglo-American in culture." During the decade between 1834 and 1844, 1841 marked the second highest amount of migration into East Texas, estimated at some 500 families arriving that year, primarily from Alabama, Tennessee, and Mississippi. In news arriving from merchants, the tri-weekly Houston newspaper *The Musquito* reported an ample supply of butter, bacon, coffee, and sugar as well as a "fair supply" of soap and whiskey. Others arriving in Texas in the early 1840s included John H. Reagan, James Hogg, J. M. Maxey, and Shapley Prince Ross and his one-year-old son, Sully. Research indicates that "the standard reason for migration to Texas was undoubtedly the hope of economic betterment."[17]

Oran Roberts upon arrival had a number of priorities, the first being finding a home for his family, the second preparing to obtain a law license in Texas, and the third, obtaining a better understanding of the political and social dynamics of his new country. While now well versed in the basics of the law, he would have to pass approval by the San Augustine Bar based on the new and evolving laws of the Republic of Texas—a mix of codes based on the Spanish land grant statutes, water rights, and local precedent as well as the traditional English common law passed down for centuries.[18] The foundation of the state's jurisprudence had deep roots, as historian James Haley noted: "The accent of this Spanish heritage would color Texas's legal history and require accommodation by subsequent Texas Supreme Courts, during both the Republic and statehood, to a degree that is unique within the American union." Many aspects of the inherited Mexican law were woven into Texas jurisprudence. An example is property protection from creditors, where the new republic adopted the homestead exemption excluding a man's home and "tools of his trade" from seizure by creditors. Furthermore, in contrast to English common law, which generally left a widow with less property and rights to the estate, a wife in Texas had the right, after all debts were paid, to one-half "of the fruit of the couple's labors since marriage."[19]

To address these dynamics, a well-seasoned group of lawyers in the region established a strong base and legal tradition. In February 1842 Roberts applied to District Judge William B. Ochiltree for an exam. The judge assigned local attorneys Royall T. Wheeler and James Pinckney Henderson to administer the review. Despite Oran's short tenure in the republic, all were impressed with his knowledge and grasp of the dynamics of frontier law and the promise that he was about to begin a successful career. His formal law license was granted on February 7, 1842—the start of six decades of legal interaction, practice, and mentoring in Texas. Furthermore, Wheeler, Henderson, and Ochiltree would become his close friends, mentors, and often unwitting opponents in the years to come. A majority of new settlers in East Texas arrived from the deep South. The economic underpinnings of the cotton-slave culture followed them to Texas. The Texas economy had just begun to expand cotton production, with concomitant increased demand for labor. The editor of the Houston *Telegraph and Texas Register* noted the transition: "Texas, by a fundamental article of her constitution, had declared the African slave-trade piracy. I believe she will willingly concur in any measures with the rest of the civilized world to make the declaration effectual. It is true she permits the emigration of citizens of the United States with their domestic slaves to her territories, because she does not desire to deny herself the valuable contingents of patriotism, courage and high faculties for public service, which characterize the citizens of the south-western states of the American Union."[20]

Other than the commercial center at the Port of Galveston, in the early 1840s San Augustine had the largest concentration of Anglo lawyers and the most robust court system in the Republic of Texas. In terms of slave ownership San Augustine ranked third behind Brazoria County. In addition to the three lawyers already mentioned, San Augustine included the legal offices of Walter Hinckley, Thomas Rusk, Kenneth L. Anderson, James C. Hyde, David Kaufman, C. M. Gould, brothers William and Richardson Scurry, W. G. Anderson, Henry Sublett, Jesse Benton, C. M. Adams and A. P. Vaughn.[21] Eager to open an office, Roberts worked from his home, placing an advertisement in the San Augustine *Red-Lander* (named for the twenty-mile-long and four-mile-wide prevailing clayey red soil running across the county) explaining that he could be found "Near Main St." Mixed in with the small retail shops and street vendors was also the office of a recently arrived young Tennessee doctor, John S. Ford, not yet known by the moniker "Rip." Ford opened his practice near Roberts, and the two new immigrants became lifelong friends. Ford, known at the time only in his local area, would practice medicine for eight years in East Texas, until he developed an interest in the law. He studied, passed the bar exam, and hung over his office a new shingle reading: "Doctor Ford—Lawyer Ford." In his memoirs, Ford recalled that "O. M. Roberts, very soon after his arrival in Texas, was recognized as a man of mark, one of the coming leaders of the people."[22]

The economy in East Texas was a constant challenge for settlers, farmers, and merchants, given the shortage of ready cash and a heavy dependence on barter. One writer noted, "Overall the population of some six thousand was rural, egalitarian, independent, individualistic, aggressive, and adaptable." For example, Roberts reverted to one of the primary sources of collateral by "hiring out" or mortgaging his slaves. As an attorney he was fastidious to contract his major transactions. In a purchase of ten barrels of whiskey at twenty-two cents per gallon from Abner Parther in December 1842, costing ninety dollars, he used his fifteen-year-old enslaved girl, Sarah, to secure the promissory note.[23] This was reminiscent of the slave Prince, owned by the Roberts family, being hired out to pay for Oran's university expenses. Sarah was retained by the whiskey seller's family as a domestic servant until the full sum was paid, at which time she was returned to the Roberts family. While it was not uncommon for distilled spirits to be bought in wholesale quantities, one observer noted, "Evidently Roberts required considerable of the *spiritum frumenti* to 'wet his whistle,' or Mrs. Roberts was a baker of fruit cakes . . . and indicates the worthy gentlemen required copious quantities!" Roberts's affinity for "spirits" seemingly did not preclude him from accepting an invitation from the Red Land Chapter No. 15 of the Sons of Temperance to be the keynote speaker at the annual Fourth of July gathering.[24]

During the next few years Roberts, who was referred to as

"Colonel O. M. Roberts" in the weekly *Red-Lander* newspaper in view of his support of the San Augustine Light Horse Company, expanded his law practice, investing the profits into city lots. His second child, a son named Oba in honor of Oran's father, was born on October 12, 1843. San Augustine was viewed as the social center of East Texas. The growing commercial center soon had three churches, a small public school, and private "universities." A number of the schools or academies, holding the "high-standing" label of "university" in name only, were little more than denominational sponsored high schools. In his 1898 history of the establishment of the University of Texas, Roberts noted: "It is certain that, by use of the term university was meant a high school of learning, and not technically a university, as understood in Europe and elsewhere."[25]

The first such school opened was the University of San Augustine, linked with the Presbyterian church, followed by the Methodist-supported Wesleyan College as well as the first nonsectarian school, Nacogdoches University. Referred to in newspapers across Texas by the honorific title of "colonel' bestowed on him in Alabama, Roberts, given his experience at the University of Alabama, was a strong supporter of education, but not education that was divisive or religiously motivated. Founders and administrators at each of the new schools attacked their competition along religious lines. Roberts, although he did not oppose freedom of religion, distrusted activist zealous people who attempted to promote sectarian religious converts for their own benefit. Roberts maintained unorthodox views of religion, even while his mentors and his wife encouraged him to be aware of his faith and "spiritual welfare." He told close friend Washington Miller, "My wife is a good Methodist. I am a sinner, and have never belonged to any church." During his career, and especially during his years as governor, newspaper editors would periodically delve into and question Roberts's so-called "infidelity"—unbelief in a particular religion. When questioned by the Galveston *Christian Advocate*, he responded, "Strictly speaking, neither religion nor temperance has a representative in our State government affairs."[26]

The primary challenge faced by all the religious-oriented schools was their need and ability to attract enough funding to sustain operations. Irritated with the most egregious and mismanaged school, San Augustine University, Roberts stepped in to lead a community effort to replace the board of trustees. In so doing, in the fall of 1845 he was named president of the board of trustees. Roberts worked to merge San Augustine University and Wesleyan University in 1847 into the nonsectarian independent institute called the University of Eastern Texas. However, its failure to maintain adequate funding resulted in its closure in 1851 and its being taken over by the Masonic Institute of San Augustine. Thus any level of education was incredible given the limited (and often expensive to settlers and small farmers) educational opportunities. Community infighting notwithstanding, in the 1840s Roberts was proud to note in his memoir, "San Augustine claimed to be the Athens of Texas." Yet, as one historian notes, the rapid growth of newspapers across Texas—which provided the only source of news other than a few imported periodicals—demonstrated a relatively high number of Texans able to read and write, despite the lack of any lengthy formal education.[27]

District Attorney

While Roberts was fully engaged in establishing his law practice, there is little doubt that—surrounded by some of the most eager, ambitious, and active politicians in the state—he maintained a watchful eye on local and state political developments. Shortly after his friend Washington Miller, the private secretary to President Sam Houston, arranged a visit with the president in December 1842 at Washington-on-the-Brazos, Roberts wrote to Miller, "For one who has enlightened views of government, the present is a propitious period to commence a political career in Texas." Such a start in politics could be launched by holding either an elected office or a judicial appointment. On February 5, 1844, at the recommendation of Secretary Miller, Houston appointed Roberts as district attorney of Texas' Fifth Judicial District. He had not solicited the position of district attorney (DA) and was named over others who had submitted formal petitions for the job. Upon taking the office Roberts faced three challenges: first, how to address his private practice while DA; and second, within days after he was sworn in, Roberts was contacted by President Houston (once again as recommended by Miller) to handle his personal legal affairs in East Texas, which due to "public concerns" had "been woefully neglected." The third challenge—among the daily duties awaiting him in the sprawling thirteen-county district, with Newton, Shelby, and Sabine counties on the Louisiana-Texas border—was being tasked with enforcing the collection of tariff duties. He addressed the first challenge by adding a partner to his law firm, Henry W. Sublett, a future state senator. In the case of the president's business affairs, he handled that request in a personal and confidential manner. The collection of the unpopular tariff duties provided the greatest challenge. An unknown farmer from Lamar wrote to the Clarksville *Northern Standard* stating he and his neighbors were all in agriculture and "we have no manufactures to protect, and therefore a tariff is unnecessary." A possible reason for Roberts's lack of enthusiasm for tariff enforcement was that the salaries of state-appointed collectors of customs W. M. Hurt in San Augustine and W. C. V. Dashiell in Sabine were $800 each, while the office of DA only paid $300.[28]

Judge Roberts throughout his life kept copious notes in journals, files of speech outlines, summaries of court proceedings, and an enormous collection of correspondence. All these are available to researchers. Often, he wrote his thoughts and observations and filed them away—and saved them. His assessments and notes, labeled as a "scrap" of his comments on life on his thirtieth birthday, provide a prime example:

> July 9th 1845—This day I was thirty years of age. Most of my life has been spent in rather a desultory unsettled manner—without any particular star to light my path. I have perhaps about learned how to learn. In this process my lot is not peculiar. The world has continually been struggling through error, superstition, barbarity, and ignorance to arrive at its present condition. Nor is it free from them yet. Still its

> progress and advancement in all the arts and sciences are predicated upon natural laws and fixed principles and for the most part in the future will not be forced to feel its way in the dark as it has done in former times.[29]

Within a few days following this journal entry, Roberts delivered an address to the Lyceum of Wesleyan College on the subject of "The Adaptation of Education to the Free Institutions of America," stating in his notes, "I understand it has been well received by the most intelligent of the numerous and respectable audience."[30]

East Texas

Experience and familiarity with the people of the East Texas region were a must. Roberts left a marked impression, described well by one writer: "Judge Roberts was of dark complexion, five foot and eleven inches high . . . symmetrical in proportions. Even in advanced age, and graceful and erect in carriage. Though his eyebrows remained black, the hair on his head and beard became white when he was thirty years old." It was customary at the time for lawyers to travel "around the circuit" in company with the district judge. On horseback, riding more than fifty miles per day between communities, and in hacks, for days at a time, they visited every county from the Trinity River to the Sabine. Roberts recalled: "When time for holding the courts arrived it was not unusual to see a dozen or more lawyers, [including the District Attorney], and judge mount their horses, with saddlebags, blankets, and tie ropes; and, thus equipped, start on their journey around the district, which embraced many counties, comprising a large scope of country. As some of them would drop out of the company at different points others would fill their place, so that about an equal number of traveling lawyers in addition to the local bar, would be found in attendance in nearly every court. This mode of practice was continued until the Civil War."[31]

The collecting of tariffs in Texas dated from when Mirabeau B. Lamar had been president of the republic in 1840. The Congress and

Lamar had debated at length the best means to raise revenue for the country. The options were a direct tax on land and livestock and businesses or a merchandise tariff on imported goods. The young republic faced what seemed to be a hopeless deficit in the treasury, a depreciated currency, and rising expenditures. Given the fact that a direct tax would have a major impact on land owners and be a burden to farmers, it was held to be "odious and unreliable." Furthermore, there was only mixed success in collecting a direct tax, while it was determined that "tariff duties were equal and just, and that they were the only taxes collectible in Texas." Thus, Congress in Austin passed the Tariff Act of February 5, 1840, in hopes of collecting duties ranging from 15 to 45 percent of the value of imported goods. District Attorney Roberts soon learned that the Tariff Act had no relationship with his office or staff duties nor expertise assigned as customs agents to ensure collection of duties. Fifth District Judge William Ochiltree insisted that the young DA exercise every measure possible to collect the required tariff duties, including having Roberts make a presentation to each grand jury upon the obligation of citizens to pay "their fare share" of the duties.

How the locals responded to the high tones and platitudes of the district attorney is unknown: "The very existence of organized society implies that its members, in the transaction of life, are governed by some system of conduct, some incentive, some motive, some principle, some rule, and that their actions are not entirely prompted by the blind chance of circumstances. Then your interest, truth, good faith, justice, honor, honesty, religion, patriotism—all sanction this obligation to [pay duties] and direct you—yea command you to fulfill it." Seemingly leaving nothing to chance and regardless of his not being an overly religious man, Roberts concluded: "Hearken to the answer of Christ when asked if it wise and lawful to pay tribute to Caesar, 'Render therefore unto Caesar the things which are Caesar's; and unto God, the things that are God's.' You must obey these sacred injunctions or renounce all title to faith or fellowship."[32]

The position of district attorney cast Roberts as a significant community leader, and he was often called on to address ceremonies.

A student of history, he was much in demand to reflect on the progress and challenges facing the Republic of Texas. President Sam Houston cautioned that efforts to pursue annexation with the United States could create the possibility of a retaliatory attack by Mexico.[33] Thus Roberts, as keynote speaker for the "Anniversary of Texian Independence" in San Augustine on March 2, 1843, was quick to caution in his address to the citizens of San Augustin that the "revolution" was not yet complete, and that vigilance was warranted:

> The clouds of war are still lowering over us, Santa Anna, whose life was forfeited by every law, human and divine, was released by the generosity of the brave. He is again in power and again he molests our borders and again he threatens us with subjugation. Ungrateful man! Nothing short of our extermination would now relieve the burden of his ingratitude. Nothing less would satiate the vindictive malice of his chagrin. Let them come! But give us *unity of action* and the minions of his power shall wilt before *Texian energy* as stubble before the fire.[34]

The obvious challenge, given Roberts's call for citizens' cooperation, was how to collect duties along the border of more than 200 miles with Louisiana. One observer noted: "The provisions to collect duties was not operative, as so many of the people in that section of East Texas were opposed to the tariff that they would connive at the violation of the Law." There were so many border crossings suitable for smuggling, Roberts realized, that even with President Houston instructing collectors to enforce the law, total enforcement would be nearly impossible. Furthermore, the *Red-Lander* noted that in addition to smuggling, the tariff drained ready cash from the economy, hampered growth of manufacturing, and discouraged emigration. Roberts's 1844 year-end report to Secretary of the Texas Treasury William B. Ochiltree said that prosecutions for smuggling "have done some good." However, those convicted of failing to declare payment of tariffs were fined one dollar for each offense, while those guilty of promoting gambling were fined fifty dollars. Roberts reported over 200 indictments, and in his seven-county district 50 persons were convicted, resulting in $1,062 in fines. As Roberts continued his DA duties, he served on the San Augustine political endorsement committee for President Anson Jones, who followed Sam Houston as president of the republic in January 1845 and continued the same tariff policies.[35]

Judge Roberts's involvement in the San Augustine endorsement as well as a petition from local supporters who had their finger on public opinion and influence were timely to any candidate for office. The nomination of Anson Jones for president of the Republic of Texas represented Roberts's first significant step into republic-wide politics, and did not go unnoticed among party leaders. Jones noted in response: "The first nomination I *received* for the Presidency. The nomination was the first *made* at San Augustine; but this was the first [of] which I had notice." Such letters were key pre-convention endorsements that determined nominations. The letter and Jones's "note" and comment follow:

San Augustine, Texas, Nov. 18th, 1843

To Mr. Anson Jones:
Dear Sir,—The undersigned Committee have the honor of informing you of your nomination as a candidate for the office of President at the ensuing election by a large and respectable meeting of citizens of the county, lately holden in San Augustine. You will much oblige your fellow-citizens in the East by accepting this nomination, and suffering them to run your name for this high station. Their selection is made with a view to their own interests, and to the dearest interests of the whole country. We may assure you that their support, founded on such a conviction, will be warm and energetic. And your success will crown their hopes with another bright prospect of their country's safety. Please accept the high esteem of your obedient servants,
O. M. Roberts
S. A. Sweet
W. Edwards
H. Griffith

A. Clark

Note.—My nomination and election to the Presidency was the spontaneous act of the *people of Texas,* and without any agency on my part. Party had nothing to do with it, unless those who wished to see the great measures of peace, Independence, and Annexation, and an economical administration of the Government, measures with which I was fully identified, carried out, might be called a party. The speculators and "war-dogs," and some in the West who misunderstood my position on the seat of Government question, opposed me, as well as the personal enemies of Gen. Houston generally. I probably lost more than I gained by my association with him. "1845."—A. J.[36]

By early 1845 it was obvious that the existing tariff law, given reports by Roberts of the estimated collection of revenue, would not meet the needs of the government. Roberts's friend Dr. John Ford had been elected to the legislature and, as a result of being a member of the finance committee, was able to keep Roberts informed as well as exchange input on his suggestions on how to collect more duties. Concerned with the continued state budget deficits, most Texans wanted no change in how duties were collected, but the Ninth Congress in July 1845 reduced the tariff to a 10 percent ad valorem tax on all articles except wines and other spirits. The opinion, espoused by Roberts, Ford, and many other Democratic leaders, was that the tariff and budget issues could be solved by the annexation as a state within the United States. Ford's position was in response to a joint resolution by the Congress of the United States to extend Texas an offer to join the Union. Texas had sought annexation after gaining independence from Mexico, but the volatile climate in Washington over considering a new slave state prevented either President Jackson or President Van Buren from taking action.[37]

Annexation

One lingering question that received little public attention during the federal debate on the annexation of Texas was an attempt in Congress to divide the massive Republic of Texas into two states—one slave and one free. President Houston in response navigated a thin line, given demands from many political and international entities. Concerned that the Treaty of April 12, 1844, was made with the intent of bringing Texas into the Union as a slave state, some, including Missouri Senator Thomas H. Benton, opposed this process. To delay or block the annexation, Benton introduced a bill in December 1844 to reduce the size of the state before admitting it. This was followed with a resolution by New Hampshire Representative John P. Hale to split the state midway from the Gulf of Mexico to the Red River. Another proposal would have divided the state from east to west, along the 32-degree parallel from the Sabine River to El Paso. The half-dozen options advocated for some two decades to carve up Texas are discussed in detail in Ernest Wallace's *The Howling of the Coyotes* (1979). However, expedient action to admit Texas as a slave state passed the U.S. Senate in February 1845, with terms of admission prohibiting future slavery in all new states formed out of territory north of the parallel 36° 30'. The debate on the division of the state did not resurface until the Texas-New Mexico boundary crisis of 1850, soon to be solved with a $15,000,000 settlement to Texas from the United States.[38]

Concerned that Republic President Anson Jones and other politicians in Austin did not support annexation under these unsure conditions, people gathered at meetings around Texas to express their support of joining the American Union. In the summer of 1845, after conversations with his former classmate Washington Miller, who was deeply involved in advising both Sam Houston and Ashbel Smith on potential British interference, Roberts was a key leader and spokesman in East Texas for annexation, expressing concern about possible "European intrigue." On behalf of the local San Augustine citizens' committee Roberts drafted a petition to the president on annexation. Miller advised that Smith remind the British representative in Galveston that the application for annexation originated with the United States and not Texas, and should it fail, Texas would consider its options with "some powerful friend" (unnamed) who might support the republic's guaranteed independence. The question of annexation quickly took on international implications as the British, concerned about their investments and commercial interests south of the Rio Grande, urged Mexico to ignore the past conflict with Texas and immediately recognize the nation's independence with the condition that the Republic of Texas would not consider annexation by another country—the USA. The New Orleans *Picayune* doubted this was possible, noting, "She [Mexico] is foiled even in glutting her vengeance, and made to bite the dust by Texas." Britain, despite its objection to slavery, felt it had a better opportunity to expand business through Galveston under the flag of the Republic of Texas, and thus viewed an independent Texas as a useful barrier to the western expansion of the United States.[39]

The British had further concerns about the lucrative trade between the Santa Fe territory and Chihuahua, Mexico, in which they felt their agents could get a foothold to open and control trade into the Midwest of the United States. This international intrigue (also including unconfirmed American motives in Cuba to use the island, considered the "key to the Gulf of Mexico," as a means to reopen the slave trade) erupted into public view with a *Red-Lander* editorial speculating: "The interior trade of Mexico would yield a handsome revenue to the crown of Great Britain, should it establish a colony west of the Nueces [River]." Annexation of Texas would secure protection for the United States, according the historian Joel H. Silbey, "to subvert the very real British designs to establish an impenetrable barrier to America's westward development." Furthermore, "If Texas became a satellite of Britain, slavery in the neighboring southern states would be immediately threatened by aggressive abolitionist activity promoted by the government in London."[40]

Five decades later, removed from the events of the early 1840s, Judge Roberts in 1892 regaled law students at the University of Texas with in-depth lectures on his assessment of the dynamics of Britain on the slavery question: "The agitation of the slavery question was started in England, and was formally commenced in America by the formation of abolition societies in the North. As early as 1833, a renowned Southern senator—John C. Calhoun—pointed out the danger of recognizing, in the general government, the overwhelming centralizing powers then so popular, and warned the country that the people of the North, believing slavery to be a sin, and a great political as well as moral evil, would feel themselves responsible for what the government, with such powers, through their vote and influence, might reform, and would petition Congress to abolish slavery."[41]

Beyond the lingering international intrigue and emerging debate over the "peculiar institution," Texans were deeply concerned with the government's financial insolvency, with hostile Indians on the frontier, and with repeated Mexican threats and invasions across the border. Roberts was tasked by Democratic leaders with drafting a resolution supporting annexation, leaving nothing unsaid on joining the Union: "There she stands a pyramidal monument of Republicanism, a living, breathing, speaking monument attesting the truth that man is capable of self-government." Thus, in early July 1845, President Jones called a meeting of state delegates in Austin to decide one question: should the nation accept recognition of independence from the Republic by Mexico or annexation by the United States. The overwhelming vote was for annexation. One lingering concern was the transition from the Spanish or Mexican legal system and land policies. How to expand westward beyond the Brazos River resulted in debates over immigration and possible new efforts to promote "colonization." The *Texas National Register*, published at Washington-on-the-Brazos, concluded: "The error committed by the Spanish Government, of granting a square league and a labor of land to a single family, created land holders of many thousands of acres, without adding to efficient labor on which the cultivation of the soil every where depends. And it is a notorious fact, that after the reduction of the quantity given from a square league to a square mile of a half of a quarter section, immigration among us sensibly increased—demonstrating that it is not to the wealth proprietor, but to the hardy cultivator of the soil that new countries owe their growth and improvement."[42]

Judge Roberts

Entry into the federal union as a state required a new state constitution as well as statewide elections, with the formal transfer of power in February 1846. Two of the key elective positions were governor and lieutenant governor, besides the legislature and county officials. The governor made appointments to the Texas Supreme Court. The new high court consisted of three justices appointed by the governor and confirmed by two-thirds of the senate for terms of six years. The incoming Governor James Pinckney Henderson, with whom Roberts had worked closely over past years, appointed as chief justice John Hemphill, from South Carolina, a veteran of the Seminole rebellion in Florida before arriving in Texas in 1838. Governor Pinckney also appointed the two associate justices: Abner Lipscomb, fifty-six, also a South Carolinian, who had "read law" in John C. Calhoun's office; and Royall Wheeler, a Vermont native who was a proponent of slavery and who had arrived in Texas in 1839. Under the leadership of State Supreme Court Judge Wheeler, the court developed a new approach to the law. As one observer noted, "The Texas judges were seemingly more interested in humanity . . . this was generous, if not outright libertarian jurisprudence." Whether these views were referred down to lower courts is unknown. Wheeler's appointment removed him as the district judge of the Fifth Judicial District, and Governor Henderson appointed Roberts, on April 18, 1846, to fill the open seat for a five-year term at $1,750 per year. Law and order in Texas in the 1840s were exercised almost exclusively at the local level, with Wheeler writing to Roberts, "I have long been of the opinion that the office of the District Judge in this county wields more influence for weal and wo to the country than any/all others combined."[43] Coincidentally, senate approval was assured, given that Roberts's old law partner Henry Sublett had been elected to the senate and served as a member of the Judiciary Committee. Sublett wrote to Roberts saying, "Your prospects are certain—there will be no dissenting vote against your nomination." Judge Roberts's first challenge, rendered more difficult by the scarcity of precedent, was to assess and develop a legal framework to meld and blend the newly created state statutes with the inherited legal fragments of actions carried forward from the Spanish and Mexican eras, followed by revolution and the Republic of Texas prior to annexation. In so doing the judge made a lasting impression upon the jurisprudence of the state. Joining the San Augustine Masonic Lodge in late 1848 further sealed Roberts's entry and acceptance into the inner circle of the local and state leadership.[44]

Oran Roberts was well suited for the job of district judge. After six years in Texas he had traveled throughout the East Texas region and developed scores of contacts, both professional and private. Within months, the concern over Mexican interference and boundaries exploded into a U.S. congressional declaration of war on May 13, 1846. Roberts's friends, neighbors, elected officials, and relatives were drawn into the war. Governor Henderson resigned his office in June and accepted a commission as a major general in command of the Texas volunteers. Lieutenant Governor A. C. Horton assumed the duties during Henderson's absence from Texas until November 1846. Henderson fought along with Roberts's older brother Ford Roberts, who served as a captain in the Texas Mounted Volunteers. Oran Roberts remained on the bench. Working with the new state government proved a major challenge as the legislature created a great deal of confusion as newly passed laws took weeks (or longer) to reach the district judges, justices of the peace, lawyers in the legal community, and citizens. Judge Wheeler was aware of the problem but little could be done as judges depended on newspaper reports and informal notices from Austin. Roberts gained additional recognition assisting the work load and providing timely advice and expertise in adjacent districts. In addition to his court duties he made numerous presentations to civic groups and Democratic Party gatherings.[45]

Judge Roberts's popularity, political contacts, and rising role in the Democratic Party caused many citizens to suggest him as a candidate. Less than decade after he was elected to the Alabama legislature and subsequently came to Texas to practice law, he was singled out to run for Congress. The population of Texas in 1850 was 212,592, including

27 percent or some 58,000 people who were slaves. While Campbell noted that "the typical Texan was not a slaveholder," the majority of the white population, for whatever reason, supported slavery long before secession. By 1850 Roberts, with a combination of his judgeship, social status, and investments, was clearly a member of the political and economic elite in Texas and moved his family twenty miles north of San Augustine to a farm in Shelbyville in Shelby County. He owned six town lots in San Augustine, valued at over $1,200, as well as some 2,000 acres in Hunt, Smith, Shelby, and San Augustine counties; he had a net worth of over $10,000, and records indicate that he held three slaves, a 21-year-old female and two children. This financial comfort was a key factor in his ability to devote more time to political activities.[46]

Congressional Bid

The years 1850–51 were a pivotal period for Roberts and his family. He had been in Texas over a decade. Settling in San Augustine proved to be an excellent decision for both his family and his career. Mentors and associates in the legal, business, and agricultural fields helped pave his way to smooth assimilation. San Augustine in 1850 had a free population of 2,087, including fifteen practicing lawyers. Roberts was financially secure, a proven civic leader, and at a critical stage to consider his options. He had been prepared well by Judges Wheeler, Henderson, Hemphill, Lipscomb, and Ochiltree, as well as by his working relationship with Sam Houston, assisted by his old college friends Washington Miller and Frank Bowdon. At age thirty-five, with a comfortable town home and farming and investment properties, he and his wife Frances and their children, Sarah (11), Obadiah (6), and Robert (4), had prospered as Texans. As one of the more accomplished lawyers in East Texas and with a taste of the political dynamics associated with the district judgeship and district attorney offices, he faced a decision as to his next step. The options included continuing for a period in the Texas judicial system as a district judge, to seek a Texas Supreme Court seat, or running either for the state legislature or as a representative in the federal Congress. The Democratic Party had full control of the election process in Texas, and his increased role in the party was noticed by the leadership. He was ready to move on from the DA's office. His friends and mentors on the Supreme Court and his close associate A. H. Evans had already indicated that he should seek the district bench. Roberts had no desire for a seat in the state legislature. In fact he had never been to Austin. The unexpected death of eastern congressional district Representative David S. Kaufman on New Year's Day 1851 helped shape his decision.[47]

District Attorney Roberts immediately recognized the opportunity of not having to run against an incumbent, and with the passing of his friend Kaufman, he announced for Congress. The exact nomination process within the Democratic Party at that time is not known, yet as happens today, recognition, endorsements, and financial backing were critical. There was little likelihood that he would run unopposed, so for the first time he would be immersed in a full-scale competitive campaign. Roberts advised the San Augustine *Red-Land Herald* that he would not stand as a candidate for the Supreme Court, and this was followed by a formal announcement in early March 1851 of his run for Congress. He also notified the governor that he would resign his district judgeship effective in mid-April. The field of candidates for the East Texas congressional seat became crowded with six Democrats and one Whig. The required level of campaigning was greater than in any political race he had been in previously. Many of the Democrats were as well known as he was across East Texas. The lone Whig, Judge William B. Ochiltree from Roberts's hometown, was a vocal and well-known lawyer and politician.[48]

The canvas for Roberts's participation began in mid-1850 and was of great local interest. What seemed a premature start to the early1851 congressional election in East Texas pitted Roberts against one of his mentors and the man who had issued his law license and sworn him into the Texas Bar—William Ochiltree, an avowed Whig. A North Carolinian, Ochiltree had practiced law in Alabama before coming to Texas in 1839. He wrote eighteen opinions while serving on the Texas Supreme Court from 1842 to 1844. The Galveston *Weekly Journal* expressed surprise that the Roberts-Ochiltree campaign was "proceeding smoothly," considering that most of the state's congressional races were marked by "fierce attacks." Ochiltree, a more seasoned raconteur—who, as one observer noted, was a master at "political tergiversations"—was quick to play his upper hand, noting that the young judge had "good sense and analytical order of mind . . . but he had too much modesty and too little voice for a congressman. Indeed, Roberts would be no more than a mere block of wood in the halls of Congress." Roberts's simple response was, first, to define his position as bringing a new approach to the state's challenges, and second, that the older opponent was little more than a "milk and cider Whig."[49] If the campaign should get heated between the two friends, the newspapers noted:

They first shake hands before they box,
Then give each other plaguy knocks,
With all the love and kindness of a brother.

Roberts's only previous experience in running for legislative office was for his single term in the Alabama statehouse. For all practical purposes, although he won a one-term seat, he was unprepared for the party politics once he took his seat in Tuscaloosa. In 1851 he was more prepared and better known across the district. His successful legal practice and his recognized ability as a judge had impressed colleagues and citizens across the region. As early as 1851 there were already rumblings of sectional concerns over "outside interference" on southern traditions and perceived rights considered important to the way of life in Texas—all of which related to owning slaves. In stump speeches and in a detailed published statement to his "Fellow citizens of the First Congressional District," he endeavored to present his position on key issues. Roberts's platform, or "Card" as it was then termed, of March 14, 1851, included the following elements: preservation of the Constitution of the United States; energetic support of the rights of the South; rigid support of the slavery question; and a conservative government fiscal policy. He concluded, "I wish your votes . . . not as a temporizing politician, but as an independent man, who would be pleased to serve you."[50]

Attacks on candidates during the 1851 campaign were numerous and frequent. Roberts's opponents used comments made publicly only months earlier about the "dubious language" in the Compromise of 1850 to indicate that he favored careful consideration of disunion if necessary to protect the South. A disciple of Carolinian John C. Calhoun, who died in 1850, Roberts honed his mentor's philosophies on his East Texas audiences to advocate against control from the federal government, while not fully or overtly advocating secession. At this early date Texans at large were not predisposed to the call for disunion, and many viewed Roberts as an extremist. What was commonly called "compromise" was in essence a series of measures in 1850, one of which was the Pierce Bill that provided for the surrender of the New Mexico territory claimed by Texas, for the consideration of ten million dollars—one half of which was to be retained under the "control of Congress" for payment of the revolutionary debt of Texas. At this early date, while discussion in general terms across the South was mixed, no firm decision had been taken on the secession issue either by Roberts or by most of the voters in East Texas. Yet the debate did hinge on where candidates stood on disunion to protect slavery. The Clarksville *Northern Standard* printed a clarification of his position: "Judge Roberts, who has been heretofore supposed to entertain an equivocal position in this respect, most clearly and positively denies the existence of an opinion in his mind favoring secession or nullification." Decades later, in an 1890 lecture at the University of Texas Law School, Judge Roberts detailed the dynamics of the debate, noting that "the subterfuge caused sectional division . . . [and] swelled the tide of public opinion in the North against the institutions of the South." This did not stop Whig Judge William Ochiltree—Roberts's erstwhile mentor—from repeatedly calling out Roberts as a secessionist in 1851.[51]

The *Red-Land Herald,* a strong Democratic paper, when reviewing the candidates, "speaks of the sportive genius of Ochiltree, the modest cultivated talents of Roberts," while the *Marshall Republican* alluded to the debate between Roberts and Ochiltree as a "brush on the political track between the young Roan Colt and Old Union"—the title opponents gave Judge Ochiltree. The *Herald* noted that Judge Roberts, "proverbial for his manly, honorable and high-toned course," and "a strict constructionist of the Constitution, is opposed to works of internal improvement of a local nature, is opposed to the protective tariff, thinks the late compromise measures should not be disturbed, and adheres tenaciously to the rights of the South." With or without Roberts's approval, a Democratic meeting was called to "unite the staunch portion of the party" to defeat Old Union. In a meeting of party leadership, most likely headed by Wheeler and Henderson, they thanked Roberts and two other potential Democratic candidates for running, and following party seniority, instead selected Speaker of the House of the Eighth Congress Richardson Scurry, a veteran artilleryman at the Battle of San Jacinto, to run and win a seat in the Thirty-second U.S. Congress. Roberts was given credit for ensuring that the grassroots members of the party across East Texas were alert not to allow Ochiltree's popularity, even as a Whig, never posed a serious threat, or might capture the seat. Following the 1851 campaign, Roberts was encouraged to run again in 1853 but declined.[52]

During the campaign Roberts met gubernatorial candidate Peter Hansbrough Bell, who in November defeated incumbent George Wood. Bell was aware of the respect and legal reputation Roberts held in East Texas. Following Bell's election, and once again at the recommendation of Miller, former secretary of state for the outgoing governor, he agreed that Roberts would make a good state attorney general. Governor elect Bell wrote to Roberts in early December 1849 of his appointment as attorney general, requesting an acknowledgment as soon as possible. Even though the appointment was apparently mentioned in New Orleans newspapers, no one from the governor's office contacted Roberts, who did not receive Bell's letter for three months after it was written.[53] In the confusion Bell indicated he was highly offended that he did not receive a reply, and the two men apparently never spoke again. There is some reason to believe Roberts was informed that others were in consideration, and he simply waited for a letter that never arrived. Also Roberts and his wife had just welcomed their fourth child, Margaret Eliza, and Frances advised against any sudden moves. The job of attorney general was filled by Roberts's friend Andrew J. Hamilton. Furthermore, the job in Austin would have required a move of his family and a cut in pay from $1,750 as a judge of the Fifth District to $1,500![54]

Judge Roberts in his "Comprehensive History of Texas" categorized the early 1850s, saying there were "no political questions agitated in Texas"—yet the rise of the anti-Sam Houston faction can be traced to this period. The Democrats controlled elective offices across the state, and the principal activity was the growth of the economy and the improvement of internal infrastructure. However, in retrospect, Roberts was candid, noting "that influences and events were occurring that contributed to make Texas rife with political controversy." National events and political actions gradually began to place the South in a defensive posture. In many ways the road to southern disunion can be traced from the June 1850 Nashville Conference of nine southern states, including James Pinckney Henderson as the sole delegate from Texas.[55] While Texas was concerned about the resolution of the Texas-New Mexico dispute on the western boundary as the Rio Grande, a focal point of North-South controversy, it was clear that there was a political and philosophical breach between southern rights unionists and secessionists—many of whom wanted to take action immediately. Both Texas senators, Sam Houston and Thomas Rusk, questioned the need for and purpose of the Nashville Convention. In contrast, the rising voices of southern extremists Louis T. Wigfall and James Henderson strongly advocated southern unity, states' rights, and slavery.[56] Thus Texas politicians, cotton planters, merchants, and general citizens would be caught in the web of national debate that was based on the assumption that the U.S. Congress did not possess the constitutional power to regulate slavery— either in the existing states or in any new territories as the nation moved westward. The titular proponent that influenced the states' rights views of Oran Roberts and southerners on southern doctrine for more than a generation was John C. Calhoun of South Carolina—well after his death. In questioning the validity of the Missouri Compromise and the Wilmot Proviso, Calhoun determined that:

> Essentially, these resolutions argued that the territories of the United States were the common property of the several states which held them as co-owners; that citizens of any given state had the same right under the constitution as the citizens of other states to take their property—meaning slaves—into the common territories, and that discrimination between the rights of the citizens of various states in this respect would violate the Constitution; therefore, any law by Congress (or by a local legislature acting under authority from Congress) which impaired the rights of citizens to hold their property (slaves) in the territories would be unconstitutional and void.[57]

Roberts was in lockstep with Calhoun—the Congress had no right to interfere with slavery, as the United States expanded westward into new territory. The South should stand firm in their position based on a strict interpretation of the federal Constitution. His political stance, years before the Nebraska-Kansas Act, was ingrained as early as 1850—a decade from any serious talk of disunion:

> The government should at once make an equitable division of the common property by a line east and west to the Pacific [Ocean] from the [existing] states—allowing the citizen to settle either side of the line according to his discretion; but with a full guarantee to those south of the line that slavery may exist, until states are formed and determine this question for themselves.
>
> The south should demand of the government to do us ample justice by its action before another state shall be severed from the common territory and admitted into the union. To deny the constitutional power of the general government to prescribe all the rules and regula-

tions necessary to the accomplishment of this object, is like denying the right of the farmer to provide for his domestic welfare.[58]

The Nashville Convention accomplished little, other than to convene the first substantive number of southern states and to agree to meet again. The debate between unionists and secessionists was brought home to Texas in the U.S. congressional vote on the Kansas-Nebraska Bill in May 1854, when Senator Rusk voted for it and Senator Sam Houston voted against it. Judge Roberts concluded, "That [vote], together with speeches and other public acts of General Houston, caused him to be no longer in harmony with the regular Democratic Party." Furthermore, "this defection from the Democratic party . . . had a marked influence upon the political sentiments of the people of Texas."[59]

The roots of disunion considerations and debate in general as well as Oran Roberts's evolving secessionist views impacted his stance over the ensuing years. These ideas had their foundation in 1850–51. Yet in 1851, shortly after Roberts wrote to Governor Bell to resign as Fifth District judge effective April 13, 1851, the Clarksville *Northern Standard* editor Charles DeMorse noted, "No man who advocates disunion or the abstract right of secession can safely calculate upon votes in this region." The circumstances leading to Roberts's resignation are unknown.[60] Notwithstanding, this frayed ties between Roberts and Sam Houston and Houston's ardent followers, who over the years prior to secession grew fewer in number as a percentage of the rapidly growing population of Texas during the late 1850s due to an increasing amount of inbound deep South immigrants. Many held out hope that Old Sam would prevail—for his devoted followers Sam "was Texas"; in the parlance of Napoleon, *létat c'est moi*—I am the State!

CHAPTER 2

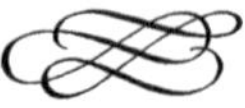

REBEL: THE IMPENDING CRISIS 1855–1865

It was the period of incipient division between the North and the South upon the great questions that arrayed them in actual hostility. The leaders of Southern thought were marshaling their forces of logic and protest on the side of strict construction, States' rights theory of the federal Constitution, and the

first sounds of that memorable conflict that afterwards thrilled the country with eloquence and argument and shook the continent with the roar of battle, were just beginning to challenge the attention and excite the alarm of conservative and observant men. Young Oran Milo Roberts was taught in that school of stoic statesmanship.

DUDLEY L. WOOTEN, EULOGY "PRESIDENT'S ANNUAL ADDRESS," TEXAS STATE HISTORICAL ASSOCIATION, JULY 1898

The price of liberty is blood, and if an attempt is made to destroy our Union, or violate our Constitution, there will be blood shed to maintain them. The Demons of Anarchy must be put down and destroyed. The miserable Demagogues & Traitors of the land must be silenced, and set at naught.

— SAM HOUSTON TO SAM HOUSTON, JR. NOVEMBER 7, 1860

BEGINNING IN THE MID-1850S, events and Oran Roberts's fanatical states' rights philosophy and his advocacy of the right to own slaves elevated him to a commanding role in the impending crisis leading toward the secession of Texas from the Union. At the age of forty Roberts became one of the leading pillars in the emerging anti-Houston wing of the Democratic Party. Given the influence of Roberts's South Carolina parentage and his education in Alabama, Dudley Wooten confirmed that Roberts aligned his political tenets with the pro-slavery states' rights movement and soon became known as a "formidable advocate of the strict construction of the Federal Constitution, and the inviolable sanctity of their domestic institutions."[1]

A major cause for the heightened excitement across the South and in Texas was the looming threat created by the rise of a new party in the North and its spread to the South—the American or Know-Nothing Party. Chief among those sounding the urgent warning was the editor of the Austin *Texas State Gazette* and the statewide leader in the Texas Democratic Party, John Marshall. Writing on the eve of the state convention in June 1855, Marshall stated that the party must take a firm stand to ensure "a TRIUMPH of PRINCIPLE—a triumph over the old Peihald [sic] Federalism—a triumph over Religious Intolerance—a triumph over secret and combined alliance with the northern Free Soilers—one of the most dangerous combinations against the South and against the peace of the Union that has ever existed in our history."[2] Marshall's editorials and his political influence in the late 1850s had a decided impact on Roberts. Decades later in his memoir, published posthumously in 1898, Roberts provided one of the best first-person assessments of the impact of the Know-Nothing Party that swept across Texas, noting that this new "political element in Texas swelled the tide of political agitation and contention." Styled after the old American Party, it formed as a secret political association in what he termed the "hot-bed of the Northern states." Roberts noted that the party derived its name from the close code of secrecy, "so that if one person should ask another what was the object of the party, the answer was 'that he knew nothing.'" The party advanced an adherence to Unionism, was opposed to uneducated foreign immigrants, and advocated a "slumbering prejudice against Catholicism." The rising concern of Democratic leaders in Texas, Roberts noted, was "in the early part of 1855 that a large body of citizens of all shades or political opinion had been drawn quietly and noiselessly into these secret societies pretty well all over the State —the effect of this discovery upon any of the distinguished Democrats in Texas was like that of a peaceful family asleep in the middle of the night being awakened to find their house on fire."[3]

In advance of the June Democratic convention, mass meetings were held across the state to bring attention against the ills of the Know-Nothings and to expound the traditional principles of the Democratic Party. Concerned with the disruption of their rallies, Know-Nothing leaders recommended that their members arm themselves. Roberts expressed amazement at how quietly the upstart party had organized without drawing more attention, except for their meeting at Washington-on-the-Brazos in early summer. Texas' social and economic diversification had largely been void of xenophobia and thus driven by European immigration and some from Mexico, which was broadly accepted to address the growing economy. Yet most troubling was that the new movement, which was gradually attracting disaffected Democrats and independents, was attacking Catholics, with the party "indirectly introducing religion into the administration of government, contrary to the spirit of the Constitutions of both the state and nation. On both grounds the party was anti-American and not in harmony with the long established principles of a separation of the Church and State." The scope of support for the new party surfaced when it briefly captured elected mayors in Austin, Galveston, and San Antonio in 1855. However, even more disturbing to Democratic Party leaders was that Senator Sam Houston was reported as a supporter of the Know-Nothing movement.[4]

Thus, at the Democratic Convention in 1855 to renominate Governor Elisha M. Pease to a second term in office, Democrats singled out Know-Nothingism as a threat to Texas and the South. The party's platform was headlined in the *Texas State Gazette* as "A Bombshell Thrown into the Know Nothing Camp"—confirming that party members were "fully aware that they have a cunning, unscrupulous and most untiring foe to deal with." The 1855 platform set the tone for the rise of secessionist sentiment among Texas Democrats. The key pronouncements included a strict adherence to the principles of states' rights; a warning to keep "more vigilant eyes" on Congress; a declaration that the federal government had no right to interfere with the affairs of a sovereign state, and that "we shall never compromise or sacrifice one iota or our defense of these rights." The delegates fully endorsed the Nebraska-Kansas Bill to allow settlers in the new territory to own slaves "and to have them protected as their property," yet showed that popular sovereignty was no panacea. The Know-Nothings, often referred to as "the Dark Lantern," were deemed "the most mischievous and dangerous enemies of free government." In a final published declaration, convention chairman James G. Swisher stated: "In this crisis, all who are not for us are against us." Senator Sam Houston's vote for the Nebraska-Kansas Bill in early 1854 was a major reason for the defection of disgruntled Texas Democrats to the Know-Nothings.[5]

The Know-Nothings selected former Democrat David Dickson as their gubernatorial candidate. As the campaign continued in the fall of 1855, Houston and Pease were publicly at odds on the issue of state-funded internal improvements to waterways and ports as well as state support of the railroads.

Houston's support of Pease waned into the fall, when he announced, "I adopt and admire the principles of the American party. I am for . . . whose principles will maintain . . . free institutions, I am for Americans ruling America." Governor Pease was reelected with over two-thirds of the votes cast. However, there were some very interesting pockets of Know-Nothing control in Travis County (in spite of the heavy-handed news media control by editor John Marshall) and in Collin, Grimes, Robertson and Kaufman counties. The most lopsided vote for Pease and the Democrats was in Bexar, Comal, Matagorda, and Medina counties.[6] One suggested reason for the commanding Democratic vote in San Antonio against Know-Nothingism was indicated in the *Ledger:* "Mexicans have stated, that they were threatened with excommunication if they voted the American ticket. They were told that they would not receive a Catholic burial, nor a burial in consecrated ground, nor their children after them. These people are not a reading people and have been imposed upon by demagogues and designing priests."[7]

The schism between General Houston and the old-line Democratic Party in Texas would never again be healed, and it brought forth the rise of factions within the fragmented party that slowly disintegrated, with the resulting breakup of the party in 1860. The Montgomery, Alabama *Advertiser* noted in September 1855 that Houston, who was still a sitting U.S. senator, "is out in a letter in favor of Know Nothingism. We are glad that he has thus formally severed the ties that bound him to the democracy of the South. Henceforth he is politically dead even in Texas. Instead of 'riding in the whirlwind and directing the political storm' in Texas, he will find himself a mere 'feather of the torrent's tide.'"[8] The political turmoil of 1855 soon opened the door for the radical fire-eater Louis Wigfall's rise in state politics with his open attacks on the Know-Nothings, Houston, and the federal government. Historian Alvy King notes that "none of the Old Hero's opponents was more obnoxious to him than was Wigfall." Judge Roberts, an invited guest of Wigfall's at many of the fall rallies, witnessed Wigfall requesting the legislature to ask for the resignation of Houston so that he could be named to the U.S. Senate as a true and dedicated "states' right senator" to represent the Lone Star state. We have no record of Oran's response to Wigfall's attacks on his old friend and mentor Sam Houston. Given his remaining support among staunch unionists, Independent Democrats, and some old Whigs, no action against Houston was forthcoming from the legislature—but the message was clear: Wigfall wanted Houston's seat in the Senate![9]

In the whirlwind of events during 1855, Roberts had been urged by political allies to run again for Congress in Texas' eastern district, his allies strongly believing he could beat his 1851 opponent Lemuel Evans, who held the seat. Both during and after the election, and especially after the threat of the Know-Nothings, Roberts maintained an active role in organizing a more solid base of support for the Democratic Party across the state. It was at this point that the states' rights faction of the Texas Democratic Party emerged. An indication of his increased attention to party affairs, Roberts contacted influential Texans to gauge the existing sentiment. Senator Thomas Rusk fully agreed with his planning, noting that "no time ought to be lost in fully organizing the Democratic party in every county in the state." Judge Roberts made numerous stops in counties to assist local leaders in organizing grass-root support, which some have noted was uncharacteristic of his general tendency for public events due to his poor speaking ability,. At the Democratic state convention in January 1856 he declined an offer to be selected as a national presidential delegate, instead supporting his old college friend, Frank Bowdon. Throughout 1856 it became increasingly apparent that the political-policy lines within the party were being drawn between those who supported a stronger focus on states' rights-induced support of slavery versus the more conservative old-line Union-Democratic followers of Sam Houston.[10]

Even before Abraham Lincoln stepped onto the national scene this rise of nativism and discourse was sown by the Know-Nothings, who worked to tie their views with abolitionists and caused Roberts to keep silent in public, unsure of the intent of this decisive movement. He noted in a private letter in August 1855, "How can anyone who abhors the oppression of Negroes be in favor of degrading classes of white people? . . . As a nation, we began by declaring that 'all men are created equal.' When the Know-Nothings get control, it will read 'All men are created equal, except Negroes and foreigners and Catholics.'"[11]

The high-water mark for the Know-Nothings was 1855–56, when Texas elected twenty-five Know-Nothing-leaning legislators. However, the slavery issue split supporters in both Texas and national elections. The vitriol within all the parties and factions set the stage for the increasingly divisive conditions between the North and South. Furthermore, to counter the attacks by John Marshall at the Austin *State Gazette,* James P. Newcomb, editor of the San Antonio *Alamo Express,* along with A. B. Norton, editor of the Austin *Southern Intelligencer,* endorsed the transition of many members of the Know-Nothings to the Unionism Party in 1860.[12] The pre-election news media in over one hundred daily and weekly Texas newspapers published a steady stream of what they felt were northern injustices to Texas and the South. The enemies of Sam Houston suddenly became emboldened. The brief but active rise of Know-Nothingism was a clear warning to the Democrats that factions they believed emanated from the North stood to disrupt the usual one-party control.[13] Attacks from perceived detractors in the North were widely circulated among the state's publishers, with this brief column on the threat of "The Isms" printed first in the Austin *State Gazette* and then statewide:

> The Washington Sentinel says truly that the North has given birth to all the 'isms.' We may add that their failure at the South has been

almost as proverbial. Not a single ism sprung up at the South; ALL of them have arisen at the North:

First. Abolitionism
Second. Freesoil-ism (very insidious)
Third. Woman's right-ism
Fourth. Agrarian-ism
Fifth. Fourierite-ism
Sixth. Radical-ism
Seventh. Native-ism
Eight. Mob-ism
Ninth. Mormonism
Tenth. Know-Nothing-ism[14]

Texas Supreme Court

In the fall of 1856 Roberts was solicited by the legal community in East Texas to run for the Texas Supreme Court but declined to challenge his friend and mentor Associate Judge Abner Lipscomb, a South Carolinian. Like Thomas Rusk, Lipscomb had read the law in the office of John C. Calhoun, who arrived in Texas in 1839 and served in the Constitutional Convention of 1845. Shortly after Judge Lipscomb won another term on the court, defeating Thomas Jennings, he died in December 1856 during the winter session of the Supreme Court. There was a sudden rush in Austin to fill the vacancy, with a number of lawyers circulating petitions for members of the bar to back their candidacies. Justice Royall T. Wheeler, even though he could not take a public position on filling the seat on the court, wrote to support Roberts and urged him to announce his intention to be a candidate as soon as possible, noting that he had the backing of Chief Judge John Hemphill, Edward Clark, Alexander W. Terrell, and Pitt Ballenger. Future governor James P. Henderson also expressed support for Roberts. In the formal parlance of the day, Roberts replied on December 20, "My friends and fellow citizens are at liberty to use my name as a candidate for that office." The special election was set for February 2, 1857, with Thomas Jennings, who had just lost, running against Roberts along with three other candidates—Peter W. Gray of Harris County, Benjamin C. Franklin of Galveston, and John Taylor of Cherokee County. Roberts was very concerned that the large field of candidates could split and dilute the votes, allowing Peter Gray in the more populous Houston-Galveston area to win. However, Roberts's greatest challenge was to win a majority in East Texas, given that Jennings could split the local voters. In addition there was a large contingent of Know-Nothing followers interested in defeating him following his constant attacks on them during the 1855 governor's race. In a close race Roberts defeated Gray by 4,740 votes to 4,394, with Jennings finishing third. Interestingly, the chief election officer, Secretary of State Edward Clark, noted that it took sixty days to tally the vote. He also reported that nineteen counties either did not vote or did not submit any results, delaying the final count. A week after certification of the election, Roberts joined the court in Tyler for the spring session.[15]

The week Judge Roberts took his seat on the bench was accompanied by headline news that would have a significant impact on events both in Texas and the nation. Full details of the monumental decision, concluded on March 6, 1857, by the U.S. Supreme Court in the *Dred Scott v. Sandford* case, did not reach Texas until April 4. John Marshall, editor of the *State Gazette,* reported that the 7–2 decision said that "Negroes, either slave or free are not citizens of the United States; second, the Ordinance of 1787 had no independent constitutional force or legal effect; and third, the Missouri Compromise of 1820 to confer freedom and citizenship to Negroes in the northern part of the Louisiana cession exceeded the powers of Congress [and] was unconstitutional, and thus void and of no legal effect."[16] One reason for the delay in the final rendering of the court's decision by Chief Justice Taney was the absence of Judge Daniel due to the death of his wife. This case had an indirect impact on a number of slave-related cases before the Texas court as well as further hardening the positions of states' rights advocates, and it fueled the sectional controversy that southerners wanted no interference in slavery from the North and federal government.[17] Roberts, in his memoirs, highlighted not the response of Texas and the South to *Dred Scott*, but the response of the North: "It intensified the already aroused sentiments of all classes of free-soilers of the North, and caused the extremists in that party, the abolitionists, to condemn the court in the most bitter terms. . . . Democrats of Texas became thoroughly aroused to the danger that beset them in the protection of their constitutional rights [to own enslaved Blacks] from what they considered the reckless fanaticism of the Northern people."[18]

Two other events had a significant impact on the personalities and events that would fester in the months and years leading up to the secession of Texas from the Union. The first was the assignment of General David Twiggs to the army's Department of Texas headquarters in San Antonio with the primary mission to control disruptions on the Texas frontier, anchored by a dozen forts. The second event that captured the headlines was the filibustering mercenaries in Nicaragua led by the so-called "Blue-eyed Man of Destiny"—General William Walker. Endorsed by Sam Houston in the mid-1850s, Walker recruited heavily in Texas and launched his operations to "conquer" Central America from Galveston. Walker's activities emboldened many who considered an invasion of Mexico to establish a protectorate dedicated to slavery—most directly fostered in the late 1850s by the rise of Knights of the Golden Circle—the K.G.C. Roberts noted: "It was only necessary for a few extremists in Texas and in other Southern states to manifest their approbation of such an enterprise to cause the Northern people to impute it to the whole South as a scheme to extend slavery."[19] In the meantime, Roberts's activities with the Democratic Party were on hold, and he turned his full attention to his seat on the Texas Supreme Court.

Court Duty

Justices Wheeler and Hemphill were pleased to have Roberts on the court and advised him that given the variety and number of pending cases before the bench, the "life of a judge of the Sup. Court was a dog's life—day & night—ceaseless labor." Since 1851 the court had rotated sessions in Austin, Galveston, and Tyler. The judicial and political acumen of Judges Hemphill and Wheeler, both Roberts's senior, proved critical in steering Texas jurisprudence during the late 1850s and then into the war years. Roberts, at forty-two years old, was an energetic addition to the court, and he wasted little time in making his presence felt. Quite possibly aware of the dissenting opinions rendered by the federal justices in the Dred Scott case, he worked in Texas to challenge the traditional narrow actions of the Texas Supreme Court to hand down only the final opinions without a response from the minority. Roberts became the first Texas justice to offer a dissenting opinion, in the case of *Cain v. The State.* Although it was in no way an attack on either Wheeler or Hemphill, he made it clear that since he was not satisfied with the correctness of the "very able" ruling, he had formed a different conclusion, "only enough to develop the principles upon which they rest." The opinion was the beginning of Roberts's lifelong effort to make the court as effective, efficient, and transparent as possible. This would be sorely tested in the months prior to and during the impending crisis faced by Texas. It was during his first tenure on the supreme court that the sobriquet "Old Alcalde" was bestowed on him. He explained its origin in a letter to the Marble Falls *Standard* in 1896: "The designation indicted him to be a high judicial officer of the state, the Spanish word 'Alcalde' meaning 'the judge' and in Mexican times the Alcalde of a Municipality [mayor] was the most commonly known judicial officer. After I became chief justice, having a gray head of hair, lawyers spoke of me as the Old Alcalde and the newspapers soon caught on to it . . . and it was generally regarded as an honorary appellation."[20]

Court cases, including many that should never have been referred to the high court, were mixed in with more substantive proceedings dealing with enslaved persons, corporate governance, and landowner disputes and right-of-way cases. Historian James Haley noted that the "Texas Supreme Court proved itself the most progressive in the South in standing guard over the rights of blacks, both free and enslaved," confirming the court's unusually strong insistence on as much equity as constitutional and statutory law would permit. The court had established this principle a decade prior to the arrival of Judge Roberts in what some convinced themselves showed "that slavery was a benevolent institution."[21] Much to surprise of many, the court endeavored to follow a strict constructionist path that sometimes was favorable to Blacks. In *Chandler v. State* (1847) the court upheld the manslaughter conviction of a white master for the killing a slave, and Judge Wheeler years later followed in the *Nix v. State,* which expanded the concept of protection to include assault and battery—be it white or Black. The first major slave case handled by Judge Roberts was *State v. Stephenson* (1857). The case involved a common form of assault and battery when a white man was accused of whipping a slave, Malissa, who was the property of another man, Linsay P. Rucker. The case was first heard in the District Court of Washington County, presided over by Hon. R. E. B. (Robert Emmett Bledsoe) Baylor, where it was dismissed on a technicality. However, the state immediately stepped in to appeal the case to the higher court. In Roberts's opinion, he rejected the lower court's notion that a "slave is property only, as a horse or any other domestic animal," thus, "we recognize in principle that the slave has personal rights and for a man not the owner to whip a slave established a *prima facie* case against the batterer."[22]

Other cases concerning enslaved people involved the obligations and rights of those who "hired-out" (rented) their slaves to others. To make extra income, planters and slave owners hired out their slaves when not needed. These contracts were made for a specific period of time. In a case before the court, a Travis County farmer, the hirer, refused to pay the slave owner his due contract fee because the slave died one week prior to the end of the contracted period, and the farmer claimed that the death allowed him (the renter) not to pay any amount. Judge Roberts ordered the farmer to pay and further noted, it was "in effect fortunate to receive any reduction in cost since the hirer commonly bore the loss in such case."

Slave hiring in Texas, apparently a widespread practice in the state, was not only common in rural areas but also a significant source of ready short-term labor in coastal ports like Galveston, both by slaves hiring out their own time and when they were hired out by their masters. In highest demand were artisan blacksmiths, pinewrights (carpenters), saddle makers, and wheelwrights. To add to the confusion of social interaction in Texas, free Blacks, poor whites, and slaves often worked together loading cargo on the seaport docks or on city construction sites. As the practice grew it also focused attention and concern on what was believed, by the late 1850s, to be a growing trend of fugitive slaves fleeing to Mexico.[23]

In a second case Roberts reversed a lower court decision when an owner allowed his slave to "hire out his own time" and reimburse the master, citing *Rawles v. The State.* Roberts said there was no offense and thus the matter was not indictable. In a third more complicated case, Roberts had to determine the status of permitting manumission "without specifying what was to become of the slaves thus gaining their freedom." While there were already Black freemen in Texas, the question was: what was to be determined and defined by the extension of freedom "within the limits of the state"? His decision was in his mind to offer justice to all involved, noting in *Boulware v. Hendricks*: "Negroes are, in this country [Texas], *prima facie* slaves. While held as such, they are slaves *de facto,* whether *de jure* or not. If they are dissatisfied with their condition, they have the right to be free, our courts are open to them . . . to assert their right. As long as they failed to do so, they recognize this *status* as slaves." Roberts concluded: "Any other doctrine would confuse the 'simplicity and certainty' necessary to both master and slave." Texas Democrats controlled the Texas legislature, responding in 1858 by passing a law requiring all free Blacks either to leave the state, or else to pick a master to re-enter slavery.[24]

These cases in no way altered Roberts's basic view that slavery, while the enslaved were both property and persons, and determined a valid southern institution and critical to the future of the "cotton" economy – driven and espoused by a combination of enslaved labor, rich farm land, and a growing international demand for cotton. Historian William Yancey offered a timely observation: "Even though this is a legal decision, one wonders how much of Roberts's personal feelings about slavery entered into his opinion. The institution of slavery made possible his education, social position, and wealth. If non-slaveholders had the right to attack any slave they saw, they would be attacking the very thing that made his success possible." One scholar noted that the Texas Supreme Court during the immediate prewar years demonstrated "a remarkable antebellum tradition of fair treatment of Blacks," citing *Calvin v. State* (1860): "The law of the case . . . is precisely the same as if the accused were a free white man, and we cannot strain the law even 'in the estimation of a hair,' because the defendant is a slave."[25]

Corporate cases before the high court were equally complicated and very political in nature. Texas cases concerning commerce were largely focused on disputes between the state and the railroads. Of the many case decisions, for example, Roberts's opinion in *The State v. The Southern Pacific Railroad Company* involved Texas law, its constitution, and the contract clause of the U.S. Constitution. The case challenged whether the incorporation charter given the railroad in another state was in fact a contract. If the charter was a contract, what was the standing of the State of Texas in passing any laws that violated the charter? In short, Judge Roberts cited rulings offered by U.S. Chief Justice John Marshall that a railroad charter "is not treated of as a contract, and was never."[26]

A second decision harked back to the early 1840s when Judge Roberts studied the mix of early laws impacting Texas for his bar exam. In *T. J Chambers vs. Josiah Fisk et al.* he discussed the action of trespass to try a title to land and gave a comprehensive history of Texas land law from the early Spanish colonial days of Coahuila and Texas. A third landmark case addressed the founders' aversion to organized banking in the state of Texas. The Constitution of 1845 prohibited formal banking in Texas, creating a serious impediment to daily commercial activities as well as economic expansion. So-called "commercial banking" was deemed corrupt and unnecessary in the state—the concern involved the issue of worthless paper money and often insolvent banks that failed to pay back depositors. As the economic growth of the state boomed into the late 1850s the moratorium on banking was questioned. The only quasi-bank formed under

Mexican law and jurisdiction before Texas became a republic, and thus an operating bank, was the Commercial and Agricultural Bank, which petitioned to transfer their charter to the State of Texas.

The bank was a small operation founded and owned by Samuel May Williams. The Texas Supreme Court before Roberts joined the bench was in the middle of two cases on banking. One concerned the authority of Williams to own a commercial bank in Texas. The other was a lawsuit against R. &. D.G. Robert Mills Company, a commercial commission cotton broker and factor in Galveston.[27] The well-established firm conducted services for customers to include loans. Second, they held accounts in currency issued outside Texas (primarily New Orleans banks). They also represented the customers in commercial transactions. The Millses were not, nor did they claim to be, a bank. The Texas attorney general felt otherwise and brought suit against the Mills brothers for operating a bank in violation of the laws of the state. The local district judge who referred the case to the high court was Peter Gray, whom Roberts had just defeated by a slim margin to win a seat on the high court. William Richardson, editor of the *Galveston Daily News,* a Gray supporter, stated that Roberts, with his roots deep in East Texas, "lacked sympathy for the commercial interests along the Gulf coast" and thus forecast trouble for the two pending cases. After Chief Justice Wheeler (who was against the bank) became ill, Roberts took over when Judge Hemphill was under consideration for the U.S. Senate and left the bench in late 1858.[28]

At about the same time the national economic Panic of 1857 (known today as a recession) began in August, numerous bank failures occurred in New York and the Midwest, which began false rumors for a brief run on deposits at the C&A Bank as well as a demand for the return of funds "held" by the Mills Brothers. The Millses reimbursed all their commercial clients who requested payment and also backed the cash needs of the C&A Bank. Calm and confidence were quickly restored. While customers, merchants, and cotton growers applauded both the bank and the Mills brothers for maintaining their business obligations during the brief panic, the two cases were delayed in the busy state docket. And there were further delays after the death of

Samuel Williams in September 1858. In February 1859 the court dismissed the Mills case and absolved them of the lower court's $100,000 fine. In March, while the Mills Company returned to their long-held operations, Judge Roberts delivered the ruling that the C&A Bank's 1835 charter was invalid due to it having been filed in 1838, three years after the inception of the Republic of Texas and the approval of the Constitution, which prohibited banking in Texas without a charter from the legislature—whose political bias was against banking! The C&A Bank was closed; still, Williams has a claim at being the father of Texas banking. The resilience and expansion of the antebellum Texas economy is nothing short of incredible given the shortage of cash in circulation and the prohibition against formal banking. The C&A Bank was the last semi-formal banking effort in Texas for the next decade. In the meantime barter and, by 1858, "services" of some 2,600 "unregulated" private money lenders operated in Texas—providing an entirely new dimension to *caveat emptor*. The Texas attorney general took no action against these rogue quasi-bank operations.[29]

Despite his serving on the Texas Supreme Court, Roberts was never far away from the Democratic political pulse of the state. As if the elections and campaigns of 1855 had not been an unsettled period of ruckus, Roberts noted that "the year 1857 witnessed the most exciting political canvas [campaign] that had ever before that time occurred." The Democratic Convention in 1857 was held in Waco, scarcely seven years after the booming Brazos River village was founded by Shapley Prince Ross. The factional political lines that were initially drawn in 1855 were further defined when Hardin R. Runnels,—a disciple of Calhoun, wealthy cotton farmer from Bowie County, lieutenant governor during the Pease administration, and vocal states' rights advocate—was nominated for governor. U.S. Senator Sam Houston, shunned by the Democratic Party, returned to Texas to challenge Runnels. Roberts noted, "They, Sam Houston and Jesse Grimes for lieutenant governor, ran under the claim of being 'old-line Democrats' independent of and opposed to the extreme states' right views of the regular [Democrats]."[30] Roberts recalls that there was general concern that Runnels could carry the state given the extensive campaign Houston launched, noting the old soldier's energy on the stump, when he "seemed exhaustless [sic]." The Old Hero drew large crowds, making at least sixty speeches to what seemed solid support. "His reference to what he had done for Texas, and at San Jacinto, which were made in that grand style of which he was pre-eminently capable, had a telling effect, especially on the old settlers. He denounced the democratic convention most bitterly, and his pronunciation of the name of the place where it was held at "Wacco" (Wack-ko) was derisively uttered to throw odium on that body."[31]

The population of Texas in 1850 (212,592, of whom 154,034 were white and 56,558 were Black) had more than doubled by 1857 to over 550,000. Most of the new influx came from the deep, or lower cotton-intense South—South Carolina, Alabama, Georgia, Mississippi, and Louisiana—followed by European immigrants.[32] Over 85 percent of the population was concentrated in East Texas, southward to the coast between the Louisiana state line and Galveston. Once established in Texas, this concentration of newly arrived slaveholders from the deep South dominated the economic, political, and social life in antebellum Texas, producing 90 percent of the state's cotton. Thus a vocal group of pro-slavery fire-eaters worked to protect King Cotton. Cotton production in Texas grew by 643 percent, from 58,071 bales in 1850 to 431,463 bales by 1860. Opposition from Lewis Wigfall, John Marshall, and Williamson Oldham was vicious, calling Sam Houston a traitor to the South—with Houston referring to Wigfall as "wiggletail." While the voting pattern of the European immigrants was mixed, a majority of the southern immigrants, attracted to Texas by land promoters like Jacob De Cordova, were connected with the cotton business. This raised concerns over northerners and recent arrivals influencing policy in the South, and thus southern immigrants voted for Runnels. Senator Charles Culberson noted that Houston was "supported in the main by the remnants of the Whig and Know-Nothing parties," and because of his vote against the Kansas-Nebraska Bill (he was one of only two southern senators in opposition), he "became politically distasteful to a considerable body of Democrats."[33]

Sam Houston lost by nearly 9,000 votes out of 56,180 votes cast. The attacks on Houston continued. In the summer of 1857 Frank Bowdon died. He was Roberts's close friend from his days at the University of Alabama and was a rising star in the Texas Democratic Party. Shortly thereafter the Texas legislature had to select a U.S. senator to replace Thomas Rusk, who committed suicide in July 1857. They selected Judge Roberts's friend and preference James P. Henderson. The year 1857 was when Roberts first traveled west of the Brazos River, visiting Austin for the first time to assist both Henderson and Wheeler. To ensure that Judge Wheeler, following Hemphill's election to the senate, would be named the chief justice, Roberts personally drafted a series of resolutions of support to ensure his speedy appointment. James H. Bell, a Unionist, was selected by supporters to fill the empty third seat on the court.[34]

Tergiversation

Disgruntled Democrats who controlled the legislature took an additional preemptive step, electing Chief Justice Hemphill to the Senate, even though Sam Houston had two remaining years in office. Any idea that this would pressure Houston to resign tremendously underestimated Houston. Sectional tensions between the North and South continued in the Congress upon his return to Washington, fueled by Houston's resolution, much to the surprise and "startled reaction" of the Senate, calling for the establishment of a protectorate over Mexico, Central America, and Cuba and "for the reopening of the African slave-trade, and the creation of additional slave States." Houston's motive, regardless of his "lame-duck" status, was not clear. Historian Randolph Campbell concluded, "Perhaps he was seeking a diversion for a nation wracked with sectionalism, or he may have genuinely wanted to continue expansion of the southwest." One result of Houston's resolution was that the topic of reopening the slave trade was publicly discussed in Texas. Houston left Washington for Texas on March 10, 1859—never to return North again.[35]

Judge Roberts became concerned in early 1858 that the Democratic Party had not done and was not doing enough to prepare for the next gubernatorial election. Governor Runnels had little impact as news of depredations on the frontier and along the Rio Grande went unsolved by a combination of ill-trained federal troops garrisoned in frontier forts and a meager force of Texas Rangers that could not fully protect the vast area under attack. The campaign of 1859 hinged on three principal questions: protection of the frontier against cross-border Mexican raids and Indian depredations, calls to reopen the slave trade, and lobbying for the dissolution of the Union. From the day Houston lost the 1857 election there was little doubt that he would run for office again. His term in the U.S. Senate had ended, but he was not yet ready to be a gentleman farmer—as he so often told his friends. Houston, under no clear party label, opened his campaign for governor in Nacogdoches among an old-line friendly East Texas crowd of friends, veterans, and local farmers. Roberts noted that "he made a conciliatory speech, in which he claimed to be an 'old-line Democrat' in favor of the Union and the Constitution and opposed to all the new-fangled 'isms' whether they arose in the North or the South, that were producing a sectional division which endangered the safety of the Union."[36] Neither Houston nor the incumbent Runnels traveled much in 1859 to campaign, leaving others to convey their messages. Unlike in his previous campaign for governor, Houston—since he was "the party"—set his own platform, promising to protect the frontier. He protested against the importation of African slaves, strongly extolled the federal Union and Texas' role in the Union, and appealed with great effect to his old comrades-in-arms, conservative farmers, and religious groups. Furthermore, he did not dodge the Kansas-Nebraska issue, clearly stating that he "owned the vote" and that was all there was to be said! Unlike in 1857, when he approached audiences on his role in national issues, Sam Houston concentrated the few appearances and interviews he made by focusing on the future of Texas and Runnel's inability to protect frontier settlers.

Houston prevailed, winning the 1859 governor's election by about 10,000 votes. However, while his victory offered some encouragement that the state could be saved from disunion, the peace was shattered by the rise of a well-organized movement to change the direction of Texas, a hostile Democratic state legislature, and a state supreme court that had no sympathy for those who did not support states' rights, popular sovereignty in the territories, and the protection of southern traditions and institutions—namely slavery.[37]

By 1859 Judge Roberts was comfortably seated on Texas' highest court (salary $2,000). He had amassed over 2,800 acres in Hunt, Shelby, Smith, and San Augustine counties and owned seven enslaved people, sixty cattle, and four horses. He had emerged as one of the leading party champions and power brokers of states' rights.[38] Beginning in the mid-1850s he proved to be a major leader in pushing back the Know-Nothings' threat and forged new alliances at the grassroots county level to expand the pro-slavery wing of the Democratic Party. Years of experience traveling the back roads of East Texas as a county lawyer paid off when he joined the Texas Supreme Court. It was evident that Texas and the South were on a path to confrontation with the northern radicals and federal government. In December 1860 Judge Roberts, in a four-part weekly series in John Marshall's *State Gazette,* provided one of most detailed accounts of Texas' road to secession. The state's path to disunion would be through defeating his great friend, erstwhile political opponent, and dedicated Unionist—Sam Houston.[39]

Judge Roberts's leadership and political clout were unmistakable. Following the death of Senator Henderson, the party wanted a staunch states' rights representative in Congress. The idea of serving in the U.S. Senate appealed to Roberts, yet a small but intense group of party stalwarts preferred that Roberts remain in Texas and on the bench, to follow through with his active role of defending and articulating the case for slavery, southern traditions, and states' rights. While he had gained many supporters across the state campaigning and organizing for the party, his place was in Texas. Having long desired the senate seat, friends of Louis Wigfall—while respectful of

Roberts—advanced their fire-eater for consideration by the legislature. Wigfall, whom Roberts admitted was "the most violent partisan in the state," was a much better speaker than Roberts, and in the face of the radical northerners in Washington, Texas also believed Wigfall was more forthright and combative. He was elected, and Roberts turned his attention to shaping the philosophical foundation for the protection of slavery. At what point Roberts decided that secession was the best path forward for Texas is unknown.[40]

As Judge Roberts worked in Texas, the newly seated Senator Wigfall more than lived up to his fire-eating reputation, quickly being censured for what was determined "arrogant speech" to the Senate. Shortly after his arrival in Washington, Wigfall placed all in the chamber on notice that the South, if needed, would seek world opinion to dictate her own terms, boasting, "Cotton is King . . . he waves his scepter not only over these thirty-three states, but over the island of Great Britain." Thus, he declared, "Queen Victoria herself must bend the knee in fealty and acknowledge allegiance to that monarch." Soon thereafter President-Elect Lincoln was under great pressure from the New York financial community as well as British investors and diplomats over any form of blockade of southern ports that threatened to cut off exports of southern cotton—over one-third of which was produced in Texas. Senator Wigfall's attitude and attacks would not be forgotten by many Republican members after the war when they refused to seat Senator-Elect Oran Roberts from Texas.[41]

One of Roberts's first drafts of his views on slavery, strongly influenced by John Calhoun, was "Constitutional Exposition of the Right of Protection of Slave-property in the Territories of the United State." While it was never formally published, the ideas and assessment articulated in this document found their way into many of his presentations and publications throughout 1860. Following his ideas on the theory of property, he concluded that any limits on the freedom of movement or ownership of slaves could not prevail. Roberts wrote essays on the rights of white citizens, on the doctrine of popular sovereignty, and the overriding principles of the basis of American liberty. Many of these positions were in response to the widely publicized Lincoln-Douglas debates in 1858, in which Douglas promoted the policy of a "Freeport Doctrine" that legislatures in the new territories could pass laws to limit slavery.[42] Roberts believed that to limit slavery in newly created territories would be a clear violation of the rights of whites in the existing slave states, and he further implied that it could quickly shift the political balance in Congress to the detriment of the southerners:

> If then it is the duty of the General Government, as the trustee of this property and rights arising out of it, to provide the means for equal distribution of the benefits to each and all the State and not to distribute then according to the mere preference of a majority, then it must not suffer such discouragement of slave labor to be affected either by its own action or by the actions of the territorial legislature, either by prohibition or non-protection," nothing the fare course forward was for the federal government, ". . . should be indifferent, impartial, neutral, as to the species of property that should be introduced [and controlled] into the territory.[43]

A series of dramatic events increased popular support for proponents of secession in Texas and across the South. The most troubling incident to white southerners was the attack by abolitionist John Brown on the federal arsenal and garrison at Harper's Ferry, Virginia, in October 1859. In addition Hinton Helper's book *Impending Crisis* "preaching revolution to the non-slave holders of the South and insurrection to the slaves" further fueled white unrest.[44] The implications of the Brown raid, heavily funded by abolition groups, according the historian Walter Buenger, illustrated "just how vulnerable the South was and how determined northerners were to destroy slavery." Roberts and his allies soon had more reason to be concerned. Shortly after news of the raid at Harper's Ferry reached Texas, a seemingly unconnected incident on the Rio Grande at Brownsville illustrated how defenseless the place was, unprotected by the federal government: the bandit Juan "Cheno" Cortina and his army of gunmen seized the town with impunity.[45] News of the murder of a number of citizens traveled fast. The *New York Daily Tribune* advised readers that outlaws threatened Texas with "fire and sword." Indian raids, on the frontier only a hundred miles west of Austin, stretched nearly a thousand miles from the Red River to the Rio Grande, further demonstrating the ill-prepared response of federal troops. Hard-line northern Republicans in Washington were not eager to assist Texas in any way with additional appropriations or troops—especially in the face of hostile attacks from newly arrived Texas Senator Louis Wigfall! In the extremely hot and dry summer of 1860, as Randolph Campbell notes, "beset for years by fear and intolerance, Texas' slave society finally gave in to near-total panic," when a series of fires in a dozen cities swept the state, known as the "Texas Troubles," fueling rumors of a threatened slave revolt that never materialized.[46]

By 1860 there seemed to be little Sam Houston or anyone could do to slow down the passage to disunion. One remote possibility was that if Houston was nominated as the presidential candidate of one of the major parties, that would dispel the need for disunion. There was a vast amount of opinion about what should happen and speculation on when it should happen. Outside forces, both abolitionists and radical "Wide Awakes" (supporters in the north) and fire-eaters in South Carolina, descended on Texas. The personality of General Houston had a major impact on the growing debate. Houston was the hero of East Texas and there had been great trust in his military and leadership ability. The split between longtime friends Roberts and Houston can also be traced to the attention given to the general's response to the resolutions and proposition from South Carolina sent to Texas as a means to ensure and encourage support for secession. The Unionist Houston was fully at odds with the secession champion Supreme Court Judge Oran Roberts. The Texas newspapers statewide wasted no time. They played a major role as the primary outlet for news, numbering over seventy newspapers across the Lone Star state, none more vocal than John Marshall at the *State Gazette* in Austin—

the de facto political voice of the disunionists in the Democratic Party.[47]

Marshall was quick to advocate the rush to secession, noting in the "Spirit of the Texas Press":

> We have always been a lover of the Union, so long as equal justice was meted out to all. But in the event of the election of Lincoln, the Union will scarce be worth preserving. Our submission to his administration will be a virtual relinquishment of our rights under the Constitution, and a tacit recognition of justice of the anti-slavery cause. This we know, the South will never do! Too much warm, generous blood flows in their veins for this! When the time arrives for action—when the tocsin sounds from every southern hill top—our life upon it, there will be no hesitation then, but with one consent they will "'take up arms against the sea of troubles, and by effort end them."[48]

Next to this column was a detailed article on "Military Preparation."

Texans and southerners generally underestimated the likelihood that the North would forcibly resist secession, or that foreign nations would not rally to support the South, and the lack of industrial resources needed to wage war successfully. These failures doomed the South's efforts from the beginning, and led to the widespread destruction of the South. Furthermore, Texans also failed to consider the impact of removing federal troops from their role in the protection of the frontier. Even so, there was not a clear path. By 1860 new immigrants from the South comprised over 80 percent of the Texas population. While some 35 percent of the farmers in East Texas owned slaves, west of Austin on the frontier, slaveholders were scarce. While cotton dominated East Texas and grew along the major river basins, Roberts in a keynote address to the Smith County Agricultural and Mechanical Society in Tyler explained that Texas also raised cattle, grew sugar, and expanded the lumber business. Texans were gradually expanding the number of cottage industries, which, while the commercial classes in Texas were small in number, were establishing a solid base of manufacturing to address the demand for agricultural and consumer goods. He noted, "Texas gave promise of making it one of the richest states in the Union."[49]

In large part concerns in Texas and the debate over disunion revolved around the future treatment of new territory, and were reflected in over a decade of filibustering intrigue south of the Rio Grande in Mexico and Central America as well as pushing westward to open new lands. Historian Robert Merry noted, "The war was, at its foundation, not about whether slavery should be allowed to continue in the 15 Southern states where it was legal in 1860—not even Lincoln in his first inaugural address contested that—but whether those states should be allowed to legalize it in the western territories and the future states those territories would become."[50]

Notwithstanding all the tension and debate over secession, the Texas economy and population continued to grow and expand. The *Texas Baptist* reported "an immense flood of immigration is pouring into Eastern Texas," seemingly unconcerned over reports of the longest and severest drought Texas had known. Only weeks before, "the upheaving of friends" of Sam Houston had gathered in Tyler, describing themselves as the Constitutional Union Convention to stop the "uprising." Ignoring Houston's supporters, the *Tyler Reporter* changed the newspaper's masthead motto to "The Lone Star of Texas, may it never grow dim." Into these unfolding dynamics stepped Judge Roberts, as Walter Buenger notes: "Still, as Roberts, a leader of the annexation movement in 1845, pointed out, even secessionists still had the emotional commitment to the United States that had played such a role in the annexation fifteen years earlier. Roberts well remembered the election of 1859, when Democratic extremism had caused his party's defeat. It had seemed previously that every time Texas's party leaders or public officials threatened the nation, they were rebuked by average citizens. *This did not happen in 1860–1861.*"[51]

The Secession Convention: "A Blaze of War"

The fall of 1860 set the stage for the secession of Texas. In October

Roberts and John Reagan had discussed the legal steps needed to call a convention. The city of Austin soon became the hotbed for the revolution as the turmoil and tempers over the 1860 presidential election pitted the Unionists against the hard-line secessionist Democrats. Some, like Judge Peter W. Gray, had concerns similar to those of Sam Houston, offering candid assessments in the *State Gazette:*, "There is no immediate danger to us in Texas, and no necessity for hasty action, at the risk of so great injury to our own cause. The matter involved is the safety of the State in the Union, or the establishment of a separate nation."[52] However, popular sentiment apparently indicated that if Lincoln won, Texas would secede. John S. "Rip" Ford, learning of the pending crisis in the capital, quickly rode from Brownsville to Austin. One observer noted that upon arriving, Ford "found the capital a scene of feverish activity, for Abraham Lincoln had just been elected President by a largely sectional vote. Up and down the streets marched groups of secessionists waving torches and carrying signs condemning Lincoln and the 'abolitionists' government. Ford became immediately an active agitator." Notwithstanding his close ties to Governor Houston, Ford had an independent streak and a record of condemning federal intervention in Texas. He was also keen on filibustering south of the border and had maintained close contact with the Knights of the Golden Circle in full disregard of any Union threats. Quick to disrupt Union meetings with chants of "damn the Union and Lincoln's Black Republicans," Ford joined the rebellious group of fire-eaters headed by Oran Roberts, John A. Green, Attorney General George Flournoy, William P. Rogers, George W. Baylor, and C. R. Johns. The *ad hoc* group of plotters (co-conspirators), ignoring Texas law and its constitution, met in Flournoy's office, and without Houston's or the legislature's authority, Roberts issued a call for a convention in Austin. To support the cause, Ford helped stage a huge parade starting at the capitol and moving down Congress Avenue, riding a white stallion and followed by bands and carriages full of supporters waving the Lone Star flag.[53]

Rumors of what historian George Woolfolk noted was a disproportional amount of "paranoia" on the course of Texas and the South followed the mysterious fires that plagued a number of Texas communities, along with the heightened implied activities of abolitionists and the election of Abraham Lincoln.[54] The full scope of Roberts's activities in the behind-the-scenes orchestration of the forces toward secession may never be known, yet among the Democratic leaders, it was clear that the planter class and the pro-secession editors recognized him as the philosophical and spiritual leader both to shape the context for Texas disunion as well as to set secession in motion. Roberts, one of the leading jurists of his era, was well aware of the primary challenge and public appearance of their rebel actions facing the challenge to achieve legitimacy in their extra-legal call for secession. Weeks of planning for the convention by Roberts were backed by the group of co-conspirators and confirmed in a public address in Austin on December 3, 1860. He followed with a detailed justification published beginning on the December 8 with four page-long installments in the *State Gazette.* Each issue had the following preamble: "Fellow Citizens: A public expression of my views in reference to the impending crisis, has been solicited by gentlemen of all parties. It is a time for all men to speak out. I shall not hesitate to express my opinions freely." It continued, "The revolutionary party of the North, have for years past advanced step by step, towards the destruction of our domestic institutions. A *single Federal gun aimed* at a withdrawing state, *will kindle a blaze of war* from the Potomac to the Rio Grande."[55]

The semblance of legitimacy to overcome the objections of Sam Houston and the Unionists was based on the secessionists' publicized claim that they acted based on tradition, backed by the law, and with the support of a majority of their fellow Texans. Guy M. Bryan, corresponding secretary for the ad hoc Committee of Safety and Correspondence, prepared a detailed letter to the public on the "situation of the State of Texas in the present unhappy exigencies," calling for immediate action, as well as stating a plan to elect delegates and support the convention.[56] Roberts's travel to Austin was delayed due to the marriage of his eldest daughter, twenty-year-old Sarah Jane Roberts, in Tyler on January 9, 1861, to Dr. Ebenezer Jones (who in 1862 became the unit surgeon for the Eleventh Texas Infantry commanded by his father-in-law). To solidify plans for disunion, the Secession Convention met in Austin on January 28, 1861, at 2:00 p.m. The first action of the delegates was to elect a president of the convention, with Roberts's old political foe for a judgeship, Peter Gray of Houston, nominating Roberts, followed by the nomination of William Ochiltree, who immediately withdrew. After a brief discussion and second vote, Roberts was confirmed by acclamation. It was apparent and should be noted that the convention participants, after years of business dealings and campaigns, were well known to one another. On taking the chair, Roberts's opening remarks, which he knew would be widely publicized, were recorded by the convention secretary: "*I bow to the sovereignty of the people of my State.* All political power is inherent in the people. The power, I assert, you now represent. The crisis upon us involves not only the right of self-government, but the maintenance of a great principle in the law of nations—the immemorial recognition of the institution of slavery."[57] In his memoirs Roberts noted the scope and seriousness of the convention:

> Nearly every grade of official position, from a justice of the peace to an ex-governor, was there. One associate of the Supreme Court and five district judges were there. The incumbent Attorney General was there. Lawyers of distinction, military men, farmers, merchants, physicians, preachers were there. Men of foreign as well as native birth, old men, men of middle age, young men, were there. More than two-thirds of the number were private citizens of local influence who had never entered public life in any capacity but who had come forward to serve their State, in this great emergency . . . which had brought them together impressed the scene with a grave solemnity.[58]

Numerous speakers followed Roberts on the opening day, including Rip Ford, who made a fiery presentation calling for immediate secession, yet "warning in grave tones that war could be the inevitable result." The over 160 credentialed delegates were a broad cross section of Texans—yet in fact a somewhat elite group not fully representative of all Texans. A large majority were born in the South;

some 70 percent owned slaves (not reflective of the fact that less than 25 percent of the Texas population owned slaves); and the largest single group by profession were lawyers at 40 percent, joined by farmers and small planters. There were few Unionists in attendance, nor were marginalized groups such as the Germans and Mexicans included, which precluded any chance to advance Sam Houston's ideas to reconsider the need for disunion. Historian Ben Procter noted: "Houston [was] relegated to the position of an onlooker." Furthermore, John Reagan said, given the critical economic dimension of cotton to the European economy, "Great Britain and France had been for forty years working to stimulate hostilities between the North and the South, looking to disrupt the Union . . . a war would enable her [Britain] to build up her cotton planting in India." The Texas convention attracted a great deal of attention from other southern states. To help ensure that Texas joined the new confederacy, commissioners from Louisiana, Georgia, and South Carolina visited the proceedings to review their secession progress and to urge quick ratification in Texas. A copy of the "Ordinance of Secession" passed by the state of Alabama, styled after South Carolina's ordinance, was provided as a sample course of action.[59]

One indication of the tremendous impact and gravitas of Judge Roberts in presiding over the revolution was that he both selected the delegates to be appointed and reviewed each working group's agenda of items to be submitted to the key Committee on Foreign Relations and the powerful Committee on Public Safety. Roberts and the organizers of the rebellion did not want to have their actions turn into an armed confrontation with federal forces in Texas and were therefore careful to limit any such appearance of overt hostile action by the Knights of the Golden Circle. Over the next few days the delegates debated the secession ordinance. One key division involved the need to submit the outcome to Texans for a vote. A secret late-evening session ironed out the details and the wording to be presented for a final vote of the delegates on February 1. Texas and Georgia were the only states to submit their secession ordinances to statewide voter ratification.

Once the canvas was complete, Judge Roberts requested that Governor Houston be notified of the final proceedings and invited to the capital chambers for the vote. The judge felt Houston's presence, regardless of his opposition, provided credibility to the final decisive action of the convention. While special invitations were issued to key leaders, anxious Austin citizens filled the lobby, gallery, and aisles to overflowing. By midday Houston agreed to attend. In what must have been an incredible scene, the Old Warrior entered to "deafening applause." Roberts recalled, "Every nook and corner of the house was occupied. As seen from the Speaker's stand [where he awaited Houston], the appearance presented [a] spectacle of faces, beaming with anxious expectations." Governor Houston was escorted and seated on the right of the presiding President Roberts, who long ago as young lawyer, in 1841, had received one of his first jobs in Texas handling Houston's private legal business affairs. Upon the completion of the roll call vote of the delegates, the ayes were 166 and the noes, 8. As the tumultuous cheering welcomed the sweeping victory, a group of the ladies of Austin entered to present the gathering a large "Lone Star Flag." Throckmorton, one of the eight who stood and cast a no vote, was confronted by loud hissing from the crowd. Throckmorton again rose to his feet and in a loud clear voice addressed Judge Roberts, "Mr. President, when the rabble hiss, well may patriots tremble."[60]

With adjournment Roberts remarked to Houston, "General, I am pleased to see you here today." Governor Houston quietly responded, "I hope we will have many happy days yet."[61]

The next morning the convention met in a closed secret session to approve the full and extensive authority for the Committee on Public Safety and their "agents" with "almost absolute power" to set siege at once to all federal property. Given his extensive military experience Colonel Ford, to no one's surprise, was given command of all Texas troops in South Texas and instructed to capture all the forts along the Rio Grande—before Texas voters endorsed the secession![62] The committee then confirmed the date of February 23 for the statewide ratification vote, with ballots boldly marked, to avoid any confusion, with just two choices—"FOR Secession" and "Against Secession." After selecting six representatives to send to Montgomery, Alabama, for the first convention of the initial six seceding states—Louisiana, Mississippi, Alabama, Florida, Georgia, and South Carolina—they adjourned. In an effort to explain that the convention's action was not a rebellion, but instead only an exercise "of the rightful constitutional functions of each state," to support these claims the convention approved a postscript to the proceedings with the release of the "Declaration of Causes which Impel the State of Texas to Secede from the Federal Union." Furthermore, the declaration was an additional effort to ensure a favorable secession vote. The declaration was ordered to be printed, with 10,000 copies in English and 2,000 each in German and Spanish, a common practice then for important state documents.[63]

In preparation for the ratification vote, Roberts on February 10 issued an address titled, "To the People of Texas." The judge, the titular leader of the Texas rebellion, emphasized that Lincoln's election threatened the social and economic status of all white Texans. This was intended to unite support from both slaveholders and non-slaveholders in favor of secession. Such support was critical given the fact that slaveholders were a minority among the free population of antebellum Texas, with Campbell noting that the number declined from 30 percent of the state's heads of household owning slaves in 1850 to 27 percent in 1860. Additionally, one question that did not gain much support, as confirmed by both Roberts and John Reagan, was why there was no strong sentiment, as suggested by Sam Houston and the Unionists, to re-establish the Republic of Texas. Nor was there any support for secession from the leading Unionist at the convention, James Throckmorton. Thus, Roberts's statement was the first detailed summary of the proceedings and actions taken by the convention. As they did not have a chance to vote on the return to the old republic, the actual preference of Texans will never be known.

Noting that the states across the South shared a common destiny, Roberts confirmed that delegates were in Montgomery to "establish a Provisional government, based upon the Constitution of the United States"—n interesting reference to the federal government, given that their goal was to separate from the Union that the Constitution guaranteed! Events moved swiftly as Colonel Ben McCulloch surrounded San Antonio, and on February 18 secured General Twiggs's surrender of the entire federal garrison, arms, and munitions.

Colonel Robert E. Lee, who had just arrived from Fort Mason, was questioned by Samuel Maverick and Thomas Devine on his "loyalty," and the next day he boarded a stage for Indianola, where he took a ship to Washington via New Orleans. "Let the brave hearts and cool heads of Texas freeman answer the question at the ballot box," Roberts concluded, with a vote on February 23—to end the possibility of "Black Republican rule."[64]

On March 2, 1861—the twenty-fifth birthday of Texas and the sixty-eighth birthday of Sam Houston—the convention reconvened with Roberts presiding to confirm the vote for secession. That action was followed by the Lone Star flag being unfurled from the dome of the Capitol. Roberts declared Texas a "free, sovereign and independent nation of the earth." He followed with an official message from Austin to Texas delegates Wigfall, Hemphill, Reagan, Waul, Ochiltree, Oldham, and Gregg in Montgomery that the "ordinance of secession by the people of Texas" was complete and ratified. In response, Houston, in one his last formal public statements, submitted to the San Antonio *Express* his "Address to the People":

> The difficulties that have surrounded me are known to you all. Fellow Citizens, in the name of your rights and liberties, which I believe have been trampled upon. I refuse to take the oath. In the name of my own conscience and my manhood, which this convention would degrade by dragging me before it to pander to the malice of my enemies, when by the Constitution the privilege is accorded me which belongs to the humblest officer. I expect the consequences of my refusal to take the oath. *I protest in the name of the people of Texas against all the acts and doings of the [secession] convention, and declare them null and void.*[65]

Newspapers across the state continued to debate the outcome of the convention and the vote. John Marshall's *State Gazette* was its usual strong voice for disunion, while the *Southern Intelligence*r and the *Clarksville Standard* condemned the rushed actions as a "gross usurpation of power." Any debate or controversy on Texas joining the new Confederacy was soon overshadowed with the coming of war. During the weeks following the Capitol meeting, Roberts received a number of calls to run for governor, and a personal request from John Ireland, to which he responded by declining due to his poor financial conditions, noting: "I have no fortune to sustain me in such a position, having not been provident in saving money," and furthermore, "I would not hesitate to make the sacrifice, did I think it necessary for the interest of the State in sustaining the cause of the South. I believe that the State could select one equally or more competent than myself." His attention was soon turned to taking up arms.[66]

Comrades-in-Arms

There was a sudden rush by Texans statewide to muster local military units. Local volunteers were gathered, greatly influenced by the organizational efforts mainly across eastern and central Texas by the Knights of the Golden Circle in 1859–1860, with each man expected to provide his own weapon, ammunition, and if possible a horse. Units carried the name and identity of their communities: for example, the Hempstead Guards, Henderson County London Guards, the Goliad and Caldwell Minute Men, Alamo City Guards, Galveston Tigers, and the Lone Star Club of Fort Bend County. In the weeks after he left Austin, Judge Roberts returned to Tyler to address personal affairs and prepare for the spring session of the Texas Supreme Court starting on April 22. After the end of the court session in late May, he turned his attention to monitoring and assisting the local military units. When the Smith County unit commanded by Captain D. F. Green, 116 strong, went to Dallas to muster with the Third Texas Cavalry commanded by Colonel Elkanah B. Greer, the spirits of the men were high, but their training, discipline, and experience were lacking. While not formally mustered into a unit, Roberts received his first look at Confederate military preparations when he accompanied the Smith Cavalry, as "a private" and as a support to the "commissary," to assist with equipping and feeding the unit.[67]

When Roberts returned home the new state legislature was considering candidates for the Confederate senate in Montgomery. Roberts's friends Judge Thomas Devine and Rip Ford (who was on the Rio Grande commanding troops) offered their support, but before he could announce his intention, Louis Wigfall arrived in Austin from Virginia, stated his intention to run, canvased the senate who selected the senators, and secured the votes needed to be elected. Many Texans assumed in the weeks prior to Wigfall's return to Austin that he had joined the army as a colonel in the First Texas Infantry and would be unavailable for the Confederate Senate. Roberts declined to run against Wigfall, who was swiftly elected. After some confusion following President Jefferson Davis's nominating Wigfall to be a brigadier general, Wigfall resigned from the army to take his senate seat with Senator Williamson S. Oldham.[68] As Roberts waited to determine what role he could play, he returned to the bench for the fall session of the Supreme Court. The judge realized that successes or failures during the first period of the war would be pivotal to southern resolve. He noted in his memoirs: "For the first two years of the war the people of Texas and other Southern States were inspired with the hope of success and incited to extraordinary efforts, with an almost universal patriotic enthusiasm in the cause, and a citizen-soldiery was incorporated into the Confederate army of as high an order of men [as] were ever muster[ed] to fight for liberty and independence."[69]

Forgoing a possible run for the newly assembled Confederate Senate, after Wigfall's win, Roberts returned to Tyler to consider his options. While he could have remained a judge or sought higher office, Roberts resigned from the Texas Supreme Court and enlisted in the military. His first efforts were to use his experience and gravitas in East Texas. He suggested that a special military "Department of East Texas" be established to help with recruiting, training, and the collection of supplies. He sent his proposal to Secretary of War Judah P. Benjamin, to Texas Senator Williamson Oldham, and to his close friend John Reagan, who was serving in Richmond as the postmaster general. Roberts also contacted a number of friends across Texas and in the army, but the young Confederate government—mired deep in red tape, and frankly not focusing on Texas—failed to respond to his plan, and the idea died without any further attention. In late 1861 came news that Brigadier General Paul O. Hébert, commander of the Confederate Department of Texas, with its headquarters in Galveston, planned to issue a call to raise thirty companies of infantry immediately. Following the adjournment of the Supreme Court in late December, Roberts went directly to Galveston to confer with Hébert. Between the opening of hostilities and his departure to the army he authored a dozen court opinions. By mid-January 1862, Roberts returned home to Tyler and the call was issued to muster a regiment of infantry in East Texas. The recruiting poster stated, "Troops Wanted—Fellow Citizen of Texas: —The great struggle of this war will be upon us in a few months. Now is the time to get ready for it. An attack upon our coast is daily expected, and at least five thousand more troops are needed to defend it. *They are needed now.*"[70]

The recruiting of troops was brisk. Letters and inquiries poured into Tyler. The new recruits preferred to serve in the cavalry on horseback. The judge's nephew, Oba E. Roberts, wrote that "if it were cavalry I could succeed better as Texans dislike to walk." By early March 1862 ten companies were mustered in and sent to Camp Lubbock in Harrisburg, east of Houston on Buffalo Bayou, the site of the first railroad terminal in Texas. The troops were officially inducted into the service of the Confederate States of America effective on March 14, 1862. On the same day Roberts was appointed a provisional colonel of the newly designated 11th Texas Infantry by General Hébert. From his first day on duty Roberts aspired to be a brigadier general, yet despite repeated appeals to the Confederate secretary of war as well as "Texas friends" in Richmond, the promotion eluded him. Roberts resigned from the Texas Supreme Court, in a letter to Governor Francis Lubbock, effective March 30, 1862.

Also located in the camp was Colonel Richard Hubbard's 22nd Texas. The initial excitement of the mustering was soon lost as poor conditions in the camp and its swampy location resulted in sickness and low morale. A shortage of weapons, uniforms, and camp equipment delayed training. An inspection by the Texas medical director confirmed that the health problems and sickness were due to bad water, poor nutrition, and a dirty camp. Roberts reported that of the 622 men in camp, 232 or 37.3 percent were unfit for duty. The challenge for Colonels Roberts and Hubbard and their officers was to maintain morale, clean up the camp, train and feed the troops, and stymie those who wanted to go home. To address the situation, Roberts was given permission in June to move his troops to better living conditions nearer his home at Camp Clough in Tyler. Once her husband's unit was back home, Frances Roberts organized the local ladies to set up a temporary hospital to nurse the sick and comfort the homesick of the 11th Texas Infantry. The first hint of war on the home front was the shortage of everyday items such as coffee, mustard, needles, and salt. Roberts conducted another recruiting drive to replace those who were ill and was aided by the new Confederate conscription law of April 1862, which extended enlistment from one year to three years.[71]

After weeks of camp duty, Brigadier General Henry McCulloch ordered Colonel Hubbard's 22nd Texas Infantry, Colonel Overton Young's 12th Texas Infantry, and the 11th Texas Infantry to prepare to move to Little Rock, Arkansas. With a large number of men still sick, Colonel Roberts was ordered to remain in camp after the 11th departed. Roberts was ready for action and felt as he was the ranking colonel among the three units, based on his date of rank, he should be in command and not left at Tyler when his unit headed north. This started a year-long series of appeals by Roberts to the higher command to rectify the confusion and allow him the command position he felt he deserved. In September 1862 he was ordered to bring the rest of the men from Tyler to Little Rock. Upon arrival, he once again appealed to be placed in command. The request was delayed, and he remained in Arkansas as the rest of the units were ordered to Vicksburg. His garrison assignment placed him in charge of a convalescent camp. In January 1863 he was granted a sixty-day leave to take his son, who was sick with typhoid fever and a private in the 11th Texas, home to Tyler to receive medical care.[72]

Following his leave in Tyler Oran traveled to the 11th Texas at their new position in southern Louisiana. With the temporary leave of Colonel Randal, Roberts was placed in command of the brigade now attached to Major General John G. Walker's "Greyhound" Division of the Trans-Mississippi Department. The units were moved down the Red River on steamboats to Alexandria, where Camp Texas was set up south of the city. When Colonel Randal returned, Roberts was ordered to sit at the court martial of Brigadier General Henry Sibley on charges of abandoning his command due to drunkenness. Roberts was joined on the court of inquiry by his friend Hubbard and two Louisiana officers. The protracted hearing dismissed the charges but ordered that Sibley never again be placed in overall command of troops.

Roberts returned to Camp Texas and rejoined his unit, which was being held in reserve until further notice as a reinforcement for Major General Richard Taylor. Fighting in southern Louisiana intensified as Union forces endeavored to gain a foothold along the Mississippi River after they captured New Orleans. By September the Union advance through Louisiana had stalled, giving the Confederates an opening to go on the offensive.[73]

By November 1 federal forces had pulled back to New Orleans, leaving a rearguard of about 1,800 infantry troops and a small contingent of cavalry near the small town of New Iberia and camped at the Chretien Point plantation along Bayou Bourbeau. Roberts had considered returning to Tyler due to "ill health." However, events quickly came to a head. Scouts reported back to General Taylor on the exposed position of the federals. Taylor then ordered Brigadier General Thomas Green, a veteran of the Indian wars, commander at the siege of Monterrey in Mexico in the 1840s, and former clerk of the Texas Supreme Court, to marshal the nearest units for an immediate attack. Quickly a composite force was assembled composed of the 15th Texas Infantry commanded by Lt. Col. James Harrison, the 18th Texas, under Col. Wilburn King, and the 11th Texas Infantry commanded by Colonel Roberts. Green placed Roberts in overall command of the units and ordered him on the night of November 2 to report to his headquarters with "your whole command by daylight tomorrow morning." All three units were awakened, packed, and marched seven miles in the dark. At first light they arrived at Green's headquarters, located in the St. Landry Catholic Church near Opelousas. As the troops finished breakfast on the church grounds, the former court clerk briefed the former Texas Supreme Court justice, ordering Colonel Roberts, in overall command, to take his 950 men south to the bayou and engage the enemy. Lt. Col. James Jones stepped forward to take command of the 11th Texas as they prepared for their first engagement of the war. The 7th Texas Cavalry commanded by Captain H. S. Smith was dispatched by Green to protect Roberts's flanks from surprise attack or harassment.[74]

The Texans under Roberts on November 3 anchored the left side of the Confederate line along the bayou. At 11:00 a.m. Green ordered the attack, with Roberts's scouts and skirmishers moving forward through a corn field, noting that "the cornstalks and weeds served considerably to conceal from view our numbers," and they probed the federal line of infantry from Indiana, Ohio, and Wisconsin. Colonel Roberts reported: "The marching in line had been very difficult on the account of the weeds, ditches, and briers in the field, and the deep gullies, logs, brush, branches, and curves of the bayou on our left. The 11th Tex Regt. encountered these curves in the bayou, and although some of the men crossed and recrossed the bayou, sinking in mud and water to their waists, it had been impracticable up to this time to keep in line all the time, notwithstanding they exerted themselves to the utmost stretch of their remaining strength to do so." As Roberts's men were breaking out in the open, the Union troops were alerted and began to have their scouts and artillery open fire almost immediately. The memoir of a "Private Porter" recalled vividly the first contact with the federals: "On the march, the men would stoop, when the shells would pass over us, whereupon Col. Roberts would cry out 'They will not hurt you, my men.' Then after a moment's reflection, he added, "Provided they don't hit you."" On the march since midnight,

Roberts briefly halted the advance to rest the men for a few minutes in a low ravine some five hundred yards from the union camp. Emerging from the ravine Roberts ordered the final charge.[75]

The headlong attack now engaged the awakened federals, and casualties were heavy on both sides. Captain (and future governor) Richard Coke of the 15th Texas was wounded in the chest. A gigantic man and a graduate of William and Mary College in civil law, Coke had immigrated to Texas in 1850, upon the recommendation of then Senator Sam Houston, and practiced law in Waco until the outbreak of the war. As the battle intensified, the unit surgeon could not respond fast enough as shrapnel raked the Confederates. Five successive color bearers from the 18th Texas were killed during the charge, and the sixth was blinded by Minié ball through his temple. Colonel Roberts's horse was shot out from under him. Unscathed, the forty-eight-year-old judge pointed the men forward. Following the intense first thirty minutes of the three-hour battle, General Green dispatched the cavalry to push the reeling enemy from the field. While Colonel Roberts's infantry bore the brunt of the battle and took most of casualties on the Confederate side, he cautiously made sure his men were not exposed to Union cavalry counter-attack in the same way that the rebel cavalry scattered and killed the yanks. Roberts in his finest (and only) hour of battlefield command led from the front and did not retreat—as his men resolutely held their forward position.[76]

When relieved from the field, Roberts, called "Old Gray" by his men, gathered his troops in Opelousas to care for the wounded. The 11th Texas received the personal attention of the commanding General Walker, who referred to the action at Bayou Bourbeau as "this brilliant little affair." General Green commended Roberts "for the gallantry of the officers and men . . . in this action." In a further honor and recognition, an officer in Green's cavalry presented Colonel Roberts and his men a Union drum captured during the fight. Roberts pointed in the direction of the retreating Yankees who professed to have their eyes on Texas: "This battle fought by Texans alone is another warning to the enemy as to what he may expect to suffer should he ever dare to meet the sons of Texas upon their own soil."[77]

Roberts and the 11th Texas returned north to spend the winter on the Red River, assigned to harass Union river traffic. His receiving neither the recognition he expected nor a promotion, along with his failing health, continued to disrupt his service. With the success at the victorious battle at Bayou Bourbeau, he had hoped to advance his promotion to brigadier general, yet he received no further recommendation from his superior officers. By January 1864 Roberts was in ill health, and he secured a furlough to return to Tyler. While he was at home recuperating, the 11th Texas was engaged in a number of actions that might have helped his advancement had he been present. Furthermore, he learned that his mentor Chief Judge Wheeler, despondent over the deteriorating course of the war as well as concerned about winning another term on the court, committed suicide on April 9, 1864. Within days friends contacted Roberts to run for the vacant court position, and to announce as soon as possible before the election became crowded with too many candidates. He confirmed his desire to run and, under a new Confederate law, applied for a medical discharge from the army. On August 1, 1864, he ran against sitting Associate Justice Bell and was overwhelmingly elected. Roberts resigned his commission and took the oath of office to rejoin the court on October 1, in the midst of reports that he was in "delicate health."[78]

Roberts and the wartime court faced critical constitutional issues regarding the rights of the Confederate government to conscript individuals. Confronted with the shortage of soldiers, the court supported the demands of the military and continued to issue rulings to expand the government power to conscript. The most controversial cases involved the exemption of ministers, foreigners who could not prove their citizenship, and state office holders, as well as regulations about substitute military service. Conflicts on the application and use of habeas corpus caused further tension across the state. At each step Roberts continued to adhere to the states' rights philosophy he championed.[79] Noting the concern with the rise of military authority at the expense of civil authority, he said,

> The [Confederate] Congress from time to time passed conscript laws, which carried to the field the great body of the citizens of the State. . . . The very old men, the lame, the blind, and the disabled, with some doctors and preachers, and the officers of the State, comprised all the men who were not in the military service in some capacity. Men in and out of the army gradually became accustomed to look to the military officers as the directors of public affairs and the arbiters of their rights and interests, and the whole country became thereby, as it were, a great military camp subject to military orders.[80]

Later that year Roberts declined an effort to recruit him to run for governor. With the surrender of Robert E. Lee on April 9, 1865, the war officially ended, yet hostilities continued into May. Within weeks Roberts's tenure on the Texas Supreme Court came to an end as the Reconstruction government under provisional governor Andrew J. Hamilton took charge. Walker's Texas Division veterans claimed one former Texas governor, Edward Clark, and three future chief executives were on the same field of battle in southern Louisiana in early November 1863: Richard Hubbard, Richard Coke, and Oran Roberts.

THE INVOLVEMENT and leadership among the returning Texas Confederate veterans had a tremendous political, social, and personal impact for the balance of the nineteenth century. These relationships formed the political and social underpinnings of the post-war era that galvanized the comradeship and efforts of Texas Democrats to regain control immediately after the war and through the Reconstruction period. These relationships began immediately after the war as Texas attempted to cope with the federal oversight. Ex-Confederates during the late 1860s had limited opportunities as the Radical Republicans controlled both the state and local government offices. Survival, perceived mistreatment, and judicial inequality, as well as the unwillingness to adjust to federal mandates, helped foment organized efforts for the Texas Democrats to retake control of the state. With the end of the Reconstruction occupation by federal troops and officials, nearly every elective and appointed political office and positions in the state was filled by former Confederate veterans. Every Texas governor from 1876 to 1908, beginning with Richard Coke through Sam W. T. Lanham in 1907, was a CSA veteran—with the exceptions of Charles A. Culberson and James S. Hogg (who was a teenager at the time of the war; his father Major General Joseph L. Hogg died on active duty in 1862).. James W. Throckmorton, governor in 1866–67, despite being one of the "Immortal Seven" who voted against secession, remained loyal to Texas and raised a company of Texas volunteers that served with distinction. Hundreds of other former Confederate officers and soldiers filled positions as state legislators, congressional representatives, department directors, sheriffs, mayors, county clerks, and judges as well as university professors and county officials. Captain Richard Coke, Major General Samuel Maxey, and former CSA Postmaster General John Reagan were post-war members of the U.S. Senate, and Colonel O. M. Roberts was elected but never officially seated in the Senate. A smaller number of veterans of the Grand Old Army of the North also played a role and held various positions. For example, Governor Sul Ross appointed a small number of Union men, including his chief of staff, former Union Army Major Holmes, and African American Union veteran William H. Holland as the first superintendent of the "colored" Texas Blind, Deaf, and Orphan School. The political dominance these Confederate veterans had in the Democratic Party before the war was fully reinstated and even stronger once they were back in control after the war. And in the case of Oran M. Roberts, orchestrator of the rebellion and secession of Texas and colonel in the CSA—he returned after the war as one of the state's leading supreme court judges, governors, and educators. Roberts's acquaintance, friendship, and political interaction with Texas veterans through the late 1890s dominated and shaped the political and economic leadership of the post-war State of Texas.[81]

CHAPTER 3

RECONSTRUCTION 1865–1877

The interest of the Southern people in slavery was not entirely determinative of the varying attitude toward the war, for some of the so-called "poor whites" and some who neither held slaves nor had any interest in the system were brave and as determined in the closing year of the war as in the opening days.

They could be continuously loyal to their state but not to the Confederacy.

— CHARLES H. WESLEY *THE COLLAPSE OF THE CONFEDERACY* 1937

Texas, having in good faith performed everything required of her, in the pacification, and resumption of federal relations, awaits the results with patient solicitude. If the war was not really waged in the "spirit of oppression and for the purpose of conquest and subjugation" she may well hope that she has done enough to entitle her to the "dignity, equality, and rights" of a State within the Union.

— ORAN M. ROBERTS TO THE CONGRESS AND THE PEOPLE JANUARY 1, 1867

THE CONFEDERACY COLLAPSED in April 1865. General Robert E. Lee's surrender at Appomattox was the beginning of the end of formal combat as units across the South and in Texas gradually received word. News moved slowly westward as General Kirby Smith in command of the trans-Mississippi Department surrendered. Richmond was in chaos. As orders went out in Texas that all military operations had ceased, Texans John H. Reagan, postmaster general, and former governor Frank R. Lubbock, his aide-de-camp, were arrested and imprisoned in solitary confinement on charges of treason, along with President Jefferson Davis. There was an interregnum of more than two months in governmental control in Texas before federal troops and representatives arrived in the state. Except for some war damage along the Gulf Coast at Galveston and Brownsville, Roberts noted, "Texas had not been scathed by the ravages of war." Soldiers left their units, many of the officers in command positions went to Mexico, and it was weeks before Texas troops from outside the state returned home—many of them sick or wounded. Judge Roberts, while awaiting the post-war federal adjustments and the status of the supreme court that were sure to come, recalled, "It is impossible to portray on paper the excitement, the despair, and the dread, mingled with the feelings of those who surveyed this passing scene."[1]

The first formal federal action in Texas came on June 19, 1865, with the arrival of Union General Gordon Granger in Galveston. After announcing that he had assumed military command over Texas, he issued the Emancipation Proclamation declaring that all enslaved African Americans were free. In many parts of the South, "an extraordinary and very perilous state of affairs had been created by the sudden and absolute emancipation," of the enslaved population, noted young Princeton professor Woodrow Wilson, of the immediate change: "bewildered and without leaders, and yet insolent and aggressive; sick of work, covetous of pleasure."[2] Gordon had no idea what to expect, yet was given practically absolute power. Shortly after his arrival he announced the appointment of Andrew J. "Colossal" Hamilton as the provisional governor of Texas with authority to organize all aspects of the civil government. A pre-war ardent Texas

Unionist, Hamilton had fled north in 1861 and accepted a commission in the Union army, rising to the rank of general. All new state and local office holders or appointees, numbering nearly 3,000, were at his discretion. Furthermore, they were required to take a loyalty oath to support of the United States, first approved by President Johnson's proclamation granting amnesty in late May 1865. Gradually a limited number of federal troops were stationed to ensure peace. Yet there were too few to be effective, given the size of the state. Former high ranking Confederate military officers and officials were not eligible for amnesty and were required to apply separately, directly to the president, for special pardon consideration. Most Confederates were eligible for pardon; for example, secessionist and Confederate officer Colonel Rip Ford temporarily moved his family to Matamoros, Mexico, but returned to Brownsville when federal officials arrived. He swore a loyalty oath and urged every Confederate in South Texas to "accept a parole, return home, and perform the part of a good citizen." Roberts, given his titular role as president of the 1861 Secession Convention and his service as a Confederate colonel, was in the group that needed approval. Refusing to apply for a pardon, Roberts found himself in limbo. Supreme Court Judge James Bell, who had maintained his Unionist stance since before the war, was appointed secretary of state. No other action was taken, and the high court sat silent. In mid-August Governor Hamilton issued orders for registration of voters and administration of oaths in preparation to calling a statewide constitutional convention.[3]

In advance of any federal review of Roberts's post-war amnesty status, and to comply with the only requirement to stand as a delegate for the upcoming Constitutional Convention, Judge Roberts took a loyalty oath in September 1865, administered by the Smith County chief justice, and then he registered to vote. Apparently no federal authority questioned this action. At some point in late 1865 Roberts joined hundreds of Confederate veterans in Mexico. Referred to in congressional reports as "Señor Roberts," he spent time in Guadalajara with other Texans, yet there is no known record of any comments by him on his brief trip south.[4] Historian Dale Baum noted, "County officials largely disregarded Hamilton's orders regarding voter registration, only requiring the payment of 'the almighty dollar' as a fee 'or a bribe'"—Roberts clearly fell into one of the fourteen exceptions and prohibited classes that required a special federal pardon to be reinstated as a citizen in good standing.[5] Roberts was elected as a delegate from Smith County. In the weeks prior to Hamilton's announcement of a Democratic Convention in Bryan in February 1866, the governor advised those who planned to be delegates that there were a number of preconditions. First, there must be a "clear and explicit denial" of the Ordinance of Secession; second, all former slaves should be allowed civil rights equal to those of the white people; and third, Texas must ratify the Thirteenth Amendment. From the moment Governor Hamilton made his demands, Oran Roberts and many former Confederates across the state voiced objections, even before the convention convened. Three groups emerged. A moderate group led by Ashbel Smith, while supporters of the secession, urged that Texans accept the outcome of the war and attempt to cooperate with federal policy in order to maintain calm in the state and to encourage economic recovery. James Throckmorton, an old-line Whig and Houston supporter, represented another group of so-called "Conservative Unionists," who had in common that they had opposed secession, but that once Texas entered the Confederacy they joined the cause. Both Smith and Throckmorton advocated that any civil rights extended to Blacks be limited to the fact they were no longer slaves. The third conservative faction of Texas Democrats were led once again by Oran Roberts, joined by hard-line unreconstructed secessionists Hardin Runnels and William M. Taylor, strongly advocating little or no change in the pre-war social fabric of Texas society, with clear demands that the formerly enslaved people be left out of the political process. Their paramount allegiance was to white Texans. In moving forward, Roberts famously noted in his memoirs, "the political government of the State was left in the hands of the white race."[6]

The Constitutional Convention of 1866 convened in Austin with sixty-three delegates. Others arrived daily during the proceedings. After some debate, Throckmorton was elected president and chairman of the convention. The three pre-convention factions prior to the official meeting were equally represented and vocal in their demands. Initially, Roberts had little standing in planning for the convention. However, to prevail over the Republicans, his plan was to unite the group of former secessionists and conservative Unionists. Throckmorton, in an effort to speed recovery, appointed thirteen committees to address a broad cross section of proposals ranging from legislation and education to public lands. Roberts cooled his vocal partisan politics to cooperate with Throckmorton and, given his legal prestige, was appointed chairman of the Judiciary Committee. From his unique legal and court experience he, joined by Reuben Reeves, Edmund Davis, and John Hancock, crafted a number of changes to the Texas legal system. The supreme court, given the approval of the relatively nonpartisan committee, was enlarged from three judges to five, and their terms were extended from six to ten years. Rotation of court hearings around the state were halted and consolidated to convene in Austin into one single session from October to June. The judge receiving the highest number of votes would be the chief justice.[7]

During the debate on the ordinance to divide the state into four equal congressional districts, the enfranchisement of all males "able to read and write," was put forward by a German contingent from San Antonio who opposed both secession and slavery. Roberts, irked by this Unionist suffrage proposal, countered with a resolution that territory be set aside for the segregation of Negroes. The proposal called for "the permanent preservation of the white race being the paramount object of the people of Texas, the legislature shall have power to pass all such laws . . . necessary and proper to secure their ultimate removal or colonization, as to give place to an unmixed white race, should it in the future be found expedient and practicable, with the cooperation or consent of the United States." With little discussion the proposal was referred to the committee on legislative affairs. Except for a few hard- line East Texas supremacists, the resolution was never addressed, as the western delegates had no interest in Roberts's idea other than the possibility of dividing the state to obtain a separate and "free" "southwestern frontier state." Roberts and his eastern allies were not opposed, feeling the new state could pay its own way for frontier defense. Yet no state materialized.[8]

Roberts, well aware of the hostilities on the frontier west of Austin during Houston's governorship in the late 1850s and during the war years when federal troops were gone, was also involved in a proposal for the Committee of Indian Affairs to cede temporarily to the United States for a period of fifty years a buffer zone against Indian attacks. The proposal was vetoed in committee.

Instead a recommendation was made to pass a resolution for the federal government to provide protection as well as a separate resolution to Governor Hamilton to appoint three commissioners to go to Washington to convey the "true condition of the frontier of Texas." Petitions to authorities in Washington did little good. This proposal was appended to the final publication of the constitution. The work of the delegates was to be codified first in a series of ordinances, "the object to readjust the state internally and externally to the new state of things the presented." The primary action was the revision and amending of the Constitution of 1845, which at the time was still regarded as in force, all of which was finally submitted to the vote of the people.[9]

There was great deal of heated partisan debate centered around the rights of Blacks in Texas. Following a vote to rescind the 1861 Ordinances of Secession, the convention limited rights for the freedmen. They had the right to sue, to enter into contracts, to hold and inherit property, and be tried in court. Roberts personally drafted the amendment in the legal code in the Freedman's Ordinance that in suits between whites and Blacks, Blacks have "the right to testify under the same rules of evidence" on their own behalf (but not against white people) and the jury and the court "shall determine credibility."[10] The official convention record noted, "Mr. R's amendment was adopted. Ayes 64, nays 17." After a long debate no resolution was arrived at on the clause in the education ordinance that gave use of the proceeds from "the school fund exclusively to white children." Provision was made for African American children in the Freedman's

Ordinance, "Providing that educational taxes collected from persons of African descent should be devoted to the education of their children"—a rather disingenuous position since the white delegates knew that recently freed Blacks had few assets to be taxed, effectively limiting local funding for their schools.[11]

The convention was followed by the legislature with the first introduction of what would be known as the "Black Codes," a means to redefine the status and position of African Americans in the post-war society as a freedmen with limited rights.[12] The state was given the federal guidelines for the Freedmen's Bureau on how to proceed. However, the legal status of the freedmen caused confusion and a split among unionists and returning Confederate veterans. Blacks were granted the right to make and enforce contracts; buy, rent, and sell real property; to sue and be sued as well as to make wills and testaments. Conservatives and former secessionists joined to limit the rights of freedmen. The new law stated they could not hold state office, serve on juries, or attend public schools, and were excluded from voting. Still bitter over the outcome of the war and post-war disruptions across the state, Roberts concurred with the new laws, expressing the view: "We never would submit to negro equality."[13] Furthermore, interracial marriage was prohibited, vagrancy laws were aimed at keeping Blacks out of urban areas, and gun ownership was limited. One major area of concern was labor contracts and regulations to prevent workers from leaving before the contract expired, which could result in the forfeiture of all wages earned. This included day labor and domestic employees. The standard labor workload for men was usually ten hours per day for no more than six days per week. Employees were encouraged when the bureau issued Circular No. 25, allowing Black tenant farmers to contract for a share of the crop rather than only for wages. Given the oversight from the bureau and military observers, historian William Richter noted, "It really mattered little what the state legislature truly intended with the passage of the Black Codes. Texas whites were not about to admit that the laws had any value at all." Although embittered with the post-war conditions, because of the demand for available labor, whites Texans did not endorse the idea of deporting all Blacks to Africa. Little is known of Roberts's activities during the last half of 1865 and early 1866.[14]

Prior to the convention Roberts drafted and released his assessment of the post-war path forward in "Objects to Be Attained in the Convention of 1866." Roberts's recommendations caused concern among many delegates and Reconstruction government officials, given his extensive role as the president of the 1860 secession convention. The vocal unionist delegates' mistrust of the "rebellious judge" had little impact on Roberts as he vigorously participated and debated key issues. The convention considered a number of his recommendations and by early April 1866 established a number of government procedures, set future election dates, determined the limits on civil litigation in regard to transactions during the war (any civil act done since February 2, 1861), but deferred to the incoming legislature the creation of rules for county elections, development of a state budget, status of public schools, pre-emption of land granted to settlers, and the need to address a labor system, aimed at limiting Blacks' self-determination. In the convention Roberts advocated taking action for "the permanent preservation of the white race," and limiting any efforts to assist any opposition political party. The delegates failed to ratify the Thirteenth Amendment, which was not endorsed by Texas until February 18, 1870. However, in one of the convention's last actions an ordinance was passed to pay the widow of General Sam Houston the sum of $1,925.00 due to the former governor for his time in office. Governor Hamilton in his closing speech expressed his strong displeasure with the delegates for not addressing the status of the ex-slaves as free citizens. While the month-long proceedings were in the hands of the loose coalition of the radical element of the Democratic Party and Unionists, Dale Baum concluded, "The convention accomplished the goals of the extremely influential but still unpardoned [by the federal government] Oran Roberts, whose rallying cry had called for 'the Certain formation of a white Man's Gov[ernmen]t' that would 'keep Sambo from the polls.'"[15]

Following the ratification of the 1866 Texas Constitution, elections for statewide offices were set for the fourth Monday in June, 1866. Due to the shortness of time between the close of the convention and the election, representatives of the "secession element" and the Union Republicans met in early April and agreed to nominate Governor Hamilton. After he declined, the Radical Republicans nominated ex-governor Elisha Pease as governor and E. H. Epperson as lieutenant governor. The opponents nominated James Throckmorton for governor and George W. "Wash" Jones, a Bastrop lawyer and former lieutenant governor. While these nominees were former high-ranking Confederate officers, their actions since the end of the war and at the convention helped bridge the divide between the anti-secessionists and the secessionists—men formerly bitterly divided in 1861. However, "At the end of the war," Baum concluded, "the basic division running through the Texas electorate thus remained in essence the same as in February of 1861." There was little campaigning and Throckmorton won easily, 49,227 to 12,168 votes, over Elisha Pease on the Union Republican ticket.[16] Roberts had been urged to run for a third seat on the Supreme Court, opting instead, given the rejection of the popular ex-Confederate by the Republicans Unionists, to support his Civil War comrade, the less volatile Richard Coke of Waco. A giant of a man, Coke had immigrated to Texas in 1850 and at the recommendation of then Senator Sam Houston was urged to open his law practice in the small village of Waco on the west bank of the upper Brazos River. He had recovered from his battle wound in late 1863 and was poised to play a major part in the post-war recovery. Calm seemed to come to Texas at last. After an adequate convention and a gradual transition to an elected government, President Johnson issued a proclamation on August 20, 1866, declaring that the rebellion in Texas was over. This was followed by both houses of the state legislature meeting in joint session to elect two senators to send to Washington. David G. Burnet was elected with little fanfare on the first ballot, but opposition to Judge Roberts's nomination by Hancock supporters, and the fact it was believed that Roberts could not qualify or take the loyalty or "test" oath for federal office, required by senators and representatives. The old-Confederate guard scuttled Hancock's bid when the *Southern Intelligencer* reported, "It seems he not only endeavored to break up the late Convention by persuading the radical member—with whom he affiliated—to withdraw and leave the body without a quorum; but also, while in New Orleans in 1864, he applied [to Union officials] for the privilege of raising a command with which to *invade* Texas!"[17] However, the election of fire-eater Roberts, on the twenty-fourth ballot over objections from Hancock, was in large part a recognition of the judge's leadership role in the recent rebellion as well as an affirmation that the "secessionist wing" of the Democratic Party still held power. Fully aware that his reception in Washington would be less than welcoming, Roberts argued that the test oath was for use as a wartime measure only and not valid, and that its use must be repealed, because its wording as it stood would disqualify nearly every southerner who had engaged in the rebellion:

"I, _____, do solemnly swear (or affirm) that I have never voluntarily born arms against the United States since I have been a citizen thereof; that I have voluntarily given no aid, countenance, counsel, or encouragement to persons engaged in armed hostility thereof, that I have neither sought nor accepted nor attempted to exercise the functions of any office whatever, under any authority or pretend authority in hostility to the United States; that I have not yielded a voluntary support to any pretend government, authority, power, or construction within the United States, hostile or inimical thereto . . . so help me God."[18]

A Representatius Man

Furthermore, the Unionists pointed out Roberts's pivotal rebellious role in the 1861 Texas secession and his strongly held white supremacist views, further evidenced in his proposal at the 1866 Texas Convention to marginalize the rights and freedom of Blacks. Nevertheless, Roberts was elected after making peace only with a few Unionist adversaries. The uproar in Austin at his election was only increased in Washington, given the open defiance by the northern Radical Republicans. Historian Carl Moneyhon raised the most obvious fact concerning Roberts and the old Democrats and secessionists: "The election of O. M. Roberts, the man who had presided over the Secession Convention, forced most Unionists to conclude that the Conservatives had not accepted the results of the war." Furthermore many concluded that Roberts (still considered disloyal) was elected "for the specific purpose of precipitating a fight over the test oath demanded by Congress."[19] In fact, the aim of the Unionists was to block Roberts completely from any position of power—this man who claimed "I was elected because I was believed to be a representatius [sic] man"—and to eliminate him from the political process. And in the short run they succeeded. The reconstruction course of reform and cooperation set by President Johnson, following Lincoln's plans prior to his assassination, gave way when the Radical Republicans, bent on retribution, took control of the U.S. Congress. The Radicals impeached President Johnson, but failed to convict him, and then passed new laws that placed the South under military occupation. "Congressional Reconstruction" divided the South into five military districts, with Texas and Louisiana comprising the Fifth District, under the command of General Philip Sheridan, headquartered in New Orleans. Major General Charles Griffin was assigned to oversee Texas. Governor Throckmorton, who had served in a difficult postwar transition role "with dignity" and what John Reagan expressed as "political integrity and moral courage," was abruptly removed from office by Sheridan using the martial law authority given him by Congress. This was followed by the removal of the entire Texas Supreme Court. Sheridan made his impressions of Texas well known often commenting: "If I owned hell and Texas, I would rent out Texas and live at the other place!"[20]

The summer and fall of 1866 were a tumultuous time for Roberts and his family. He no longer received a salary as a sitting judge, and his law practice had received little attention, or incoming revenue, while he attended the convention in Austin through mid-April 1866 and prepared for the statewide elections. He returned home during the summer and then went back to Austin in August for his senate election. Frances and Oran had five of their seven children living at home, Robert, 22; Margaret, 18; Peter, 13; Fannie, 10, and one-year-old son Oran Milo Roberts, Jr., as well Frances's father Peter Edwards. To raise money Roberts sold a 209-acre tract in Smith County and their home in Tyler, moving the family to a nearby farm. Once they were settled, Roberts left Tyler for Washington City—as it was known then.[21]

Senators-elect Roberts and Burnet—along with the four Texas congressional representatives, Colonel George Chilton, Benjamin H. Epperson, A. M. Branch, and Claiborne C. Herbert (Branch and Herbert former Confederate congressmen)—traveled in mid-November by stage to Shreveport, then down the Red River to New Orleans to board a train to Washington. In preparation for being seated in the Thirty-ninth Congress, members of the Texas delegation of six representatives were urged to arrive in Washington before the opening of Congress on December 3. Governor Throckmorton, despite their political differences, urged Roberts to be careful in Washington and to use extreme caution when facing the Radical Congress. He noted that Roberts would be no stranger and was well known in the national capital for his past activities, and most northern Republicans viewed the old-guard pre-war secessionists who were still in power in Texas with contempt. Upon his arrival Roberts met with Alabama classmate Clement C. Clay, Jr., a former Confederate and now United States senator, at the Willard Hotel. It was clear that most in Washington disapproved of the Texas Convention and of Throckmorton. Furthermore, they were incensed that the southern states were sending hard-line secessionists as their selected representatives to Congress. The likelihood of being seated in Congress in this hostile environment was a political long shot. The *New York Tribune* attacked Roberts for his disunion role in the Secession Convention, his service as a colonel in the Confederacy, and his recent role in the Texas Constitutional Convention, where he had objected to the need of a loyalty oath and worked to limit the rights of Blacks.[22]

The closest Senators Roberts and Burnet got to their senate seats on the floor was as onlookers in the remote visitors' gallery. The snub in Congress was etched in his mind; over a decade later while Roberts campaigned for governor in the fall of 1878 in Corsicana, an attentive reporter noted: "In the course of his remarks he referred to his former election as a U.S. senator, and in this connection likened himself to Moses while on Mount Nebo, viewing the promised land he was never permitted to enter . . . and while a credentialed senator from this state, he was only permitted to enter the gallery and look down upon the seat he was destined never to occupy."[23] When Senator Reverdy Johnson, a Union Democrat and friend from Maryland, presented their credentials to the chamber secretary on the floor of the Senate, they were tabled, and from that moment forward ignored. Hopes of being recognized were further dashed when President Johnson's annual message to the Senate noted that the body had the right to reject any new member at will. One primary reason for the immediate rejection was that Texas had failed to ratify the Thirteenth Amendment. When Governor Throckmorton learned of Washington's distaste for Texas over its failure to ratify the Thirteenth Amendment, he notified President Johnson that there seemed to be no rush, "on the grounds that it had already been adopted by the requisite number of states [27] and had been embodied in the constitution of Texas by the [Texas Constitutional] Convention."[24] Nevertheless, with the new Radical Republican majority taking over the Congress, Roberts and other southern representatives there that opening day, hearing the demeaning speakers in the chamber attack the South, had little or no hope of being seated.

Representative Schuyler Colfax of New York wrapped up his biting remarks on the floor of the House, quoting John Greenleaf Whittier, "No black laws in our borders, No pirates on our strand, no traitors in our Congress, No slave upon our land."[25]

Seemingly undeterred by their rejection in the Senate, Roberts and his Texas colleagues conducted a series of meetings with senators and cabinet officials and made numerous visits to the White House to confer with President Johnson. In addition to determining their status in Congress, Roberts, at the request of Governor Throckmorton, presented a request to Secretary of War Edwin Stanton for an investigation of the federal army's activities on the frontier as well as federal troop incidents like the burning of the city of Brenham on the night of September 7, 1866. Another allegation was the "palpable 'white wash'" of federal troops' indiscretions across the state. Throckmorton failed to ask the federal government for an investigation of the widespread violence against Blacks. No action was taken. By the end of December it was obvious that the Texas delegation would not be seated. In addition to representing Governor Throckmorton on state business, Roberts also facilitated outstanding pardons "of particular individuals in Texas." Amid rumors that the Radical Congress might confiscate the property of wealthy southerners, Roberts was retained by Matthew Cartwright, William W. Holman, Dr. Lewis V. Greer, and William Ingram of East Texas, to secure their pending federal pardons. Roberts wrote to Cartwright from Washington that "he had the four pardons in hand . . . and we just got through yours in time," it being "about the last signed by both the President and Secretary of State William Seward." Roberts told the East Texas men that he did not believe Congress would "undertake to confiscate property." Yet with the incoming Radical Congress attacking President Johnson and repealing many of his actions, it was timely to have the pardons secure. Prior to leaving Texas for Washington, Cartwright told Roberts "to be liberal as to any terms [cost]"—concerning payment and fees, and for rushing the pardons through prior to any change in the law, "I was told . . . that about two hundred dollars apiece [sic] was the customary fee." The pardons were recorded at the county courthouse and after each man took the amnesty oath their citizenship was restored, their political rights reinstated, and property made safe.[26]

Rebellious Spirit

Eager to have the Texas position heard, Roberts drafted one of the most interesting detailed documents—a "letter"—reviewed and read by the members of Texas delegation in Washington, to articulate his views on federalism, race relations, the progress of Reconstruction, concerns that the recovery process in the South was being subverted by the Radical Congress, and most important in conclusion, the reasons the Texas delegation should be seated in the 39th Congress. Southern delegations from other states lodged complaints but none as detailed as Roberts's. The letter, addressed "To the Congress and People of the United States," was finished on January 1, 1867, and hand carried to the White House and to the Congress. This is the most detailed document of the period "published as a sort of protest," that argues the position of the South in general, and Texas in particular. The unseated Texan delegation were guests of the Democratic Party dinner at the National Hotel to celebrate the fifty-second anniversary of Andrew Jackson's victory at the Battle of New Orleans. As they prepared to depart to Texas, Roberts's letter was published on the front page of the *National Intelligencer* on January 10, 1867, and reprinted widely in papers across the South. This document is further supported and annotated by a book of notes, possibly from his trip to Washington, found in Roberts's papers at the University of Texas and published in 1908 by the Texas State Historical Association as "The Experiences of an Unrecognized Senator."[27]

Senator-elect Roberts was both candid and straightforward in addressing the rejection of their seating in Congress, their objectives, and the vitriol the members of the Texas delegation experienced in Washington. There was clearly and publicly an enormous disposition among northerners in general and the "radicals" in particular to attack the former secessionists in Texas and the South. The comments and justifications coming from the titular leader of Texas secession, orchestrated by Roberts, must have given many capital politicians pause. One historian noted, "It should be remembered that not only in Texas but in the Southwest generally sharp disagreements between man and man were customarily settled as often by personal conflict . . . it was the rough way of the frontier, and Texas was pre-eminently a frontier State." Thus, the claim that Texans had a disposition for a disloyal spirit and thus were rebellious was acknowledged, noting that violence had occurred, and that Unionists in Texas had kept a watchful eye over recent events. The Texas delegation argued that this so-called rebellious spirit was not grounds for refusing to seat the Texans.[28] Roberts was concerned that the bigger prospect of increased federal oversight and a rejection of the fundamental doctrine of perceived states rights' was in dire jeopardy:

> The whole question at issue of state rights might as well be given up—for that power alone is sufficient to centralize the government and perpetuate power in the hands of the minority that are in office. Although the President [Johnson] had often used the term *loyal* in this connection, I had supposed that he by that term [meant] to designate those who had returned to their allegiance by taking and observing the amnesty oath which he had himself prescribed as a test of loyalty.[29]

Oran Roberts was candid, albeit highly partisan, on the conditions and attitudes in the South. There are "many disappointed men and violent partisans . . . who are continually seeing things around them in a distorted light . . . who seem to be endeavoring to bring her people in as bad odor as possible before the public mind." Northern newspapers and carpetbaggers flooding into the South spreading rumors and slander added to the hysteria that Roberts indicated was exaggerated. Conditions were gradually returning to normal, with the critical problem that the disenfranchised Blacks lacked fundamental rights. Many Confederates who left home after the end of the war for Mexico, Central America, and Brazil were slowly returning. He failed to mention the large contingent of southerners in Argentina, most of whom never returned. Roberts was sure the South wanted to be a loyal part of the future of the nation, appealing to the patriotic links among all Americans: "Texas will stand by the flag of the United States against any nation on earth, and the descendants of the heroes of San Jacinto will contest the palm on any field where the country's foe may be met with descendants of the heroes of Bunker Hill."[30]

Prior to the publication of his detailed stance on the "rights" and place of both Texas and the South in the post-war political and social environment, Roberts had occasion to have a long chat with one of his pre-war political foes, Andrew Jackson Hamilton. A Unionist, Hamilton had departed Texas in early 1862 to serve in the Federal Army, only to return as the appointed provisional governor of Texas for a year beginning in the summer of 1865. He then returned to Washington to work on affairs for the Republican Party. Upon Hamilton meeting him in the halls of Congress, Roberts said Hamilton told him that he had wasted his time in Washington, because he would never be seated in Congress. Roberts's indignant reply was, "Jack, let me just tell you something! Me and my sort will in the near future control the destiny of Texas." And in time, he would be proven right.[31]

Judge Roberts and the elected Texas representatives returned without being seated. Roberts received a hero's homecoming welcome: "our people feel like he did all that could be done, under existing circumstances, while in Washington, and that in him they have an able and watchful representative, who will ever labor earnestly to promote their best interests."[32] Within a few weeks of the publication of Roberts's address in Washington the entire South was placed under federal military rule. The repercussions of the increasingly radical Congress further spread to Texas, with General Sheridan ordering in late July 1867 that Governor Throckmorton be "removed from that office" due to being "an impediment to reconstruction." He was replaced by former governor Elisha M. Pease, a Unionist whom he had defeated two years prior by more than 23,000 votes [when Blacks were not allowed to vote]. Roberts noted that the increased enforcement by the military government during reconstruction was forced "over a subjugated people." Pease quickly replaced all the officers in the state's executive offices and disloyal county officials as well as removing all the justices from the Texas Supreme Court. After over a year racial violence continued under Throckmorton, in spite of an increased vigilance by federal troops. Governor Pease was little more than an ineffective place holder and there was little or no respect among the former Confederates for the Republican appointed officials forced on the counties. The federal

Freeman's Bureau established to help protect and educate the Blacks provided ineffective.[33]

The Wilderness Years

Following the renewal of his law license, Robert attempted to restart his law practice. Not only were Roberts's legal activities drastically curtailed, but his political activities were as well. As with the executive branch, General Griffin, under new mandates during the Congressional Reconstruction, issued new procedures or "Circulars" for civilian trial by jury. Additional oaths were required and freedmen were allowed to sit on juries for the first time. Furthermore, local military officers were authorized to intervene in any court when they decided local authorities were not impartial. Protests among both judges and lawyers, especially after allowing Blacks to sit on juries, soon shut down many proceedings due inability to seat a jury, with Griffin trying to replace the civilian courts with military tribunals. An appeal by local judges and lawyers to Griffin was denied, and the courts and legal activity came to a halt. Violence across the state in late 1867 to intimidate Blacks and keep them from voting or participating in local affairs surfaced in Marshall, Waco, and Caldwell as well as San Augustine County and may have been a reason for Roberts's decision to move his family to Gilmer. Neither the Freedmen's Bureau nor the federal troops had enough resources to be stationed in every county, which meant they could not prevent much of the racial confrontation. Along with scores of ex-Confederates, Roberts was openly hostile to the bureau, in what the judge termed was "an almost constant harassment of the citizens of the country," that usurped the jurisdiction of civil officials. Only in the area of providing a limited amount of common school educational programs did the bureau have some lasting impact. The Freedmen's Bureau in Texas was phased out in December 1868.[34]

In late 1867 Roberts contacted Professor Morgan H. Looney, the founder and headmaster of the Looney School in Gilmer, Texas. A regional school, it attracted some 200 students yearly from a hundred miles in every direction. Such segregated academies, especially ones with a good reputation among whites, were highly respected as a means for education in the South. While not accessible to all, they were generally well supported by local communities and often were the only source of a formal education for their children. Courses were offered for both children and adults in English grammar, composition, Latin, Greek, and mathematics, while advanced classes for adults were offered in history, government, ethics, and science. Looney, while local church attendance of one's choice was encouraged, was a strict disciplinarian and any contentious arguments about politics or religion were forbidden. The school was the leading business enterprise in the little town of Gilmer and residents earned extra income boarding students. Roberts proposed to teach law, agriculture, and bookkeeping.

Looney, pleased with the addition to the staff, felt Roberts's presence would attract enough students to justify his salary.[35] Excited at the arrival of Roberts, Looney sent out thousands of circulars on the judge's plans to teach at the school:

> As professor of Law, Agriculture, and Scientific Bookkeeping, we have secured the service of Hon. O. M. Roberts, formerly Judge of the Supreme Court, Chief Justice of the State, and United States Senator-elect from the State of Texas. He is [so] well known to our citizens that not a word of comment is needed here in reference to his character as a gentlemen, a scholar, a lawyer, and a statesman. The course of Study in the law department will be, Blackstone's and Kent's Commentaries; Stephen's Pleadings; Greenleaf's Evidence; Story's Equity Jurisprudence; and other ordinary text-books on special subjects. The study of each work is to be accompanied by lectures on the Jurisprudence of Texas.[36]

One of Roberts's main objectives for joining the Looney School in the unsettled economic, social, and political environment was to place his young children in school—Margaret, 18 years of age, Peter, 13, and Fannie, 10. In addition to teaching, Roberts maintained his law practice and routine interaction with the local lawyers. He spent over a half-day in class and the balance of the time in his law office or in the limited access to court. In addition to the work in classrooms and law, he delivered weekly lectures on the law and Texas history, held symposiums on scientific topics, and periodically published newspaper articles. Roberts proudly noted years later, "Everything considered, it was a model school, under the direction and supreme control of one man, and many were the young women and men who received a good substantial education." After three years of teaching law classes, Roberts turned out to be a mentor for a number of future successful lawyers, among them Judge Sawnie Robertson of the Supreme Court, Attorney General John D. Templeton, Judge George Aldredge, and Governor Charles Culberson. Most likely the most successful school of period closed in 1870, when Looney departed to Arkansas to take care of his sick wife. As he prepared to depart Gilmer, the Marshall *Weekly Harrison Flag* noted, "he is well known to almost every one in Texas, either personally or, by reputation."[37]

Even during his absence from the public eye while teaching in Gilmer, Texans were entertained with stories about the Old Alcalde. Told once, they soon were reprinted statewide. While never an active farmer or rancher, other than maintaining an occasional garden, Roberts was always close to agrarian issues and concerns—which made stories connecting him with the land even more entertaining. The following first appeared in the *Dallas Herald* shortly after his election as governor:

A student at the Gilmer School shortly after the close of the war told [the] story of Judge Roberts encounter with a sow. All eminent men, like the renowned Horace Greely, at some period in their lives, conceived the idea that they are practical farmers, and on a large or small scale, try their hands at the business. So it is with Governor Roberts. Attached to his residence, near the public square in Gilmer, was a large garden upon which the governor was wont to bestow quite a deal of his time and labor in the way of planting fruit trees, cultivating vegetables, etc. Among other things the governor had a very fine sweet potato patch which he seemed to [take] pride in. There was, however, a certain sow which ranged the town commons, that had taken a fancy to the same potato patch, and had a habit of breaking through the pickets and helping herself to the sweet potatoes.

The governor stood it very patiently but seeing that the sow was likely to get more than her share of the potatoes, he set to work putting a stop to her depredations. Upon arriving home one evening after the adjournment of his law class, he found the sow in the patch at her favorite business. For one time, during a residence of over two years in that town, he seemed to get thoroughly mad. He summoned his venerable father-in-law, Mr. Edwards, who lived with him, to his assistance, to make war upon the mischievous hog. He first carefully examined the enclosure until he found the aperture through which the animal entered. He then armed himself with a [fence] rail with which to deal the hog a deadly blow, and instead of taking a position a little to one side and in convenient reach of the hole, he planted himself immediately in front of the same so as to have as he thought a fair chance at the sow as she ran out. He then told his father-in-law to turn his dog loose upon the hog and "let her come." The dog [chased] the animal around the garden a time or two when she rushed for the hole.

So frantic was the frightened animal that she did not even recognize the distinguished obstacle in her way, but with the speed of lighting she dashed through the hole, but in so doing she was compelled to pass between the legs of the governor, which threw him five or six feet in mid-air, with his rail yet elevated in his hands. He was dressed in a fine suit of dark cloth, as was then his custom, which [was] literally torn off him. The sow in making her escape, besides the damage done the governor's person, demolished three panels of the garden fence and went on her way rejoicing unhurt. Gathering himself up as best he could, the governor declared that many a time in the capacity of a judge he had had occasion to punish men for malicious mischief in wounding and killing hogs, but if he always felt as he did then he never would do so again. The incident so amused Mr. Edwards, a very sedate man, he delighted to tell all of the governor's *rencontre* with the old sow—and most heartily would he laugh over it.[38]

The Klan

The seemingly quiet environs of Gilmer did not reflect the racial tension in other parts of the state. The federal army occupation and the Freedmen's Bureau demanded, by whatever means, political and social equality for Blacks. Tribunals set up by the bureau, according to Roberts, were only interested in the rights of Blacks. By early 1868 violent outbreaks, many unconfirmed, resulted in Roberts noting in his memoirs, "The Negroes having been set free, with the prejudices of race still prevalent, were encouraged by secret societies, camp followers, and by some republicans to assert and maintain their equality with the whites everywhere and upon all occasions."[39] The inability to settle the issue of equality of the two races, given their history and the intractability of many whites, according to the judge, was the primary reason for the rising conflicts. The white response included the appearance of the Ku Klux Klan. As one writer noted, "Roberts's writings [in his memoirs] proved that he viewed this organization as one wearing a 'white hat,' literally and figuratively," further noting:

> Just when the dread of the impending catastrophe had reached its highest pitch, in many towns in sections where Negroes were numerous there would suddenly appear at bedtime a body of from fifty to one hundred men on horseback, dressed in white flowing shrouds and tall paper hats, with their faces paper-covered and with their horses covered with white sheets, marching into town in military array and passing from street to street, speaking to each other in low, guttural, indistinct tones, and the negroes visiting and passing in the street seeing them started to their homes at full speed, and, if intercepted along the way, darted into the first house they came to and remained there until after sunrise the next morning. The next morning after this parade was witnessed in any part of the country

the whites and blacks were at peace, the same as they were in slavery times, and occupied socially very much the same relations they had toward each other.[40]

Roberts attributed the Klan to a "groundswell" that did not have much impact, during that period, in Texas. This view of post-war race relations in Texas has since been clearly discredited.[41] As time passed after the 1866 Convention, where most agreed that freedmen should be adequately protected in their person and property, whites and Blacks became more combative. In Roberts's view the main source of social destabilization was the Freedmen's Bureau. This opinion has also been discredited. One major altercations and Black-White confrontations was at the cotton depot town of Millican in southern Brazos County during June–July 1868. A detachment of federal troops from Brenham arrived on July 15 to quell tensions, yet the unease continued into the fall. There were a number of Klan-like organizations that professed to represent the rights of the whites, yet instead harassed and attacked Blacks. There is no evidence either that Roberts was a member of any such organization or that he condemned such activity.[42]

In July 1869 the attacks on Oran Roberts became personal when he was notified that his son Robert Roberts, 23 years old, had been arrested by Freedmen's Bureau agents in Tyler and charged with attempted murder. According to historian Leila Bailey, Robert was caught up in an alleged race riot related to the arrest of a white man for assaulting a Black woman. Then the man attempted to avoid arrest by shooting at, and missing, the local Freedmen's Bureau officer, Lieutenant Gregory Barrett, popular with Blacks but unpopular with whites. As the incident unfolded outside the bureau office, Robert was working as a clerk in a dry goods store near the courthouse. When the owner saw the riot he called on Robert to get a gun to keep rioting freedmen in the square and out of the store. In the chaos, as Robert stood in front of the store, the gun was allegedly taken out of his hands by Richard Long, who then turned and ran into a bureau agent who confronted him. Then agents arrested Robert and sent both men and Thomas Meadows to the stockade in Jefferson, Texas.[43] There is little doubt that all in Tyler knew who young Robert's father was, and some whites believed the incident was created to discredit and harass Judge Roberts. A former Roberts law clerk, F. B. Sexton, wrote to the judge convinced that his son's charges were directed toward him, writing in early August 1869:

It was quite superfluous for you to assure me that he [Robert] had nothing to do with the matter charged against him. It is apparent my dear Judge, that the whole force of the blow is aimed at you. It is a mode selected by mean spirited local radicals and petty tyrants to punish you of the Supreme Court when white people held the governing power, for commanding with distinction a regiment and brigade in the Confederate service and etc. . . . It is a species of devilish torture resorted to by those now in power to bring you over to radical views and opinions."[44]

Judge Roberts at once came to the defense of his son as well as the so-called "accomplices" before the military commission. The hearing was little more than a sham and "show trial," much to the disgust of the local citizens. In November 1869 the son was acquitted of all charges.[45] The attack on his son only encouraged Roberts to work diligently behind the scenes to resurrect the old Democratic Party—a political label or term temporarily abandoned; they were now calling themselves "Conservatives." Efforts were expanded to determine how to restore the leadership and organization of the party to rid Texas of the Radical Republicans and limit the rights of Blacks. The Conservatives emphasized in their platform that the "Africanization of Texas" must be prevented to advance further their claims to white supremacy. Tensions ran high as the former Confederates worked to regain power, with the pro-Davis and Republican Party newspaper, *The Representative*, in Galveston, noting: "They imagine they live in a miniature Confederacy—they have no idea that the South has ever lost any of the prestige of its former glory, and any man differing with them in politics is in danger."[46]

Governor Davis created a State Police force to suppress attacks on freedmen, recognizing the limitations of the federal troops. His administration attempted to spur commercial activity with the support of internal developments, mainly expansion of the railroads. The railroads were a bone of contention to the Democrats, who complained about the public "land-give-away," coupled with northern financial backing and the heavy-handed corporate interests, yet the investment showed sizable results. By the early 1868 the Houston and Texas Central Railroad (H&TCRR), began to open central Texas from Houston, north through the Brazos Valley, to Millican and to Dallas–Fort Worth and on to the Red River. From only 341 miles of railroad in 1865, rail track mileage doubled to 711 miles by 1870, and doubled again to 1,600 miles by 1873. Railroad spurs or "taps" were added to Brenham and on to Austin, Waco, and east bound to Nacogdoches. Bisecting the cotton-rich area of Texas, some two dozen counties along the H&TC increased their production of cotton. In addition, increased agricultural production spread westward across the state. While rural Texas still dominated the landscape until the turn of the century, civilization was coming with the growth of new towns along the railroads as well as more varied services, such as mercantile businesses, gins, cotton mills, corn silos, and storage faculties. The diversification of agricultural products was critical given the declining price of cotton—at the same time that production increased—throughout the period, and reminded all of the need for farmers to be more diversified and self-sufficient. However, Texas would remain the "cotton kingdom" even as the geopolitical-economic dynamics placed the state's farmers in direct competition with the British textile industry, for example, which was investing heavily in cotton plantations in Egypt and India. "The recovery of agriculture and commerce [in Texas]," noted historian Carl Moneyhon, "represented the most significant economic trend" during the post-war years.[47]

The "Semicolon Court"

After five years of U.S. military authority over the governance of

Texas, the federal authority ended on April 16, 1870. The ensuing civilian state government resumed under the Texas Constitution of 1869, which guaranteed Black rights. Radical Republican Governor Edmund J. Davis remained in office and held onto power with his carry over appointees. One key power base was the Davis-appointed Texas Supreme Court, membership of which was reduced to three judges under the new state constitution of 1869. The new civil court was first considered an improvement over what Roberts declared was "the previous ignominy and ruin" of Republican rule and the federal military courts.

The independence of the new justices appointed by Davis was soon questioned. Roberts and other close political observers of events in Austin were optimistic that the time would soon come when they could take back control of Texas. Judge Roberts, as was later repeated by Charles Ramsdell (following the conclusions published in 1898 by Roberts), roundly condemned Davis for his "tyranny" and "aggravating and oppressive injuries suffered under the military government." The full story of Edmund Davis did not appear for more than a century and a half—not until historian Carl Moneyhon's detailed biography addressed the governor's misrepresented and misinterpreted legacy.[48] However, any meaningful change and resumption of white power would have to come from the reconstitution of the old-line Democratic Party and its victory at the ballot box. Shortly after the blanket 1872 congressional amnesty of all Confederates amending the Fourteenth Amendment, the Democrats had their first chance to unseat the last vestige of Radical Republican rule with the election of 1873.[49] With the lifting of the onerous loyalty checks under the Ironclad Oath, Texas Democrats were able to flock to the polls en masse. Believing he controlled the local election monitors in each county, Governor Davis stood for reelection. The Democrats acted swiftly to meet the challenge. One of the primary election issues was a fierce stance to halt the large subsidies to the railroads and, above all, to take back control of the government.. The Democrats wanted no candidate with friendly railroad ties, such as John Ireland or Charles DeMorse. Advocates of prohibition surfaced, and while this was not a full-fledged issue, the Democrats deflected any debate on the impending fight between the "wets" and "drys" to a stance that the state had no business intruding in this private matter. For a while, that position stood—the aim was not to let any issue deflect the primary object of winning. Thus, the clear safe choice to nominate as governor was the well-spoken Richard Coke, former associate justice of the Texas Supreme Court, Secession Convention member, and heralded battle-wounded veteran. Coke quickly raised support in every quarter of the state. The campaign resulted in a sweeping victory for Coke and a humiliating defeat of Davis, 85,549 to 42,663, signifying the end of the Radical Republicans and the beginning of the "Redeemers." Additionally, the Democrats won a majority of seats in both houses. Not accepting the outcome, Davis and the Republicans immediately challenged the results in a number of cases statewide. Most understood that this was a hollow challenge to alter the overwhelming electoral results—until the high court received a petition of a writ of habeas corpus from a jailed inmate, Joseph Rodríguez, held on a warrant for voter fraud.[50]

The Radical Republicans were not going easily. While early reports indicated that Davis would abide by the results, his Radical supporters demanded that they fight to hold control of the Texas government and, if needed, appeal to Washington and President Grant to send military support. One way to disrupt the outcome was to file objections aggressively to declare the election invalid. The case filed was a straw man, involving the mock custody of a certain Rodriguez for voter fraud, as a fabricated test case to go before the justices of the Texas Supreme Court, all appointed by Governor Davis, to rule on the validity of the election—judges Moses Walker, John McAdoo, and Wesley Ogden. Remotely connected with voter fraud, the intense and heated debate before the high court involved the meaning of a clause in the state constitution that had a phrase punctuated with a semicolon and stipulating the number of days the polls should be open at the county level. Texans across the state were stunned and livid when the court ruled the election of 1873 as invalid. Immediately judges across the state, including O. M. Roberts, Reuben Reeves, Richard

Walker, and James H. Bell, published detailed articles on the groundless court action. Once again, Judge Roberts was at a pivotal juncture of Texas history. The obvious injustice in the decision in *Ex parte Rodríguez* stirred outrage, with the Houston *Daily Mercury* noting: "A manifest sham and collusion from the beginning—such a case as a court, mindful only of its rightful duty and proper duty, would have regarded as a fraudulent effort to make use of its jurisdiction—it could only have been sustained by the court to give effect to the schemes which set it on foot."[51] The following urgent message was sent from Austin:

Austin: Jan. 5. --- The Supreme Court have decided the election unconstitutional. Rodriguez has been discharged. --- Telegram.[52]

As Davis sat barricaded in his first floor capitol office claiming he would remain in office until the end of April 1874, angry armed mobs converged on Austin. Colonel Rip Ford, Generals W. P. Hardeman and Henry E. McCulloch, and Travis County Sheriff George Zimpleman, all combat veterans and deputized to have legal authority, took charge on the capitol grounds, as Roberts recalled, to "use their influence in controlling the agitated crowds . . . all experienced in managing affairs of difficulty." The governor telegraphed President Grant for assistance to maintain him in office. The seasoned Union general realized that after eight years of occupation and economic disruption, it was time to return the South and Texas to local control. Grant's reply in mid-January 1874 was that no federal help was forthcoming. The *Galveston Daily News* was bold and dismissive in its assessment of Washington's reaction: "The people do not feel scared by such a threat, and entertain the opinion that Grant has had enough of making war upon the peaceful States." With no rescue in sight and to avoid possible violence, Davis was forced to leave the capital in ridicule and disgrace. A court reporter's footnote to the judicial opinion of the Reconstruction days concluded: "We may properly say, that the question before the court in *Ex Parte Rodriguez* received its final practical solution as a *political* and not a *judicial* question."

Governor Coke and Lieutenant Governor Richard Hubbard, along with the new legislature, were sworn into office and ratified the results of the election.[53]

A decade after Richard Coke and Oran Roberts faced the sting of battle in 1863, on January 24, 1874, Governor Coke named his unreconstructed comrade-in-arms as chief justice of the Texas Supreme Court. The Roberts Court would recast the Texas judicial system into a new post-war order in its rules of practice. The court once again rotated locations, with Roberts confirming that the term was "synchronized with the festival and frolic of Momus or Mardi Gras" in Galveston. A contemporary friend who practiced law in the port city and future biographer of Roberts was sure the judge was aware of the scope of the annual celebration, noting, "It was a season of revelry and riotous fun. By common consent all city ordinances against minor offenses were suspended and the city, so to speak, was wide open." The return of local and county celebrations across the state marked the beginning of a new post- war era—yet the recent past was not forgotten. The white-dominated Democratic Party was firmly dedicated to exercising maximum control. Historian Gregg Cantrell concluded: "With its brief but radical experiment . . . the Republican Party was irrevocably fixed in the minds of most white southerners as the party of 'Negro domination' and the 'horrors' of reconstruction." A renewed generation of white Texans, styled as "Redeemers" would usher in an era of growth, government reform, and economic development in response to over a decade of stagnation, all the while undercutting Blacks' fundamental rights. An excellent snapshot of the mid-1870s period was captured by *Scribner's Monthly* reporter Edward King, in his periodic articles first titled "The Southern States of North America," and later edited into the stand-alone volume "Texas: 1874" describing Texans rebuilding after Reconstruction.[54]

CHAPTER 4

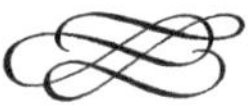

GOVERNOR 1878–1882

> *Standing in this place on the 4th day of March, 1861, as the president of the seceding convention, and acting by their authority, I proclaimed Texas a free and independent State. I did it in good conscience, believing it to be right. I now, with the same good conscience, as the governor of the State, declare Texas to have been in good faith reconstructed into the Union by the voice of its own people—marching steadily on with her sister States in the new progress of national development, and standing ready to vie with any other state in advancing the prosperity and defending the honor of our common country.*
>
> — ORAN M. ROBERTS INAUGURATION, JANUARY 21, 1879

IN THE SUMMER of 1876 the sixty-one-year-old chief justice of the Texas Supreme Court was living a tranquil life. The appointment to the court afforded Judge Oran Roberts, in essence, a life appointment that required only infrequent tenure in Austin and at district trials held across the state when the court was in session, thus allowing him ample time to spend with his family on his farm outside Tyler. In the immediate years prior to the end of Reconstruction he had operated the small law school in Gilmer. In 1873 Roberts was approached to run for governor, yet in the terms of the *Galveston Daily News*, *"he abstained to support his long time friend Richard Coke"*—with the triumphant friend appointing him as chief justice shortly after the election. The full behind-the-scenes story of how they agreed on who would run in the gubernatorial election will never be known, yet the agreement arrived at was years in the making, and their bond had been sealed long before on the battlefield in southern Louisiana on November 3, 1863, as the two comrades-in-arms charged headlong into the Yankee line of fire.[1]

During the period from early 1874 to mid-1878, Roberts concentrated his time on the Supreme Court, his family, and occasional political activities. Joining him on the court as associate justices were close political allies and friends William P. Ballinger, Thomas J. Devine, Reuben Reeves, and George Moore. With the demise of the Davis government, the Redeemer Democrats and the courts shaped and dominated state policy well into the early twentieth century. The Democratic plan was to join the political agenda strategically to the encouragement of economic development. Three immediate items dictated the changes necessary: first, a legislature that was business-friendly but not overindulgent with the railroads; second, modification of the state constitution on matters of education and taxation; and third, a fully engaged and functioning Supreme Court.[2]

Judge Roberts's role and challenge was to help navigate a middle ground between those in favor of subsidizing railroad expansion and those in the Democratic Party and the public who objected to what they viewed as unwarranted, excessive handouts. The high court thus had to deal with a number of pending cases involving railroad land claims and objections to any further granting of additional portions of the public domain. The proceedings were further aggravated by the fact that many of these claims derived from railroad companies owned and controlled by northern industrialists. Among the matters referred to the court, the two leading cases that defined the state's role in economic development and land grants were *Bledsoe v. The International Railroad Company* (1874) and the opinion arrived at in *Keuchler v. Wright* (1874) right-of-way dispute demands of the El Paso and Pacific Railroad. The high court, the legislature and the public, as well as Governor Coke and state Attorney General William Alexander, were split over the railroad issue. To smooth the waters, Roberts, as chief justice, wrote what court recorder Alexander Terrell termed a "separate" opinion to validate a reasoned strict constructionists' assessment of the existing statues and constitutional covenants. Roberts's separate opinion was reminiscent of the Texas Supreme Court's first dissenting opinion in 1857, written by the young first-term judge in *Cain v. the State*. "The International [railroad] controversy suggests how contested public promotion of economic development could become," according to historian Patrick Williams, "but its resolution perfectly illustrates how Redeemers ultimately managed the conflicting demands of retrenchment and development." Any notion of railroad preference when Roberts became governor was dashed as he reviewed and approved most applications for railroad land grants, not taking them at face value, and rejecting many incomplete requests—for example, writing to the owners of the Denison and Pacific Railway that no land would be conveyed, as "Your report is herewith returned that it, said road, may be made to conform to the law of 1876, page 153."[3]

The big winner in the handling of the railroad-subsidy debate was Judge Roberts. Unlike most court decisions, which held little interest for the general public, the judge's reasoned and clear assessment of the need for balance was popular with most Democratic Party leaders and voters. While not overtly attempting to draw attention, he had in fact placed his stamp on the "Roberts Court," generally unbeknownst to the rank-and-file Texans, with the *Central Law Journal* noting that his detailed yet concise rulings "stamp him as one of the foremost jurist of the country."[4] What followed was the Texas legislature's call in early 1875 for a convention to craft a new state constitution. While Roberts as a sitting judge could not be a delegate in the proceedings, before the convention met starting in early September, he was consulted both on procedural issues as well as on key portions of the proposed platform, not just those involving the judiciary. The result was a vastly decentralized government, including a reduction of the powers of the governor, and cost cutting in all state operations. Not surprisingly, and in agreement with Roberts, the court was reduced from five to three justices for a term of six years with annual salaries fixed at $3,550. The convention ended in November 1875, with February 15, 1876, scheduled as the date for voters both to approve the Constitution of 1876 and to elect statewide officers. Passing by a margin of more than two to one, the constitution took effect on April 18, 1876. Roberts was elected as chief justice and Gould and Moore as associates, along with the new constitution reinstating three court sessions per year in Tyler, Austin, and Galveston.[5]

Soon after the February 1876 election Roberts was called on to resolve and advise on an election-office tenure issue not addressed in the new constitution. Shortly after Richard Coke was re-elected governor he decided to run for the U.S. Senate seat held by Republican Morgan Hamilton. The state senate still selected the U.S. Senator, and Coke was elected over three other candidates. At issue was the timing needed to resign as governor, when to announce, and when a formal resignation would have to go before the legislature to be approved. Hard-line Democrats did not want Coke to resign until the end of Hamilton's senate term in March 1877. Coke did not want to create an adversarial situation in the legislature, and therefore asked Roberts for a solution. It was suggested that he craft a "proclamation," simply declaring his intention to resign, with Roberts advising that "you are not bound to tender your resignation" to any specific body or department. Roberts's advice was followed to the letter. Coke resigned on December 1, 1876, and Lieutenant Governor Richard Hubbard was sworn in as governor.[6] In spite of the heavy caseload before the Redeemer Court, Roberts spent late 1877 and early 1878 re-crafting the rules and procedures of the court to ensure "distinctness and certainty." Rumors circulated that he should stand for governor, yet he refused.[7]

In the process of deciding weighty supreme court cases, there was always the random case referred for review by Roberts, such as the jury charge sent to him by a circuit judge:

> If the jury believes, from the evidence, that the plaintiff and the defendant were a partner in the grocery, and that the plaintiff bought out the defendant and gave his note for the interest, and the defendant paid for the note by delivering to the plaintiff a cow, which be warranty 'not breachy' [not apt to break fences or be wild], and the warranty was broken by reason of the breachiness of the cow, and the plaintiff drove the cow back and tendered to the defendant, but the defendant refused to receive her, and the plaintiff took her home again, and put heavy yoke upon her to prevent her jumping the fence, and the cow, attempting to jump the fence, by reason of the aforesaid yoke, broke her neck and died; and if the jury further believe that the defendant's interest in the grocery aforesaid was not anythings, the plaintiff's note was worthless, and the cow good for nothing, either for milk or beef, or for 'green hide,' then the jury must find for themselves how they will decide the case, and don't know now how such a cussed case should be decided.[8]

Even with periodic rumors, there is no indication that Roberts had any interest in running for governor in 1878, as illustrated by the fact that for the past decade he had forgone attendance at the annual gathering of the state Democratic Conventions. Roberts had received inquiries about running, but he did not want to challenge his friend and Smith County neighbor, Richard Hubbard, the incumbent. Hubbard in his first term was generally favored to land the renomination. Political undercurrents across the state were brought on by a mixture of events, primarily the vocal rise of two landmark movements—the Greenback Party demanding fiscal reform and the inception of the Patrons of Husbandry or Grange—that posed the first substantive post-war challenge to the Democratic Party in the state. Hubbard was known to his friends as "Jumbo,", holding the distinction as the heaviest Texas governor, tipping the scales at over 400 pounds. By early June 1878 he was gradually losing support of the major newspapers in the state, led by opposition from the Austin *Weekly State Gazette,* in addition to the Dallas *Herald,* Sherman *Courier,* Houston *Age,* and Dallas *Commercial.* The *State Gazette,* which had the second largest circulation statewide, was alleged to have "mercenary motives" in dropping its support of Hubbard. A well-informed and skilled orator, Hubbard maintained a respectable gubernatorial administration, in spite of charges of financial irregularities he inherited from previous administrations and of supporting the expansion of railroads, enhanced frontier defense, and the need for tax reform. The primary challenger who emerged in the weeks prior to the mid-July Democratic State Convention was former governor and sitting Texas Congressman James W. Throckmorton.[9]

Delegates to the generally well-scripted and planned Democratic Convention were in for a big surprise. Typically two- or three-day gathering, the convention in 1878 dragged on for over a week without a party nominee. Prior to the convention, in addition to Throckmorton declaring as a candidate, former governor and sitting Senator Richard Coke endorsed Colonel William W. Lang, Worthy Master of the Texas State Grange and successful Falls County farmer. This support was based on the results of the local McLennan County Democratic caucus in Waco that resulted in selection of hometown favorite Coke, backed by his political ally Sam B. Maxey. The Democrats determined that the fusion of "grangers and greenbackers" who backed Lang as the leading candidate would be a winning combination. Lang addressed Grange and Greenback assemblies across north Texas to test the level of support—due primarily to the fact the Greenbackers had no declared standard bearer.[10] The rise of these two political movements in all probability cost Hubbard the swift nomination. The politically active editor of the Austin *State Gazette* wondered if Coke and Maxey were "using Lang for the purpose of favoring a dark horse." Yet there is no known mention prior to the opening proceedings at the convention of Roberts, or anyone else, as the "dark horse." Division within the Democratic Party was clearly present in the days before the convention met at the Millett Opera House in Austin on Saturday, July 13, 1878.[11]

Incumbent Hubbard arrived confident that he had the necessary two-thirds of the delegates' votes to secure the nomination on the first ballot. Some 1,488 delegates from 140 counties (four to five counties had not arrived) cast votes as determined by their local caucuses prior to meeting in Austin. There were two types of voting delegates: "instructed," obligated and bound to vote for the designated candidate selected at the county caucus, and "uninstructed," delegates who generally supported the candidate for whom they voted but at some point could be released to vote at will. While the two leading contenders had similar political views, a rancorous opening floor debate between Hubbard and Throckmorton engaged the two governors over claims and counter-claims of failures of each administration's fiscal policies "with palpable evidences of waste and improvidence" while in office. These claims were noted in the news media for the rank "electioneering ardor" and dexterous attempts to swing delegate votes. In the late afternoon prior to the first vote, a Coke surrogate placed William Lang's name before the meeting as a candidate. What followed, given the requirement to have a two-thirds majority, was the beginning of scores of ballots and a deadlocked convention. Vote totals were little changed following the first three days of votes, as shown in the following tabulation.[12]

1878 Democratic Convention Votes

		July 13	July 16	July 16 (3rd vote)
Hubbard	instructed	355	366	366
	uninstructed	392	*	339
	total	747		705
Throckmorton	instructed	337	204	304
	uninstructed	187	*	281
	total	524		585
Lang	instructed	142	103	103
	uninstructed	70	*	95
	total	212		198
* released uninstructed vote total			715	
Grand delegate total votes:		1,483	1,488**	1,488

Source: *Galveston Daily News*, July 13 and 16, 1878.
**Five votes difference due to late arriving delegates.

After a brief squabble between those representing the majority and minority committee reports the convention platform was reconsidered and adopted. The convention leadership hoped that during this cooling off period to iron out the platform, the delegates could coalesce to secure one nominee with the needed two-thirds of the votes. Late on Tuesday the 16th the fortieth ballot was taken and the convention remained deadlocked. The only significant change was that from the floor Texas fifth district Congressman Gustave Schleicher received 121 votes and John Ireland 84 votes. Late in the day chairman Jacob Waelder gaveled the meeting closed for the day, noting that there would be no change in the rules and, if needed, "balloting will be kept up indefinitely." The proceedings were statewide news, and it is presumed that Judge Roberts was kept informed by the Tyler, Marshall, and Jefferson newspapers.[13]

By the fourth day of the meeting, given the poor accommodations and the fact that temperatures in the un-air-conditioned opera house exceeded 100 degrees, delegates tempers were also rising, and many suggested that the sensible move on the part of the convention leadership would be to adjourn and immediately move to Galveston. Rumors spread within the convention that Lang would soon withdraw. The Hubbard and Throckmorton camps both agreed that "the probability of a dark horse entering the contest is lessening hourly." The majority of the Lang votes would probably go to Throckmorton, and thus the ensuing vote tally did little or nothing to break the deadlock with Hubbard. Convention officials visited with each county delegation to determine if votes had changed or what could be done with "uninstructed" delegates to effect a change. Indications were that Hubbard was gaining some strength but not a majority. Another dozen ballots followed with only a slight change—Hubbard 680, Throckmorton 561, and Lang 240.[14]

By Friday, following the impromptu departure of some 200 delegates, there was a "little more elbow room . . . yet a great number remaining still had the inevitable hum and confusion." The departures were the result of the poor housing conditions in the capital and rumors of a yellow fever scare—which most blamed on warm whiskey, "raw kitchens" (restaurants), and hot weather. On Saturday after thirteen ballots, Throckmorton withdrew and Lang restated his momentary interest in running, but withdrew when a dark horse, not a compromise, former Supreme Court Justice Thomas J. Devine, was introduced. This move had little impact. On the eighteenth vote of the day the deadlock continued, with Hubbard receiving 907 votes and Devine 592—to win nomination required 1,002 votes. Following a recess all proceedings came to a stop when news arrived that the notorious train, stage, and bank robber Sam Bass had been cornered and killed at Round Rock, Texas. The delegates passed a hasty resolution that the next legislature pass a bill giving suitable recognition to those who had made the capture. On the Monday the 22nd, on the twenty-sixth ballot of the day, Devine pulled in front of Hubbard, 787 to 721. Tensions and frustrations increased in a number of squabbles on the floor. In one incident the *Daily News* noted: "In a dispute over the vote of Brazos [county] members one of the delegates, William King of Bryan, called another delegate from the same county, Colonel Page, a liar and said he would whip him." By late evening the caucus was no closer to a solution. As delegates slowly began to return home, not waiting for a final vote, rumors on the street included a change in the balloting system and the introduction of a new—acceptable—"'dark horse.'"[15]

Certain that no candidate would gain two-thirds of the votes and following a late night negotiation, the competing camps agreed to withdraw all floor nominations and to appoint a commission of 32 members. To prevent another contentious week-long deadlock, previous nominees could not be placed in nomination. The compromise was accepted, and Hubbard, Throckmorton, and Devine withdrew from the race. This did not prevent behind the scenes maneuvering. The commission, comprised of only a token number of the delegates, drafted a list of the most prominent Texans. Only those on the new ballot recommended by the commission would receive votes—no write-ins were allowed. The first ballot of the select committee resulted in: John H. Reagan 15; W. P. Ballinger 2; John Ireland 5; R. Q. Mills 3, and O. M. Roberts and Charles Stewart 1 each! The *Daily News* noted: "After the first ballot the Devine delegates, believing the Hubbard delegates had conferred and agreed upon one man, Judge Reagan, whom they voted for solidly the first round, while their men scattered, held a caucus, and determined to make the nomination by voting for Judge Roberts." Furthermore, the caucus members gathered behind closed doors were aware that the "Old Roman" Reagan, whose nomination by the commission was made in deference to (and in honor of) his party seniority, most likely would not accept due to his age and his current obligations representing Texas in the U.S. Congress. This did not preclude him from receiving commission votes and did not slow the proceedings. The second ballot showed Reagan 9; Ireland 1; Mills 2; Roberts 16, Culberson 1; Stewart 1. The third ballot resulted in Roberts 19 and Reagan 11, and the fourth ballot Roberts 18; Reagan 13; and Mills 1. Oran Roberts, having repeatedly received the majority of votes, was declared the unanimous choice, and the high commission adjourned.[16]

The convention was reconvened. William S. Herndon of Smith County placed Roberts's name in nomination and the rules were suspended to accept it by acclamation. Joseph D. Sayers of Bastrop was confirmed as the nominee for lieutenant governor. In addition to the selection of Roberts and Sayers at the top of the 1878 ticket, George McCormick of Colorado County was tapped to run for attorney general, Stephen H. Darden of Gonzales County as comptroller, former governor Francis R. Lubbock for treasurer, and William C. Walsh of Austin for general land office commissioner.[17]

Legend has it, according to historian Kenneth Hendrickson, that Roberts was at his farm in Tyler when notice of his nomination arrived, and he rode to town "on his fan-tail spotted pony," to meet with friends at a local saloon. He borrowed fifty cents to send a telegram to determine if he would go to Austin to accept the nomination. Given the extended length of the convention, delegates were ready to adjourn and thus, it was agreed that he would by return telegraph send a message to confirm his acquiescence. Again, he borrowed a few cents from his Tyler friends to send the following telegram:

GENTLEMEN OF THE Convention—I cheerfully obey the voice of

the people who have called me through you to the democratic candidate for governor of Texas.
Should I be elected, it shall be my endeavor to advance and protect the rights and interests of the whole people of our great state. Without attempting to develop any State policy at present, I beg to refer you to my past services in the various positions with which I have been honored by the people as the best assurance I can give for my future conduct.[18]

The day Roberts's gubernatorial nomination was announced statewide, the story of his candidacy was nearly overshadowed by newspaper headlines on the capture and death of the outlaw Sam Bass.[19] After over a week of political wrangling in Austin, Roberts's nomination came as a surprise to many Texans. Some newspaper editors also expressed questions and suspicions about the process, and many argued that the judge was not the "selection (or 'voice') of the people." Many of the editorial comments came from partisan papers that had endorsed Hubbard and Throckmorton. Given the last minute modification of the convention selection process, noted the editor of the *Galveston Daily News,* the judge was not the "foregone choice of the party and the people, but only the exhaustion and despair of the factions after abortive attempts to select a nominee." A month later A. H. Belo, the publisher and owner of the *News,* tempered the paper's earlier assessment, noting that the nomination of Roberts was "unexpected and without solicitation." Many questioned what they felt was the unjust treatment of Governor Hubbard. However, any criticism must be tempered with the fact that Roberts, who was well known in legal and political circles, did not seek the governorship, and furthermore, it must be assumed, the leading Democrats both selected the potential Texans put before the 32-man commission and also voted on the final selection. Nevertheless, historian Alwyn Barr concluded that many old-line Texas Democrats were well aware of the risks of any further disruption and thus they avoided a possible party crisis. "Roberts's background and apparent lack of political ambition made him an ideal compromise candidate. Texas Democrats had resorted to a figure and a philosophy from the past in their failure to evolve a new consensus on state administrative policies for the future."[20]

In the weeks following the nomination of Roberts, newspapers filled columns with reflections on the rushed nomination. Interestingly, months earlier in January 1878 a letter to the editor of the *Galveston News* speculated that "Chief Justice Roberts for governor and Col. Joel Robinson, of Fayette County would be a good slate—but the Judge has no aspirations in that direction." The Graham *Leader,* a strong supporter of Throckmorton, concluded, "All should remember that the unity and harmony of the party are infinitely more important than the election of any man, however well qualified."[21] Newspapers and their readers relished the smallest insight into the political and personal stories, and circulated the latest vignette, often never corroborated. The *Galveston Daily News,* the leading paper in Texas, employed a staff to comb as many papers as possible to help fill its daily issue with letters and stories about Roberts and observations of Texans. Thus, it was routinely quick to reprint news on Roberts. For example: The *Capital,* the Greenback organ at Austin, called Judge Roberts's letter of acceptance "too gushing," said he was not the choice of the people, and repeated the following anecdote, embellished to suit its own notions of propriety:

The wise and prudent nomination of the Hon. Oran M. Roberts, sometimes called "granny Roberts," recalls a pleasing incident of the good old ante-bellum times, when money was plentiful and whisky [sic] sold for twenty-five cents a gallon, and war Democrats, copperheads, kuklux [sic], loyal and radicals, had no special application to members of either the national Republicans or Democratic parties, the lawyers of Austin gave a bar dinner, memorable for its success and the excellent toasts proposed and drank to by the joyful party.

On this occasion Judge Roberts being called on for a toast, arose with his intellectual countenance beaming with ineffable wisdom and oriental profundity, and said: "Gentlemen, I will propose to you a toast, not original with me, but a scintillation of my [slave] boy Jim. Some time ago he came into my room, and after making me a fire, asked for a dram. The bottle was on the bureau, and I told him to help himself, which he did by pouring out a glass of whisky [sic], saying: 'Master, may your shadow never grow less,' and then swallowed it down. Jim's toast struck me forcibly as being unique and original, therefore, gentlemen, allow me to propose, in the language of boy Jim: 'May your shadows never grow less!'"[22]

1878 Campaign

One of the biggest questions following the Austin convention surrounded the speculation concerning Roberts's plans to depart the Texas Supreme Court in advance of the fall campaign. The timing of the date of his resignation from the bench involved the appointment of a new judge who would serve until the next general election in 1880. Concerns that he remained on the high court until the November election and after his pending election would appoint his successor were allayed when he announced his resignation as chief justice on August 9, to become effective in early October, in time for a judicial candidate to be elected at the ensuing November election. In the face of rising opposition to the Democratic Party from the Republicans and Greenbackers, friends and supporters were eager to start Roberts's campaign. Candidates were well aware that local economic conditions influenced voters. As the campaign opened, farmers in the midst of a lingering mid-year drought and were eager to commence with cotton picking as it was commanding the per pound price of 11 cents for middling class fiber, with early reports that "the hot weather, which has been productive of so much discomfort, has been of great advantage to the crops."[23]

The Democrats' concerns were well-founded, given the divisions in the party during the July Democratic Convention, followed by the rise of the Greenback Party, and the increased activity by and demands of farmers and the Grange. Within weeks the Greenback Party, following an organizational meeting in Austin in March 1878, convened their first statewide convention at Turner Hall in August at Waco, with 217 delegates (some sources report nearly 300 delegates) from political clubs or local chapters across the state. Unlike the often confused and delayed Democratic Convention, the Greenbackers' main focus was on their platform and the hasty approval of a nominee. The opening keynote was given by former governor E. J. Davis. While a noted and dedicated Republican, he stated, "he would cheerfully vote for their ticket [as] . . . it is absolutely essential that the Democratic Party in Texas be broken up [and defeated]." The upstart Greenbackers had attracted a large following across the state and were gradually recruiting to their party disenchanted Grangers, urban workers, ex-Democrats and ex-Republicans as well as a strong following of African Americans. The platform, with many issues taken from the Grange and the Democrats, emphasized assistance to public schools, property tax reform, regulation of the railroads, increased coinage of silver (to expand the money supply to help reduce farm debt), a balanced state budget, protection on the frontier, a more equitable land policy limiting the donation of public lands to railroads—and one unique plank: "we hold that the importation of servile labor from Asiatic Countries should be prohibited under the severest penalities [sic]." Roberts's grasp of economic conditions as well as understanding of the highly debated "free coinage" of silver proved decisive in winning votes.[24]

Historians of the period have for years wondered about the actual impact of the Grange in Texas. The following item brings into question and sheds light on the organization's overall impact at the ballot box: "The Waco *Telephone* says there are 36,000 Grangers in Texas of whom 10,000 are females, leaving 26,000 Grangers who are voters. There are 210,000 voters in Texas, 150,000 of them are Democrats. The Grangers compose less than one-eighth of the voting population of the State."[25]

Greenback Party

To address the Greenback Party candidates, a prominent railroad and land developer in the Brazos Valley, William H. Hamman—a forty-eight-year-old attorney and signer as a delegate of the Democratic minority report in Austin a few weeks earlier—was unanimously nominated as the party's gubernatorial standard bearer. James S. Rains, a farmer from Kaufman County, was selected as the nominee for lieutenant governor. For the Greenbackers to be successful they needed to attract as many farmers as possible. Forty percent of Texas farmers were either tenants or sharecroppers, and most carried a heavy load of debt. Thus General Hamman launched his campaign in Austin on August 24 with a headlong attack on the currency issue and farm indebtedness: "Money is an agent of transfer, a medium of exchange. We can not barter or trade without it. We are compelled to have a medium of exchange . . . paper money has another capacity. Its greatest quality is its debt-paying capacity."[26]

The response from Republican-leaning newspaper editors was equally swift, with the conservative Brenham *Volksbote* instantly attacking both the Greenbackers and the Democrats: "In the principle of unlimited issue of paper money, we can see nothing in the future but misfortune and ruin, and even the dangers of Democratic supremacy can not induce us to join the Greenbackers, which is nothing more nor less than getting 'out of the frying pan into the fire.' The new party would undoubtedly be made up for the most part of Democrats, and we would then have a government of Democratic Greenbackers with a Republican tail hanging to it, while the republican votes would be of as little weight and influence as heretofore."[27]

By late August the Democratic campaign was in full swing. The platform held many of the same objectives as those of the Greenbackers, yet with decidedly different views, being pro-railroads, in favor of improved schools but concerned about the funding, against any fiscal quick-fix by denouncing "fiat money," and favoring no increase in the rate of taxation. The Democrats' primary weaknesses included opposition claims that they had failed to reduce taxes and had not done enough to assist public education and frontier defense. However, the responsibility for education (still under-funded) had been deferred to local communities. Many East Texas voters were not concerned about the frontier and wanted state funding directed to the expansion of railroads in their region. The small West Texas constituency had little voice in the 1878 election. Furthermore, most Texans had little awareness of either party's platform, and thus, as in most elections, responded to the personalities and reputations of stump speakers of each party. Local and regional influences were pivotal. Over 90 percent of the state's population and voters were east of the 100th meridian (roughly I-35 today) and concentrated in about 140 counties. One strong suit of the Democrats, in spite of the rancor and parochial factionalism during the Austin convention, was that all the former Democratic contenders lined up to support Judge Roberts. A further defining aspect was that the leading contenders for the gubernatorial nomination represented and influenced constituencies in different parts of the state and before different organizations. Hubbard and Reagan were strong in East Texas, Coke was a well-known leader in the Brazos Valley, in north Texas Throckmorton organized grassroots support, Devine represented the small but important "west" Texas canvas, and Grange Worthy Master Lang aligned his membership in support of Roberts. All these men, joined by Senator Charles Culberson, endorsed the judge. These politicians, while competitors, shared a common bond as former officers in the late Confederacy. Richard Coke led the charge with headlines in the Austin *Weekly Democratic Statesman,* "Governor Coke will make most effective speeches against the heresies of Greenbackism."[28]

To a man, those stumping for the Democratic ticket proved to be better speakers than Oran Roberts. One guarantee for an enthusiastic crowd was to schedule campaign stops in counties celebrating the "First Bale" of cotton of the season. From the Red River to the Rio Grande, Roberts and his supporters attacked Greenback supporters at the local level. As noted earlier, despite Roberts's training as a debater at the University of Alabama, the popular judge "had none of the arts of public speaking." Following a two-and-a-half-hour speech in Sherman, one reporter noted: "He did not arouse much enthusiasm." However, his friend Norman Kittrell remarked on one exception. While on the campaign swing up the Brazos River, "the host committee at Waco had placed a generous-sized pitcher of water on the speaker's stand and without the old gentleman's knowledge, they had 'spiked' it pretty freely with something which was stronger than water." The day was warm, and during Roberts's presentation of more than an hour long he drank freely and "towards the close of the speech he felt considerably exhilarated," giving what all noted was the Old Alcalde's most enthusiastic and spirited stump speech of the fall campaign![29]

Roberts proved to be an election strategist astute at neutralizing the Greenback threat, as he had been in restructuring the Texas court systems and setting procedures. The theme on the campaign trail was fourfold: highlight the northern roots of the fledgling Greenbacks; blame Republicans' misrule for the economic downturn in the state and criticize the Greenbackers for their monetary policies, raise the threat of African American participation in the political process, and emphasize the misleading guidance and endorsement from the bankrupt policies of former Republican governor E. J. Davis—whom many white Texans considered a traitor to the Lone Star State. William Lang was critical in organizing the farmers in the Grange. Among the hardest issues to manage and articulate clearly to the Texas voters were the concerns with and solution to the economic downturn as well as the need to show that a Greenback demand for a fiat flood of paper money, greenbacks, was not the solution.

In response to those demanding the issue of irredeemable Greenbackers, Roberts reminded voters: "To issue two billion of paper money, never redeemable in coin, and receivable only in payment of government dues (which is what is meant by 'absolute greenback money') would, if it was practicable to be done immediately, which it is not, produce a redundancy in the circulating medium of the country that would so depreciate it that it hardly be money at all . . . it would have ruinous consequences." While support of the Grange proved important, many expressed concern about the increased political activities that failed to address the original purpose of the organization, with the Corsicana *Observer* noting: "The movement has 'no political significance' in fact it is believed that the Grange has in some measure been prostituted from its original beneficent purpose by allowing politics to slip in, and the intention now is to revive the organization, purge it of all extraneous influences, and renew it as an organization for the benefit of the farmers." The week before the statewide elections, Governor Hubbard boasted to a large crowd in Galveston: "the Judge would be elected by 100,000 [vote] majority."[30]

Campaign travel was generally done without any protection or escorts, and Roberts had extensive contact with people along the campaign trail across the state. He engaged any voter who approached him, and the German newspaper in San Antonio published the following story on the eve of the election:

Several drummers [traveling salesmen] were dining at a restaurant in Paris. Judge Roberts, with a friend, was there. One of these modest drummers—they are always acutely, sensitively and painfully modest —said to the judge:

"You ought to suppress robberies and murders and crime. There is too much of it in Texas, and always has been. Northern and eastern people are afraid to come to Texas, and will not do so freely until the existing condition of things is changed."

Judge Roberts answered that in all new counties, sparsely populated and rich and prosperous like Texas, where it cost nothing to live, where the spontaneous products of the country supported life, where people advertised in the newspapers and on trees that the poor can have all the beef they want if they will only save the hides—in a country like this there will be adventurers and lawless desperadoes.

"Yes," continued the drummer, "there is so much of bloodshed and violence that good northern people are afraid to enter the state."

The judge was growing a little impatient. He was addressed in this manner by a person he had never seen before, and turning to the young man from the swine and oleomargarine city of Cincinnati, the judge blandly suggested:

"See here, my young friend. I came to this state thirty-five years ago. I have been sober and industrious and attentive to my business, and traveled everywhere in Texas by day and night, and nobody has ever once harmed me in any manner. *If your friends of Cincinnati fear they can't do and live as I have they should stay in Cincinnati*."[31]

The last weeks of the election resulted in some violent outbursts by zealous Democrats who disrupted Greenbacker rallies. Yet the outcome was never in question. Roberts polled 158,933 votes (67 percent) to Hamman's 55,002 (23 percent), and the dark horse Republican on the ticket, Antony B. Norton, drew 23,402 (10 percent)—a 100,000-plus-vote victory over Hamman, as predicted by Hubbard! Roberts overwhelmingly carried the rural-farm vote and had little opposition from urban labor organizations or pockets of Black voters in a few East Texas counties. The Greenbackers won a few seats in the legislature, but like the upstart Know-Nothing party years earlier, did little to impact the hold of the Democrats over all levels of the state and local governments. The Texas Supreme Court was in good hands with the election of George F. Moore as chief justice. Roberts recommended Robert Gould to take his seat on the court. Furthermore, the ebb and flow of political movements in Texas resulted by 1878 in another effort to represent the concerns of farmers and "to elect good men."[32]

In the immediate days following the election, Roberts admitted he had conducted a campaign across the state "more extensive than he had at first expected to make." However, he gained an immense grassroots firsthand look—the first since his days as an East Texas circuit judge in the late 1840s and early 1850s—at the economic conditions and the concerns of common Texans. His years of legal and judicial experience researching and reorganizing the Texas courts and drafting opinions brought an entirely new approach compared to those of the former gubernatorial administrations' *laissez-faire* attitude and their unaccountable policies of state government and failure to hold state officials accountable for their actions. The state government was filled with "Redeemers," most of whom he left in office. Key positions were held by elected officers under the new constitution, such as the attorney general and comptroller, over whom he had little power. Furthermore, he came into office without any allegiance or obligations to any faction of the Democratic Party. In a move that most likely no other previous Texas governor-elect attempted, he initiated a month-long examination in Austin of the conditions and problems facing the state government, as well as an analytical review of the budgets of the state departments. The study included a review of the laws relating to the various departments and their funding and "other objects within the usual scope of the legislature." Roberts was urged just to review past departmental and legislative reports. Instead, he would forgo this deflection of his questions and investigation to hold additional meetings with the attorney general, comptroller, and heads of the Texas Land Office and the treasury department. These were followed by numerous meetings with legislators. His objectives were to learn as much as possible about the state operations prior to his inauguration and prior to submitting his recommendations to the legislature. First he was told the state had not had a balanced budget in over thirty years. Administrators and legislators blamed the financial shortfall on the irresponsible actions of the post-war Radical Republican administrations.

Roberts also learned that the "state had not been able to pay current expenses with current annual revenue collected." Then he was told the estimated outstanding state debt was $300,000—and it was soon revealed that the true amount was nearly $500,000 [equivalent to $15.5 million in 2024]. The governor-elect concluded that the state had "no means on hand to pay it [the debt] . . . thus, a most difficult problem was presented." The state debt dated further back than just the cost of the war and the Radical Republican administration that followed. John Reagan in his *Memoirs* (1906) wrote: "When General Houston, in 1841 was president of the Republic, he said, in his message to the Texas Congress: 'There is not a dollar in the treasury. The nation is involved in ten or fifteen millions: we are not only without money, but without credit.'"[33] Facing the financial disruption, Roberts was reminded of the political platitudes of the election process drafted at the state convention and the most recent Democratic platform, which called for the following:

- public bond debt of the state must not be increased
- taxes must not be increased over fifty cents on the dollar
- annual expenses must not exceed the annual revenue

- laws must be vigorously executed
- public schools must be maintained
- provisions must be made for convict work only at the penitentiaries[34]

Many wondered if the Democratic platform was in spite of or in reaction to the urgent need to address the state's lingering poor condition and fiscal debt crisis. Staffing to support his goals to lift the state out of prolonged debt was critical. To fill appointed positions in a score of state agencies, commissions, and boards Roberts received over 400 letters, petitions, and endorsements from possible office seekers. Recommendations arrived from citizens as well as his political cohorts, such as Coke, Hubbard, Lang, and Lubbock. Close friend Colonel and Doctor John 'Rip' Ford was appointed superintendent of the "Deaf and Dumb Asylum" in Austin. The pre-inauguration examination by Roberts resulted in a series of detailed "messages" on specific topics, which he submitted to the legislature between January 27, 1879, and early March. Key topics included the judiciary, state finance conditions, the proposed state university and support of the existing Agricultural and Mechanical College and the college for "colored youths," the asylums, frontier defense, the budget deficiency and plans for state revenue, needed railroad regulations, and one last legislative message "on a number of minor subjects." In a show of unity Governor-elect Roberts accompanied Governor Hubbard when Hubbard made his last public speech, and they made a joint appearance and presentations to the Texas Sheriffs' Convention. Sheriff Peter F. Ross, older brother of Waco state Senator Sul Ross, chaired the meeting.[35]

Following an inaugural ball of 1,200 guests at the Austin Opera House, any doubt about Governor Roberts's resolve and determination to grapple with the deteriorating condition of the state's finances was quickly addressed. As one newspaper noted, "any conclusion that Judge Roberts who numbers about sixty, must be incapacitated by age for vigorous and enterprising public service, can be very briefly dispatched." Roberts would convert his conservative political positions and fiscally prudent philosophy into a full restructuring of both state spending and the identification of new revenue generation sources that did not increase taxes on the farmers. He made clear that he would not tolerate deficit spending and that the path to state solvency would be based on a "pay-as-you-go" principle and, not surprisingly, that "everything must go according to the law."[36] "In the present Constitution of the State there is a limitation plainly expressed as follows," noted Roberts. "The legislature shall not have the right to levy taxes or impose burdens upon the people, except to raise revenue sufficient for the economical administration of the government, which may include the following purposes: the payment of interest on the public debt, the erection and repair of public buildings, for the benefit of the sinking fund, for the support of the public schools and asylums, for the payment of officers of the government, for the enforcement of quarantine, and for the protection of the frontier."[37]

The week before Roberts took the oath of office, he advised the state's departments, commissions, and agencies that he expected a detailed written report and review of their budgets with plans to cut and streamline operations. Panic spread through the state government, as few state employees wanted budget cuts. Comments in the reports were telling: the attorney general's office pushed back, saying "the business of this office cannot be efficiently done with less force." "Now is not the time to cut," State Treasurer J. R. Lubbock warned. The secretary of state questioned whether such a request was lawful. V. O. King, insurance commissioner, requested an increase. Only W. C. Walsh, commissioner of the General Land Office, agreed to cut his $2,695.79 annual budget by $233.30 by reducing staff. The Executive Department was no exception, with the governor reducing expenses from $34,735.75 during the late 1878–79 Hubbard administration to $21,465.17 under Roberts—a reduction of $13, 270.58.[38]

Roberts's mandates immediately ruffled the feathers of many Democratic legislators and agencies that had not been held accountable for years. The only agencies Roberts singled out for continued support were what he called the "charitable institutions," for the deaf, mentally ill, and blind—issuing an executive order on February 6, 1879, to protect their annual funding.

As one observer noted: "Despite his prudence and sincerity, Roberts was neither infallible nor without his critics; these apparently are built-in perils which attend all men of decisiveness and action." Roberts had a very small staff of his son Robert, private secretary, and his son-in-law Hugh Spain, executive clerk. In addition to budget cuts and new sources of revenue, Roberts made it clear that those delinquent in the payment of taxes would be found: "Any man who is able to pay taxes, and willfully fails to do so, is receiving protection, and if a citizen participates in the rights and privileges of citizenship without rendering a consideration to the government therefor, he imposes an undue burden upon other persons, which is a gross injustice and should not be tolerated in this or any other State."[39]

Roberts's initial budget targets and plan to reduce state spending included reducing the interest charges by renegotiating the outstanding bond debt—held, much to his disgust, by New York bondholders. Possibly Governor Roberts, who was well read, was aware of the Texas financial assessment written by William M. Gouge in 1852 as a harbinger of debt coming due, with Gouge warning even at that early date that the shortfall of revenue and the state public debt were not sustainable (they were only partly reduced over the ensuing years by the gradual disposal of frontier lands). When the Democrats regained control in Texas on January 21, 1874, they inherited a state government debt, from Republican (and earlier Democratic) rule, of an accumulated total of $3,614,568 [today equivalent to $112 million] —with the state comptroller's office reporting to Governor Roberts that "they had no certain knowledge of the estimated amount." The state faced a cascading financial disaster that was going to come due in 1882.[40]

This situation demanded immediate action, yet resulted in a slow methodical process as a result of opposition in the legislature. Notwithstanding the pushback, Roberts, working with the latest official published bond data from the U.S. Secretary of the Treasury, negotiated a reduction from 10 percent bonds issued under former

Governor Davis's administration. Bonds were retired and replaced with new bonds costing only 5 percent, with an immediate windfall to the state and annual saving of $55,721.70. In January, as Roberts prepared for office, the treasury department called in (redeemed) $150,000 of the 6 percent bonds and substituted 4 percent bonds in their place. The *Galveston Daily News* noted, "It is [a] rather remarkable fact that more bonds were retired during the last month than during any whole year previously." State treasury officials were surprised at Roberts's level of expertise. What they did not know was that he researched the flow and execution of treasury notes and bonds prior to a major campaign presentation in August 1878 in response to the financial plank of the Greenback Party.[41]

The second action, considered a drastic act by many legislative opponents, was to adjust the pension structure for Texas veterans. While this could have been political suicide, given the large number of veterans and their supporters, Roberts clearly outlined the budget situation and recommended cutting their benefits from $150 to $100, but the legislature chose instead the substitution of grants of up to 640 acres of land in the place of cash payments. These land grants were in West Texas and were criticized by recipients as being of little or no value. His third action during his first six months in office proved the most controversial—a review of public school funding. Even before he was through his first year as governor, speculation on the governor's "pay-as-you-go" policy was cast as Roberts's plan "to land him in the U.S. Senate." The governor's key ally in the legislature to enact his budget plans was Senator (and future governor) Lawrence S. Ross, chairman of the Senate Finance Committee.[42]

While the governor was a lifelong advocate of education, he advised the legislature that the state could not, in the short term, continue spending nearly 30 percent of the budget on public schools. In the pre-inaugural weeks, knowing harsh budget reductions were in the offing, his view on education was made clear: "Good schools are the jewels of the State, the only nurseries of general popular culture, whether a republic or a monarchy. The school is the measure by which the degree of popular culture of the different nations, is ascertained and fixed; the better the schools, the higher the material and intellectual strength of the people." Exploring every avenue to fund education, Roberts ordered the attorney general and the comptroller's office to launch a full-scale effort to collect the indebtedness dating from 1859 from railroad companies that had been advanced loans from the Texas Public Free School Fund. Some debt was collected, yet a major court battle resulted when it was discovered that railroads had made payments "in worthless and unconstitutional Confederate currency," some of which arrived at the state treasury more than a month after the surrender![43]

In a politically astute move, prior to the convening of the Sixteenth Legislature, Roberts attended the annual meeting of the Texas Teachers Convention in Waco to advise them on the critical nature of the fiscal challenge facing education and to hear their recommendations on how to improve the schools in the face of the current budget shortfall. Once convened, the legislature failed to heed the governor's recommended reductions and passed a school bill that Roberts abruptly vetoed in the last hours of the regular session. In the face of growing criticism, which he said "produced a violent excitement," Roberts went to the news media to explain in detail the veto and called a special session for June 1879.[44] Knowing the schools might have to shorten normal terms, reduce teacher pay, and raise additional supporting funds locally, the legislature relented, meeting the governor's demands. The education appropriation was cut from one-fourth of the general revenue to one-fifth—then cut further by the legislature to one-sixth. Roberts received the unqualified support of one of the state's leading educators, Rufus Burleson, at that time president of Waco University. In support of the governor's veto Burleson noted: "The present so-called system of public free schools in Texas, without the organization and supervision which are indispensable to both efficiency and economy, is generally a failure, and on the whole a prodigal waste of public money."[45]

Those who suffered most were poor Black and white students who had little or no access to education. To cut state spending further, state employees had their salaries reduced, including the governor.

The state centralized purchasing to prevent waste, and Roberts started a liberal pardon or "commutation" policy to reduce the number of inmates and expenses in the state prison system. While the system was a closely monitored program, along with efforts to improve interstate extradition, there were risks of repeat offenders he was willing to accept. Roberts was attacked by newspaper editors across the state for pardoning a number of Blacks whom he felt had been convicted unjustly. Every pardon request was brought to him, by pardons clerk Peter Roberts, and Roberts personally reviewed and inquired into all the circumstances involved with each case—often noting that he worked until midnight reviewing documents. Not all Blacks or whites or teenage minors were pardoned after his review. Citizen protests against the pardon actions that released inmates resulted in a number of towns "hanging the governor in effigy." Teenagers between thirteen and sixteen years of age, most in prison for petty theft and burglary, were pardoned after three months of good conduct. A report from Cameron noted that "the people awoke to find the effigy of Governor Roberts suspended from an oak tree in the courthouse yard. It had a corn-cob pipe in its mouth and it was labeled 'Old Commute.'" Detractors claimed it was an "abuse of power" and that his actions were causing the country to "go to Hell." The governor calmly replied to a friend, "I can't help it. If the country goes to Hell, under my rule, it will have to go According to the Law." In fact his predecessors pardoned many more: Coke, 133; Hubbard, 188; and Roberts only 100 inmates. The *Galveston Daily News* wasted little time in lampooning Governor Roberts's stance on incarceration:[46]

A Bad Case

"How is your son coming on!"

"Oh, I'm having a power of trouble with him" "What's the matter now?"

"Well, you know I couldn't send him to school, because, thanks to Gov. Roberts, there are no free schools, and I could not afford to send him to private school."

"Yes, I know that is so."

"Well, I sent him away from Galveston out to the frontier, and as luck would have it he was convicted of horse stealing and got five years in the penitentiary."

"That was bad."

"No, it wasn't, for you see at the penitentiary he could learn a trade and become a useful citizen."

"Well, that's good."

"No it ain't, for Gov. Roberts has pardoned him out on account of his youth and ignorance."[47]

The Mansion

Frances Roberts brought the "down-home" way of life in East Texas to the governor's mansion. In addition to doing her own sewing, cooking, and gardening, much to the surprise of the local ladies' society, she hosted a "big levee" (Irish for party) for the members of the legislature as well as the visiting Texans. One writer recalled: "Pigs, chickens, turkeys, salads, cakes, and pies galore took the place of the dainty sandwich or refreshing ice of today. Coffee was made and served by the gallon and the doors of the hospitable old mansion were thrown wide to the public—such was the democracy of the Roberts' regime." One legislator of the time remarked: "Mrs. Roberts is rather plain and I don't know how I will like her." After he attended the first levee he was heard to say, "Old Mrs. Roberts will do. I never ate such a supper." Delightful chamber music was provided by the band of the blind asylum. She regularly hosted the governor's frequent visitors, Judge Gould, Dr. Ashbel Smith, Judge John Reagan, and Colonel Santos Benavides from Laredo. After a return to the border, Benavides often sent Mrs. Roberts presents, including a cage of parrots.[48]

The governor's mansion was home to some sixteen full-time residents, including family, friends, and domestic help. It was the largest home Roberts had ever occupied; moving in, he "felt like a mill-pond trout suddenly turned into the Atlantic Ocean ever since he has occupied the vast empire called the 'governor's mansion.'" Three Roberts children resided there: Robert, 34, a local merchant; Oran Jr., 19, student in the Texas Law School, and Maggie Roberts Spain, 28, and her husband Hugh and their two children, Thomas and Hugh Jr. Hugh Spain first worked in the governor's office as the executive clerk and later was named by the governor as acting secretary of state during the second Roberts administration. The 1880 U.S. Census listed two house guests, Medicus A. Long and Annie Hooper, along with four servants—three of whom were Swedish immigrants. The eleven-room two-story Greek Revival-style home had no bathrooms and a remote kitchen.[49]

Retrenchment

Governor Roberts was not alone in following a Redeemers' "retrenchment" approach to cutting spending on education and public services. Massive budget shortfalls, resentment of the Radical federal policies, and poor judgment were not collective sentiment in Texas alone.

Throughout the South public education suffered—Virginia, Mississippi, Alabama, Louisiana, and Arkansas were crippled by reduced school funding. While the reasons may have been many, one key factor was the demand for new farm labor taking precedence over the local advocacy for common education. Even young children worked on the family farms. The labor was needed to boost the agricultural production coupled with getting beyond what C. Vann Woodward termed a "general poverty and depression" that further set back recovery. The average length of the common school term fell by 20 percent. Thus, while Roberts and the Texas legislature only planned a pause in school funding for only two years, Woodward concludes: "Even if the Redeemers had abandoned retrenchment and championed the cause of the schools, they would not have been able to provide an adequate system of education."[50]

At no time did Roberts say he was against public schools. His goal was to address the state's financial crises in the short term in order to provide for added appropriations in the future. To accomplish this, in addition to making deep budget cuts, he and the legislature crafted a number of means to increase revenue without any added tax burden upon existing permanent property. The legislature was cooperative in passing a smorgasbord of corporate, professional, and user taxes—some successful and some short-lived—all with the intention of increasing state revenue. New levies were placed on telegraph companies, insurance firms, passenger railroad services, and gas companies, with a tax on traveling "drummers" (commercial salesmen) as well as the first one percent tax on gross receipts of rail, stage, and steamboat companies engaged in passenger travel within the state. To ensure that the farmers understood the new consumption tax structure did not impact them, a joint resolution was passed for a special exemption from taxation on supplies used on the farm. Furthermore, long before Governor James Hogg claimed credit for regulating railroads in the 1890s, Roberts noted: "Railroads—while they would help to settle the country in the shortest amount of time—require regulation, as individuals can not cope with corporations." The first major attempt to introduce a railroad commission bill occurred in 1881, but railroad lobbyists and land speculators killed any legislative action, claiming such regulation was unconstitutional. In addition to a continuous stream of lobbying from the Grange, Roberts received visits in Austin from railroad magnates Jay Gould and Collis Huntington to influence any legislation and regulation of the railroads.[51]

Texas State Budget Estimates:
March 1, 1879 to March 1, 1880

Total state estimated expenses: $1,901,753
Revenue estimates
Total revenue from existing tax: $1,600,000
Three months tax from bell punch tax: 20,000
Six months tax from passenger tax: 10,000
Six months tax palace car tax: 1,000
Six months telegraph tax: 1,500

Six months drummers tax: 5,000
Other misc. taxes on trial: 10,000
Total State Revenue: 1879–80: $1,647,500[52]
Note: These revenue figures were prior to the increased in public land sales.

While the scope of Roberts's seemingly harsh attacks on educational funding caused a backlash, few were aware of his strong stand to make sure that the indigent and needy in the State Lunatic Asylum (known today as MHMR) were cared for. In his message to the legislature, notwithstanding the tight budget and needed cuts, he recommended "that enough of the surplus revenue of the State be appointed to enlarge the Asylum so as to afford a proper treatment of the inmates, and for the reception of every lunatic in the State" that would "require an outlay of about $300,000."[53] The concerns to be addressed were not the staff or leadership, but rather the poor conditions provided at the institution, which in 1881 housed 378 patients.

Furthermore, fire had damaged one of the facility's buildings. The superintendent submitted plans to implement a proper mental health care system for 650 patients. Roberts, like he did in his governor-elect days, launched with the assistance of the asylum superintendent and staff a critical assessment of expenses to identify ways to economize. Senator Ross, as he had assisted the governor with the education budget, was again a champion of this oversight and funding. The result was better control over supplies to evaluate both the pricing and quality of products. In addition, when those interned had a family with means, the family should help contribute to their relative's expenses; the care of veterans should be a high priority and their state assistance could be a means to pay for health-care services; and cottages should be added on the grounds of the institute for staff to free up an additional space for thirty patients in the main facility. To improve the existing facilities the state agreed to fund improvements to the sewage system, water supply, and fire protection by providing ten fire extinguishers. The governor and Mrs. Roberts routinely attended concerts by the patients at the asylum.[54]

Roberts faced pressure from the hard-core Democrats in his party about cleaning out Republican appointees and uncooperative Redeemers who had lingered in appointed state and county offices. An appeal from Shack Roberts, a Black Republican state representative from Harrison County, asked for the governor to leave the situation alone in the short term.

Furthermore, according to Campbell legal entanglements concerning jurisdictional issues in Harrison County involving the Supreme Court were an additional reason to take a wait and see approach. Any question of Roberts's ability to manage the Texas government was quickly dispelled by mid-1879. An often mentioned aspect of the Texas Constitution of 1876 was that the state had a "weak" governor style of government. However, there were three critical areas in which gubernatorial oversight and action proved decisive: budget and tax recommendations, the veto power, and last, the power to make appointments. The governor managed these aspects masterfully. Note has already been made of his pay-as-you-go fiscal policies, which set the tone.

The third significant impact was his power to appoint. Having presided over courts, assisted legal clients, and made campaign stops statewide for over two decades, Roberts had a firm grip on and knowledge of the leading political, educational, and business citizens. By the early summer of 1879 Roberts began the appointments to dozens of state agencies; for example, public cotton weighers, port pilot commissioners, state customs officials, hide and animal inspectors, notaries public, border extradition agents, and college board members. The most impactful appointments, given his judicial background, were the appointments by the fall of state district judges and district attorneys. He knew them and they knew him, helping create and galvanize a strong grassroots network by the end of 1879 across the state.[55]

One new state tax that caused much uproar was the "Bell Punch Law" applied to the saloon sale of all liquors. All dealers in "spirituous, vinous, and malt liquors" in quantities less than a quart were required to pay a special occupational tax based on the amount of single order drinks sold. Each establishment paid an annual tax of $250 and a tax of two cents on each drink. Special state-sponsored cash registers were provided by Austin at a cost of $10. The law went into effect in October 1879. Each time a customer paid, the register would be cranked and a bell would ring, thus tracking the number of drinks sold. The tax collector visited monthly, but he registers system quickly became unpopular and was easy to circumvent. Furthermore, penalties to mandate tax collection in most saloons failed. Thus the law proved a failure and was repealed in 1881. The best financial projections still left a $250,000 revenue shortfall for 1879–80. Beginning in 1881 the temperance movement supported passage of the first prohibition amendment in the senate, yet it failed in the house.[56]

The management of the vast public land domain in Texas occupied much of Roberts's time and his negotiations with the legislature. In 1879 the legislature approved designating, surveying, and selling 3,050,000 acres of the public domain for the building of a new state capitol. The governor issued an executive order requesting the legislature to resolve the "unorganized" land designated to organize a dozen counties in the northwest corner of the Panhandle adjoining the state line with New Mexico.[57] An additional 50,000 acres were set aside to pay for expenses of the capitol project. The formal start of planning for the new capitol began on April 18, 1879, with the appointment of a commissioner to contract, design, and plan for the new building. Governor Roberts further ordered that the one million acres of land previously appropriated for the proposed "state university," provided for in the state constitution, be surveyed in preparation for the possible generation of additional revenue. After these allocations, the Texas Land Office estimated that there were still 17,392,000 acres of vacant land. During the waning hours of the specially called session the legislature passed a bill to sell large sections of West Texas and the Panhandle that had not already been marketed. The new legislation, called the "Fifty Cent Law," so named because of the price of the land, called for not less the 160 acres and not more than 640 to any one person, and land was reduced in price from the normal $1.50 to fifty cents per acre. Half of the proceeds went to the school fund and half to retire the public debt. While the new law did not end state homestead programs for the small farmer or rancher, it did open sales to speculators and large corporations, causing complaints.

Even Roberts in his memoir noted: "The land was estimated at fifty cents an acre, though worth a great deal more." Roberts was not without his supporters, as the Austin *Texas Mule Ranger Weekly* championed the state's economic vitality and growth with articles like: "Texas—Now and Ten Years Hence," noting, "Texas is an empire, producing all the luxuries and necessaries of life, and capable of sustaining 30,000,000 people. Texas produced last year one fifth of the [nation's] cotton crop and next year, no doubt, she will produce 1,250,000 bales."[58]

Furthermore, the low price of land—even though it brought in needed revenue for the state—triggered the first significant opposition by Democrats against Roberts when both the General Land Office Commissioner Walsh and Lt. Governor Sayers (already unhappy with the cut in school funding) publicly attacked the land policy and urged its repeal. However, in spite of attacks on the railroads and land speculators, Roberts knew that one key to opening the Texas frontier was to expand rail service south to Laredo (and into Mexico) and west to El Paso. In the 1882 legislative fight to restore local public school funding, opponents to the governor challenged any future reductions, pointedly reminding the chief executive that two decades earlier, when he presided over the Secession Convention, "during the last days of the [1861] session, [they] voted themselves full compensation and made it retroactive!" As land speculation swiftly grew, and the state lacked the ability to monitor pricing properly, ensure proper surveying, or gauge the intent of the buyers, the law was repealed in 1883. This did not impact any of the other large tracts of land previously set aside for funding the capitol or the proposed state university.[59]

Frontier Troubles

Governor Roberts inherited an unsettled dispute on the northern frontier with Oklahoma Territory over Greer County along the Red River and constant disruptions in South Texas along the border with Mexico. As he entered office there was a steady outcry from Texans in these regions to curb the attacks and violence. The problems of scores of Texans being killed and thousands of livestock being killed or stolen were not new on the frontier, dating from the limited action during both the previous Coke and Hubbard administrations. Details of years of hostile attacks on the southern border and frontier were provided to the governor by Adjutant General John B. Jones.[60] Other than from newspaper accounts and rumors, few in East Texas, including Roberts, had any idea of the magnitude of the frontier depredations that continued unchecked. The farthest west he had traveled across Texas was to Austin (and never west of present day I-35), with the *Galveston Daily News* noting: "he is not well inclined towards frontier protection." One wonders whether Roberts's plan to sell land west of Austin was not a veiled effort to increase settlement of the region in order to reduce the incursions of Indians from the north and Mexican bandits from the south. No known documentation on this appears in the records, yet the dynamics of the problem tend to support this conclusion.

Notwithstanding the continuing cost to the state and federal government of over $400,000 annually in attempts to provide frontier defense, the efforts failed to calm the region fully. The federal outlay for protecting Texas was two million dollars, with each federal soldier costing $1,000 yearly. As with the frontier defense in the decade prior to the Civil War, federal troops in 1879, numbering 3,922 officers and enlisted men, were garrisoned in a string of forts reaching to El Paso and the New Mexico border. That averaged one inexperienced federal soldier for every 100 square miles. And the army's inability to maintain the initiative over rugged terrain due to the Indians' agility was only magnified when the Indians obtained repeating rifles. However, while the operations and deterrence of the army on the frontier have often been questioned, there was no question about the tremendous economic impact on the nascent frontier economy. Working with the U.S. Army commander in Texas, Major General Edward Ord, Roberts quickly became involved in appealing to federal officials in Washington for increased assistance. The governor-elect was in correspondence with General Ord prior to his inauguration to determine the scope of the frontier problem.[61]

Roberts's main challenge, in addition to obtaining adequate appropriations from the state and Washington, was the ability to cover the vast West Texas region effectively, which required well-trained and frontier-savvy mounted troops. Newly minted West Point officers were not trained or prepared for frontier duty, having been indoctrinated on European fixed-base siege and fortification tactics.[62] While the largest groups of Indians in Texas had been relocated from the Brazos Reserve to the Oklahoma Territory in the late 1850s, small bands of Comanches, Kiowas, and Lipans would leave the reservation near Fort Sill and roam south of the Red River on the pretext of hunting. With the depleted herds of buffalo, raiders along the frontier stole cattle, horses, and mules from settlers. Further west in the Trans-Pecos region Mescalero Apaches, often joined by Indians from Mexico, under the leadership of Chief Victorio, raided and killed with impunity—taking refuge in Mexico. Far from the Pecos, citizens in the Texas Panhandle petitioned the governor to send help to protect them not just from attacks and the "reign of terror" by Indians but also from roving bands of thieves and escaped convicts who robbed and murdered. Roberts and Texas Adjutant General John B. Jones directed Captain George W. Baylor to the region to command a unit of Texas guards and join with the troops at Fort Davis.[63]

Jones advised the governor that "citizens had a fight with Indians within fifty miles of the Capitol of the State," resulting in "frontier settlers moving back considerably towards the interior." By mid-1880, some forty companies of Texans comprised the Frontier Battalion. It was estimated that as many as 2,000 Indians frequented Texas to "hunt." Hostilities were such that the governor requested the army to authorize a special armed escort from Fort Elliot in the Panhandle to protect the team surveying the 3,050,000 "state capitol acres" in the Panhandle. While federal troops cooperated in returning Indians to Fort Sill and attempting to prevent their return to Texas, it was apparent that like earlier troops stationed on the frontier, they were ill-trained to stop the hit-and-run raiders. Following a letter of protest from Senator Coke to Roberts demanding that all hunting by Indians in Texas be halted, General Ord advised Governor Roberts that any hunting parties "on the border of the staked plains" would be escorted by troops to protect settlers. However, many hunting parties circumvented any army escort. In the case of Mexico, Roberts, not the State Department in Washington, handled border affairs and executed a treaty of extradition with the governor of Coahuila.[64]

Ex-cathedra

A smallpox epidemic in the fall of 1879 created a scare requiring the temporary quarantining and closing of the Port of Galveston, with an ordered inspection of all passengers and freight items, particularly those inbound from New Orleans. Roberts faced an equally acute problem of yellow fever on the lower Rio Grande—with Mayor Thomas Carson reporting over 500 cases in Brownsville during August. When ships and local health officials failed to abide by the governor's quarantine guidelines, passengers and crews were ordered to remain "quarantined on their vessels indefinitely if needed." Tensions ran high in Galveston when Dr. A. P. Brown, health inspector, wrote to tell the governor there was a "threatened 'running the blockade' with all N. O. men declared they will do if interrupted in traffic, when talking to me on this subject—they seem perfectly indifferent to human life." Roberts responded that the port inspectors would do all possible including the use of armed guards.[65]During the years prior to Roberts taking office there was a significant increase of violence along the Texas-Mexico border, primarily on the upper Rio Grande. With only a few federal forts to patrol over 1,400 miles, tensions were high. General Ord reported the challenge in combating Indians on both sides of the border in a vivid assessment:

The Indians, by their thieving course, have already depopulated some portions of the country. Lipans, which had thrived for over a year in the vicinity of Santa Rosa, a Mexican town, under the protection of the townspeople, who profited by the traffic of plunder brought by Indians from Texas. These relations are peculiar. Apaches are usually at war with the people of both countries. They have, however, friendly leagues with certain towns where they trade, and receive supplies of arms, ammunition, etc., for stolen mules. The people of San Carlos, who have amicable relations with the Comanches, make the town a depot for arms in their annual incursions into Mexico The Indians we have so continually complained of are a terror to the country.[66]

Articles in northern newspapers began to circulate stories, like the one in the Cincinnati *Enquirer,* that there was an active "war party" in President Rutherford B. Hayes's cabinet that "ostensibly would make the punishment of cattle thieves and [bandits] a mere pretext for plunging the country into a war of annexation [with Mexico]." These were some of the same claims used by Sam Houston twenty years earlier to justify filibustering in Mexico. However, Hayes, a five times wounded Union general, did not agree, publicly professing peace with Mexico. He did, however, change the rules of engagement by authorizing General Ord's troops on the border with permission, for the first time, "to pursue the marauders, if need be, across the border" in hot pursuit. The politicians in Washington were primarily being lobbied to enter Mexico by railroad lobbyists who "were anxious" to expand commercial operations south of the border. Proposed routes included one to the Pacific from Texas through Laredo via Monterrey to Topolobampo as well as a second line down the east coast of Mexico, with reports that Texas Senator Richard Coke in Washington supported this plan.

The strange aspect of this saber rattling was that Ord in Texas had not been advised of such plans, and in fact was in the final stages of working out a border protection plan with Mexican General Jerónimo Trevino, in charge of the northern region, for the two armies to cooperate to capture bandits and to move any hostile Mexican Indians into the interior of the country. Furthermore, Ord advised Trevino, who in turn notified President Porfirio Díaz, that the cross-border hot pursuit, "if needed," was "no insult to Mexican sovereignty if such an incursion into Mexican territory happens." After months of delay President Hayes recognized the Díaz government, but Mexico still refused to treat seriously the expanding border problems as long as the hot-pursuit orders remained in place. Hayes wanted no war with Mexico, regardless of the interests of the railroads. Private correspondence between Texas State Representative Guy M. Bryan of Galveston and Hayes confirmed this, noting that "while some are exasperated or have suffered raids of Mexicans and Indians," they wanted to find a way to "be a go*od neighbor.*" Governor-elect Roberts learned of these details shortly after the election. However, any protests about U.S. incursions by Mexico were eliminated in March 1880, when the U.S. secretary of war rescinded the order of all army cross-border pursuits south of the Rio Grande.[67]

Unbeknownst to those scheming in Washington with eager railroad lobbyists, Governor Roberts maintained a valuable back-channel contact with President Díaz through his friend Colonel Santos Benavides. A native of Laredo and former Confederate commander in South Texas, Benavides was selected by Díaz to be his envoy to keep the Mexican dictator abreast of political events in Texas, on the border, and in the United States. A commercial dispute concerning Mexican boatmen's right to have free access for their ferry on the Rio Grande between Brownsville, Texas, and Matamoros, Mexico, soon involved the U.S. secretary of state as well as Roberts in Austin and authorities in Mexico City.[68]

Colonel Benavides noted in a February 1880 letter to President Hayes's Secretary of State William M. Evarts, "At an early date I had the pleasure to communicate these views [of Díaz] to Governor O. M. Roberts, and I have the honor of his reply." Furthermore, "Addressing you, as I do, outside of the pale of strictly official correspondence, I speak without the formality and reserve of diplomatic form." Benavides was a citizen of Texas, and his confidential facilitation included routine contact with both the U.S. Army under General Ord and Mexican generals Servando Canales and Trevino. While scattered incidents continued along the border, the tension of expanded hostilities was greatly reduced. The economic development in South Texas helped bring calm. The stabilizing of the national government in Mexico by Diaz was further evidence of better relations. The lower Rio Grande valley anchored by the twin border cities of Brownsville and Matamoros seemed to be less volatile, as shown by the reporting in 1881–82 of the gross value of trans-border commerce of $5.2 million, an increase of 20 percent over the previous year. A further indication of improved conditions was the arrival of the first passenger train in Laredo on March 8, 1882, carrying Civil War hero William Tecumseh Sherman, who represented the International and Great Northern Railroad. This had a profound and lasting influence on the town, soon to link the border by rail to Monterrey and Mexico City.[69]

Robbed the Gallows

The frontier situation faced by Texas for decades was also the source of a possible financial windfall due to the state. Since the Civil War, Texas had petitioned the federal government to reimburse the state for frontier expenses. Roberts's administration, with the help of Representative Ashbel Smith in the Texas House and Senator Richard Coke and Representative John Reagan in Washington, followed up on claims for over $500,000 dating from 1854. The most decisive attempt to collect from the federal government occurred a year before Roberts took office, with a detailed report to the secretary of war that was referred for the fourth time to the House Committee on Military Affairs for payment. Once he was governor, Roberts again pursued federal payment during his administration. This was followed with Texas Representative Reagan introducing a joint resolution in April 1879 to pay the accumulated claim due to Texas of $1,629,615.69. No documents supporting this accounting have been found. Once again the audit documents of expenses, frontier unit muster rolls and rosters, and damages were either lost or tabled in committee. The records in the *Texas Indian Papers* and additional filings of requests and formal bills or resolutions in the U.S. House for payment by

Reagan in 1880 led some to assume Texas was fully reimbursed. However, in fact, settlement on claims between the state and federal government for frontier defense was not approved until 1908, when Congress allowed a final payment to Texas in 1911 of only $104,426.74.[70]

Oran Roberts's first term as governor proved consequential. His simple message of pay- as-you-go, the passage of a broad array of revenue-generating laws, and the power of the veto were the hallmarks of the implementation of his fiscally conservative principles. Approval by Texans was generally forthcoming, yet there were always detractors who questioned his success in tackling the state's failed fiscal policies by attacking and cutting appropriations to public education and many of their other pet programs. At sixty-four Roberts seemed little concerned about the vacillating comments and criticisms that routinely appeared in the press. Gratuitous assessments of the governor's approach to a new era of state government in Texas were noted in the New Orleans *Times,* the out-of-state paper that was most widely circulated in Texas (imported through Galveston):

> The Man [Roberts] ancient in years and holding to the fossilized and forgotten doctrines of the Paleozoic age of politics discouraged immigration, made war on the public schools, vetoed the customary appropriation to pay interest on the State debt, broke down the State force for the conservation of public order, and by extraordinary abuse of the pardoning power, robbed the gallows of its dues and the State's prison of its usefulness.[71]

In a highly anticipated and most detailed fiscal and legislative report, Roberts released his message to the incoming Seventeenth Legislature on "Appropriations and Expenditures under the Control of the Governor," which recapped his first term and outlined his priorities going forward. He reviewed both successes and failures. Concerning the Bell Punch Law, which he felt had failed, he noted, "It is notorious that the law was not generally executed." The failure, even after aggressive prosecution of violators, was that both saloon keepers and local sheriffs did not want to enforce it. Public land sales had been slow but did provide a ready stream of revenue, in spite of fraud from illegal surveys and straw-man deals. While many complained of his pardon policy and commuted sentences, he expanded cash rewards, ranging from $75 to $1,000 and totaling over $16,500, for criminals arrested, and more than 100 fugitives from justice, primarily for offenses of murder, were arrested in his first years than in the previous two administrations. When "drummers" evaded the payment of taxes, Roberts recommend that fines be increased and traveling salesmen be required to have a license to do business. Finally, he indirectly thanked the legislature for approving funds for repairs long overdue to the governor's mansion, noting, "There should be a roof put on the house that would turn the water on the outside of the walls, instead of on the inside, as it does now!"[72]

Criticism in newspapers seemed to have little negative impact on Roberts, given the high regard for him among the power brokers in the Democratic Party, the way the bar of the state applauded his judicial approach to fiscal affairs, and a growing respect from Texans—especially with farmers and local school educators—who felt he was their champion. The San Antonio German language *Freie Presse,* which only a year earlier had attacked Roberts's veto of public school funding, now applauded the governor, noting, "We hear of nothing but the immaculate wisdom of Roberts, to whose wonderful financial genius we are indebted." Focused on the future, and ignoring media comments, he entertained aspirations for the U.S. Senate (after having being snubbed in 1866). However, there was little doubt that Roberts would run for a second term in office. A small faction of Democrats expressed support for Lieutenant Governor Sayers, supporting his claims that it was unjust to cut public school funds and frontier defense. He also took exception to the Bell Punch Law and the fifty cents law. Sayers was backed by the radical *Globe-Democrat,* which attacked Roberts as "a Bourbon of the Bourbons and has done infinite damage to the state."[73]

The often opinionated *Galveston Daily News,* its circulation approaching some 150,000 statewide, submitted a laudatory editorial on the governorship of Roberts, noting that he had "been a series of surprises . . . his opponents have been more than surprised and they have been perplexed and disconcerted." In regard to public education, "The governor in this connection broadly recognizes that to educate the rising generation is in no sense a charity, but is in every sense a great, constant imperative duty imposed upon the government of the state. It is important to be assured that the governor is on the right path . . . it is better and nobler for any man, occupying such a position as that [of] Gov. Roberts, to be inconsistent and right than to be consistent and wrong. There are occasions when consistency is not only a blunder in statesmanship, but a crime in morals."[74]

The 1880 fall campaign started in the spring and Roberts focused on his record, ignoring Sayers's comments—and what the *Galveston Daily News* termed opposition amounting to little more than "lightning-rod peddlers." Roberts's land program to increase state revenue included encouraging immigration not only from the lower South but also from Europe. Conservative-minded Texans embraced his message, with Roberts concluding: "The people of Texas are now beginning to see their way out of the former gloom of financial embarrassment . . . that all our leading interests have reached a solid basis. That gives promise of future prosperity in the operations of the state government, and that each and all of them may now be safely promoted in harmonious co-operation." While Roberts promoted economic growth as a means to increase state revenue, the party debated the need to encourage migration to Texas, possibly fueled by the Greenback Labor Party denouncement of the importation of servile labor from Asiatic counties. By April 1880, county caucus meetings across the state canvassed elected delegates that "unqualifiedly endorsed Gov. Roberts."[75]

Governor Roberts wrapped up his campaign tour with the keynote address to the Texas State Teachers' Convention in Mexia, outlining the gains made in restructuring public education, the support of a state university (free from any sectarian government), and his pledge to increase school funding in the next legislature. With the teachers' unanimous endorsement he awaited the state Democratic convention in Dallas. The convention platform called for increased school funding, maintaining tight fiscal oversight, reducing taxes, improved protection of the frontier (to include an effort to be reimbursed by the federal government), regulating railroad freight and tariff rates, and a pledge to endorse the establishment of the University of Texas. Roberts, with the added support of the Grange, received the required two-thirds votes on the first convention ballot to secure the nomination, and in the largely Democratic state this was tantamount to securing re-election. While some in opposition claimed he was a "demagogue" in his approach to limit funding to local schools, the Dallas *Daily Herald* predicted that the Old Alcalde would be swept into office, "Jingling his 'cash balance' and telling how he pays as he goes." Former Republican Edmund Davis represented his party, and William Hamman was once again nominated by the Greenbackers. With efforts by the opposition to forgo a "fusion" challenge, Roberts easily won with 166,101 votes (63 percent), compared to Davis's 64,382 (24 percent), and Hamman's 33,721 (13 percent). The Democrats, with the waning showing of the third party efforts (except for Greenbacker George Washington "Wash" Jones winning the Fifth Congressional District seat) were in firm control of all levels of the state and local governments.[76]

Roberts's second inauguration occurred on January 17, 1881, nearly twenty years to the day after he had orchestrated secession and carried out an insurrection against the United States. Roberts addressed a joint session of both Texas houses, intent on having a better working relationship by singling out the importance of the work ahead: "It is only by wisdom of the legislature, the harmonious co-operation of the executive officers, and the patriotic aid of the citizens, that I can hope to equal to the grave responsibilities imposed upon me, in the effort to make Texas what she should be in the near future—the great and prosperous State of the American Union."[77]

The Seventeenth Legislature approved an increase in funding for public schools, to one- fourth of the state's budget. Given the increased revenue from the sale of public school lands, ad valorem taxes were reduced from fifty cents to forty cents per one hundred dollars valuation. One observer noted that "the old man is honest as the day is long—is stingy with the public money to a point bordering on the miserly—has a horror of going in debt." The poll tax was reduced, and the controversial Bell Punch liquor tax was repealed.[78] In a seemingly unnoticed or unheralded action, Roberts continued championing increased funding for the state-sponsored lunatic asylum and veterans' programs. Opposition newspapers such as the Clarksville *Standard* were never short of criticisms, such as: "Governor Roberts is neither sugar nor salt, notified especially a saint or a sinner, but he has acted like an old Texan, who feels that he is a white man, with the free spirit of original manhood which first settled Texas and made its Republic, which threw out its flag and demanded recognition of the world. Most of his critics in this case seem to have little comprehension of such spirit." Little did the *Standard* know he represented Texas' interests in a number of matters that never became news. A case in point is his support of a petition from merchants in El Paso in a letter to U.S. Secretary of State Blaine to protest the implementation of the 40-mile-wide free trade zone by Mexico authorities along the Rio Grande that in effect would harm business in Texas and harm revenue to the state.[79]

President Garfield

In July 1881, following the attempted assassination of President James A. Garfield, Roberts gained nationwide notoriety when he refused to issue a statewide proclamation for a "Day of Thanksgiving" in honor of the wounded president. The recognition was advocated and promoted by governors in the northeastern states. Roberts's rejection of what the *Galveston Daily News* termed "a religious activity for the 'blessed deliverance'" of Garfield during the president's attempt to recover was in line with Governor Roberts's "eminently practical" views of not mixing up the state with the appearance of church or religious affairs. Other than his objection to state-church conflict, quite possibly Roberts harbored some personal objections to the former Union Army general officer who had fought at both Shiloh and Chickamauga as well as having been a sitting U.S. House member from Ohio in 1866 who indirectly blocked Roberts's seat in the Senate. The response from across Texas was mixed, with the *Wills Point Local* leading the opposition: "Gov. Roberts' action in the thanksgiving matter wherein he tried to create the impression that the people of Texas were a heathenish, God-forsaken, skeptical and unthankful set, drove the last nail in his political coffin, notwithstanding the opinion of his bootlicking element to the contrary."[80] In contrast, the Clarksville *Standard,* which opposed the governor on many issues, expressed support: "We think that Gov. Roberts did exactly right in declining to follow in this line of monarchial [sic] precedents . . . the governor was not placed in Austin to do any man worship or suggest any." Unmoved by newspaper editorials across the state, Roberts and Texas issued no proclamation, and on September 19, 1881, Garfield died due improper medical treatment.[81]

Capitol Flames

Tragedy struck at noon on November 9, 1881, when smoke was discovered filling the hall of the third floor of the state capitol. Governor Roberts was in the building. Smelling smoke, he stepped out into the hall. At first the extent of the fire did not seem critical, but within an hour the building was a total loss. In the inquiry called by the governor and chaired by Travis County Justice of the Peace Wilson Gregg, Roberts was the star witness to events. At the time smoke was detected, Roberts was in the southwest corner of the representatives' hall, holding a meeting of the Board of Capital Commissioners on the plans for and design of the new capitol. Attendees were J. H. McLeary, William Brown, W. C. Walsh, F. R. Lubbock, L. N. Norton and Judge Joseph Lee. As the governor went to investigate he was confronted by a man running up from the basement "coked with smoke." Roberts, Joseph Lee, and Secretary of State Bowman ran downstairs in the direction of the billowing smoke. The door to the room with the fire was closed. They broke down the door and discovered the fire almost engulfing the storage room. Bowman scrambled to have his staff remove government documents. Backing away from the fire, they had trouble closing the door, but Roberts recalled that "somebody standing near him, got down and crawled to the door and pulled it to." With the alarm out to the fire department, the staffs in the other state offices removed records and left the building. The legislature had previously turned down funding to place water hydrants near the capitol, so the fire hoses had to be secured from locations on Congress Street, and given the long distance, the water for fighting the fire had little or no pressure, and the building burned out of control. Roberts noted that as the fire spread, "I walked down to my office and found my sons [Robert and Peter], gathering things and I remained in there until the last thing was taken out . . . seeing fire and smoke above the transom, and seeing it flashing up in the room on the walls, indicated the extent of the fire." At the conclusion of the hearing, Roberts agreed with the investigators that the fire started from sparks in a flue. With the inquiry complete, the governor concluded, "my opinion is that it caught from some pure accident, without anybody intending it." There were no injuries, and planning for the new capital continued within a few days after the governor relocated his office to the Supreme Court Building.[82]

THE UNINSURED LOSSES at the capitol—including the library, some supreme court records, the state geological collection, furniture and fixtures in the legislative chambers, portraits and paintings—were estimated at $220,000. Governor Roberts met with Senator Lawrence S. Ross of Waco, chairman of the Senate Finance Committee, to review the loss to the state. Oran Roberts was determined to maintain concentration on the tight budget controls. All state departments were relocated, and the loss did not delay the plans for the new capitol. Historian Louis Wortham concluded, "By the time Roberts went out of office the finances of the state were on the road to full rehabilitation." In spite of the capital fire, an atmosphere of calm and goodwill prevailed between the executive and the legislature as Governor Roberts turned his full attention to public higher education and especially the establishment of the long awaited University of Texas.

IT WAS the normal cooperative and competitive practice of newspapers to exchange articles as well as debate politics and personalities around Texas, often targeting Oran Roberts. He told one interviewer that "those who write for papers seem to know more about my future course than I know myself . . . and such reporters are essentially officious and unreliable intermeddlers, who are likely to spoil the game before the cards are dealt!"[83] As one of the most highlighted subjects, his future was always in question:

> The Waco *Telephone* asks: "Does Governor Roberts expect to live out the century as governor?" To which the Jefferson *Democrat* replies: "Our impression is he does not, but the mass of the people find that it is especially annoying to the Republicans and the pseudo Democrats, and the so called Independents, they may insist on his being governor until 1900."[84]

CHAPTER 5

PUBLIC HIGHER EDUCATION 1879–1883

The time may come, as I hope it will, that we may be able to have a class of young men who will come to that school to learn agriculture and mechanics practically for their own use of them, as well as for spreading its improvements over the state. And when it is found that by attending that school it will be learned how to produce two ears of wheat and corn and two bails of cotton by the same labor and capital that have been heretofore producing but one, then it will be understood that most extensive and the most beneficial to our race that has engaged the educators of any previous age. It can and will yet be done.

— OLAN M. ROBERTS, MAY 21, 1879 GOVERNOR AND PRESIDENT, BOARD OF A. AND M. COLLEGE

TEXAS HAS ALWAYS HAD education as a major priority, yet the state failed to fund and staff schools adequately. Oran Roberts had both a major role in the fostering of local public education, in what were then known as "common" schools, as well as a significant impact on the inception and growth of public higher education in the state. Judge Roberts's early experiences with educational programs during his career provided a general foundation for his role and impact on schooling in Texas. He was one of the very few of his generation to receive a university education, and his time at the University of Alabama was critical in shaping his formative years. Shortly after arriving in the Republic of Texas he became active in the advancement of education in East Texas. His concern was that private parochial institutions were tied more with religious ideology than with providing basic education. This led to Roberts's involvement to redirect the teaching priorities of the schools in San Augustine, resulting in his selection as the chairman of the local school board. The third event was during the early years of Reconstruction, when he taught in a small private school in Gilmer, Texas. Yet his most challenging experiences with education were the angst and necessity during the first term of his governorship in 1879–1880 to cut funding to common schools and then, as the state's financial situation improved, to fund and restructure a more robust educational system across Texas. The jewel of his legacy would be championing public higher education.[1]

In a four-year period as governor between 1879 and 1883 he put his stamp on the first four public institutions of higher learning in the state—Texas A&M, Sam Houston, and Prairie View universities, and the University of Texas. Roberts's engagement with education likely surprised many in Austin who were concerned with other issues and priorities. However, as a seasoned and respected jurist he knew well the covenants in the constitutions of Texas, which set forth the conditions of creation, endowment, and governance needed to support such endeavors. The state's primary champion of education in Texas, Rufus C. Burleson, reminded the governor, "The highest interest of Texas—socially, politically and financially—all demand efficient [public] schools."[2]

Governor Roberts is most closely identified with the opening of the University of Texas, but in fact he played a pivotal role in the three earlier public institutions of higher learning in Texas, all of which predated the inauguration of the state university in Austin. Texas' first venture into public higher education began with the opening of the Agricultural and Mechanical College of Texas in 1876, followed by the establishment of Prairie View Normal School in Waller County in 1878 and Sam Houston State Normal in Huntsville, Texas, in 1879. As both the governor and president of the board of directors of each of the first three institutions during their formative years, Roberts guided the often reluctant Texans, legislators, and collegiate faculty during these difficult years.[3]

Land—the public domain—was the pivotal asset and source of revenue for the cash-strapped state treasury as well as the primary source of funding for public education. The largest need and demand for public higher education funding in 1879 was for the A&M College, with Texas Comptroller Stephen Dandry writing to board member Anderson Peeler to confirm that revenue from bonds in the University Fund would be in addition to any appropriation from the legislature. One dynamic that was part of Roberts's aggressive plans to raise revenue for the state without raising taxes was the rapid population growth of the state, doubling from 8 million in 1870 to 17 million in 1880. New settlers moving west and needing a homestead fueled this growth![4] Roberts in his memoirs, published in 1898, offers the best review of the governor's approach to the public domain, to assist education:

Previous to the administration of Governor Roberts, the manner of selling school lands was to limit the sale to one person to one hundred and sixty acres, and to require the purchaser to settle upon the land; and pre-emptions of the same amount were allowed upon settlement. Many thousands of acres were being used for pasturage by stockmen without buying the lands or paying for the pasturage on them. The policy was, therefore, adopted and acted upon of increasing the quantity permitted to be sold to a single purchaser, and to extend the time for payment, and not to require actual settlement upon the land. The proceeds of these sales were required to be invested in the bonds of the State or of the United States, for the benefit of the free public schools.[5]

Sam Houston Normal

One exception to Governor Roberts's approach to address the state's fiscal deficits with a pay-as-you-go program was to lay the groundwork for expanded access and improvement in public higher education. His veto of funding for local common schools during his first year in office proved only for the short term, as in his inaugural address and first messages to the Texas legislature he stated his intentions to foster public higher education. With the return of Democratic rule to the legislature, his support of plans to establish teachers' training schools, proposed in the party platform, received renewed interest. The improvement of local "common" schools required more qualified teachers. Fully aware of the impact of a conservative state budget, Roberts in his address to the legislature in early February 1879 presented a plan that provided state appropriations with a match of $6,000 of philanthropist funding from the George Peabody Educational Fund. Furthermore, the Huntsville community, which desired to have one of the new normal schools, also had to make a matching contribution of $14,000 to the establishment of the new school as well as providing a valid title to the defunct Austin College site.[6] Before there was an official state search for a site for a new school, a group of Huntsville's leading citizens, led by attorney Leonard Abercrombie, contacted House Speaker John Cochran with a detailed proposal to convert old college campus grounds in the city into the "Sam Houston Institute." Speaker Cochran, in advance of any would-be competitors, pushed the bill through the House, and it passed by three votes. On April 21, 1879—San Jacinto Day—Governor Roberts signed the bill formally establishing Sam Houston Normal Institute, placing it under the control and monitoring of the State Board of Education in Austin, consisting of the governor, comptroller, and secretary of state.[7]

Governor Roberts demonstrated his interest in public higher education by working with the legislature, private philanthropists, teachers' associations, and local communities to extend more opportunities to Texas students. His work with Prairie View for Black students as it was reorganized in early 1879 indirectly helped advance the legislative approval and opening of Sam Houston Normal Institute. The governor and Representative Roger Q. Mills from Corsicana, a former Confederate colonel and twice wounded veteran, were the keynote speakers for the formal opening of "Sam Houston" on October 10, 1879. Texas State Representative J. E. McComb of Montgomery, who championed the enabling legislation in Austin, stated that "an efficient system of public schools was now the paramount consideration with the statesman of Texas; that in regard to public improvements and all the material interest, Texas was far on the road to great developments." Early recruiting accounted for the sixty-eight students who registered, with a signed pledge to teach "for a term of years" in Texas common schools after graduation. While Roberts was often portrayed as a "stiff-necked" and somewhat aloof stump speaker, he received special notice by the *Galveston Daily News* for his hour-long "speech-making," his presentation at the college's opening: "His remarks were interspersed with quaint and humorous allusions that kept the audience entertained," J. J. Lane noted, "Governor Roberts co-operated heartily with them in the enterprise." The irony, most likely not apparent to most in attendance that day, was that Roberts was front and center at the dedication of a school named for his one-time friend General Sam Houston, who had then become his arch enemy some two decades prior—and that Roberts made no disparaging remarks about his old friend. Prior to completing his visit to Huntsville and returning to Austin, the governor and guest speakers had dinner at the residence of Colonel Thomas J. Goree, superintendent of the state penitentiary.[8]

Within a few weeks Roberts would return to central Texas to deal with altercations at the A&M College near Bryan.

The Crisp Affair

From the inception of Texas A&M in the early 1870s, the governor of Texas was the chairman or "president" of its board of directors. Governor Richard Coke had the honor as the first board president and presided over the dedication and opening of the college on October 4, 1876. Shortly after the college's inauguration Coke resigned his gubernatorial office to become the junior U.S. senator from Texas, passing the governor's office to Lieutenant Governor Richard B. Hubbard, who had been an ex-officio member of the A&M board since its inception. Once governor, Hubbard encouraged the legislature to provide a larger appropriation to the fledgling college because experimental farming, equipment, and machine shops cost a great deal more than classical and literary classroom instruction. Those increases in agricultural funding were not to weaken the literary features of the college. The literary or "classical instruction" features of the college and the absence of an adequate level of focus on "agriculture and mechanics" instruction would to result in both internal disruption as well as external attacks from groups concerned with the mission of the college during these early years.[9]

Texas A&M's first president, Thomas S. Gathright, was a friend of Hubbard's, and the governor had been involved with the president's selection as well as the recruiting and approval of the first faculty. Born in Georgia in 1829, Gathright began his teaching career in Alabama, before moving to Mississippi to open a private school for boys called Summerville Institute. During the Civil War he successfully argued in a petition to Governor Charles Clark in Jackson that his work should exempt him from the Confederate draft in 1861. Governor Richard Coke, in the search for a president of the soon to be opened A&M College of Texas, first offered the post to Jefferson Davis, who declined the offer, and then offered it to Gathright, who accepted in the summer of 1876. During the college's first two years, first Coke and then Governor Hubbard supported Gathright. However, Hubbard became a lame-duck governor in 1878, failing to receive the Democratic nomination, which fell to Judge Oran Roberts after a ruckus and a convention stalemate. While Roberts had made no known comments about Texas A&M, Gathright was concerned with the abrupt change in the governor's mansion. He wrote to new faculty member Louis McInnis, noting, "I greatly regret his [Hubbard's] defeat, and think our College lost its best friend." As noted by historian Henry C. Dethloff, "Texas A&M had indeed lost a sympathetic political ally at that moment." Roberts's long and careful study of the Texas Constitution, his judicial experience, as well as his experience at the University of Alabama rekindled his desire during his earliest days in the governor's office to focus on the eventual establishment of the constitutionally mandated "University of Texas." Surveying the role of first three public institutes, Roberts concluded: "There is largely a wide demand in our state for just such scientific and practical industrial education and if there exists a demand as wide for a broader and more liberal literary and professional culture than existing colleges within our [state] limits can supply, then the time has come for the establishment of the State University."[10] However, Roberts's attention to addressing the fiscal crisis in the state delayed any immediate action on his part or recommendation to the legislature. In the meantime, ample attention was given to the troubles at Texas A&M.

Governor Roberts in his first inaugural message on January 21, 1879, confirmed Gathright's concerns that all portions of the state government including funding for the college would come under detailed scrutiny, noting that his administration would "retrench expenses from the top to bottom." Furthermore, he alluded to the support of the college as one of the "burdens" of the state that needed close examination. The college needed to conform with the mandates of the Morrill Act of 1862 to produce graduates for agricultural and mechanical jobs—Texas needed skilled laborers rather than people schooled in the classics. Roberts, after commending the directors and faculty for their persistence in advancing programs at the college, given their limited resources, noted that he would recommend all funding possible, but it depended on the status of the overall state finances. Vocal members of the Grange had expressed their concerns to the governor on the misguided path of Texas A&M, which offered classical studies, and the lack of agricultural instruction. Furthermore, Grange members would not be satisfied until an experimental farm was established.[11] Ironically, the reason for this lay with the college's board of directors chaired by the governor, who set the curriculum and who hired the faculty. The *Austin Weekly Democratic Statesman* closely followed the growth of and debate over the programs of the college, noting as the Sixteenth Legislative session opened: "Farmers say they can instruct their children in plowing and digging and rail-splitting, and that they expect the learned gentlemen at Bryan to teach the youths how to utilize soil and the chemical value of the contents of the bat cave on Capital Hill."[12]

Three weeks after his inauguration Roberts delivered one of his first messages on public education. It chastised those who had gone before him for not acting on the creation of the state university. From this early date in February 1879, despite the budget crisis, Roberts begin to lay plans and garner support for the university. In this report, he opened: "I beg leave to submit some views for consideration upon the University of Texas." He then recapped with a synopsis of actions dating from 1839, when fifty leagues of land were donated and set apart for an endowment for the future university. He noted, "When, about forty years ago this liberal donation was made, it could hardly have been anticipated that at this remote period there would be no university in Texas," further stating that if no action were taken, "It may be forty more [years] before Texas will have a university, when its founders and most of their children shall have disappeared from the stage of action." Thus he recommended to the legislature that an additional one million acres of state land be set aside and the policy to sell the land be changed to allow a more rapid disposal "as the value of the land grows with the growth of the empire," and an increase in the university fund, so that "we may expect in a few years to have a university."[13]

In no way did the governor attack Texas A&M or question its funding under the federal Morrill Act. His primary concerns were, first, to delineate the college's mandate to teach "agricultural and mechanical arts" distinct from the mission of the proposed university, and second, to urge the legislature to take action on establishing the university as soon as was practical. Roberts's next messages of budget cuts and audits of all departments imposed a halt on any new action requiring large appropriations. The A&M board in its report to the governor detailed its concerns over the mandate placed upon the college: "It is undeniable that not enough has been done to carry out fully the main objects of the grant and for this short-coming the directory [board] can only justify the main objects by positive deficiency of means, which they hope may be furnished to the successors. Could they have used for agricultural development the money put into the new dormitories, much might have been done, but without dormitories we could not have scholars and without scholars we could not build up a great State institution of learning, and those who have applied for instruction so far have not demanded instruction in agriculture or mechanics."[14]

Following the submission of Texas A&M's annual report to the legislature, published along with other key state reports in the *Galveston Daily News* and *Austin Weekly Democratic Statesman,* the college directors, in hopes of shedding light on the funding needs of the institution, requested that the legislature appoint a visiting committee of representatives to the campus. The committee of two senators and three House members arrived on March 3, 1879. The committee found 167 student-cadets in good order and conduct of military discipline. The shops, dorms, stables, and classrooms were crowded but adequate. As Dethloff notes, the faculty were quick to present a series of "agricultural classes," which were conveniently in session during the campus legislative tour. The notable inadequacies included the shortage of laboratory equipment, no library, shortage of farm implements, and a major need for a campus hospital. The committee recommended to the legislature that funding equal to the interest accumulated in the University Fund be made available to the college to address the deficiencies mentioned. The college received broad support from O. N. Hollingsworth, secretary of the State Board of Education, recommending that twenty thousand dollars be appropriated to "establish a course of practical instruction in agricultural."[15]

As Roberts turned his attention to the state budget in early 1879, Texas A&M worked to implement more agricultural programs with assistance from the only college agricultural instructor, Rev. Carlisle P. B. Martin. Professor Martin, who had previously developed and taught agriculture courses at schools in Georgia, was hired and the *Galveston Daily News* considered him "one of the ablest agricultural educators in the South." Like all the faculty at the newly created land grant schools, Martin was hampered by a shortage of textbooks, and the complete lack of laboratories, livestock, barns, or farm equipment for instruction. Martin borrowed implements from local Brazos County farmers, instituted a campus-wide tree planting program, opened up a 30-acre school-managed farm for demonstration work, and received board approval to "hire" cadets to work on the farm. In 1917 Clarence Ousley, the first director of the Texas Extension Service, noted that although Martin was a minister of the gospel and popular with both students and farmers, his "knowledge of agriculture must have been entirely *empirical* . . . as was the knowledge of most educated gentlemen of the time." This momentarily curbed complaints from the Grange, aided by the fact that Professor Martin was a past Master of the Montgomery County Grange north of Houston, and "silenced sticklers for the [letter of the] law [Morrill Act] of Congress."[16]

Roberts closely followed events and progress at the college. To ensure a smooth transition to conform with Morrill Act, he requested that Gathright submit a detailed reorganization plan for the college. The governor sought more control of all public higher education, recommending a bill whereby he and not the legislature would appoint the board of directors (with the approval of the Senate). Not surprisingly, Gathright and his "classical" faculty supported classical studies and were slow to recommend that budgeting at the college be directed to agriculture and mechanical arts [engineering]. Gathright emphasized that the state needed both agricultural and classical studies—it was performing many of services and offering the classes that would eventually be taught at new state university. Roberts viewed Texas A&M, even as enrollment grew, as little more than a technical or adjunct branch (as described in the state constitution) of the yet to be established "university." Henry Dethloff noted that the scope of Roberts's plans regarding the founding of a university was not known by or acknowledged by Gathright at that time. Other than securing more university funds via land sales, Roberts, whose first-year focus was on the state budget review, made no formal recommendations to the legislature at the time for organization of the new university, other than his brief inaugural comment.[17]

The outwardly calm image of the college near Bryan was short-lived. Following less than remarkable commencement exercises in June 1879, there was an undercurrent of campus unrest due to poor attendance by elected officials from Austin and a lingering drought. Governor Roberts and the representatives were occupied with the special legislative session that had been called and did not attend the commencement. Notably, none of the graduates completed a degree in agriculture or the mechanical arts. Martin's demonstration farm had failed in the heat and prolonged drought, and Gathright thus had cause to be pessimistic when the legislature approved only $7,500 for the upcoming year. Only three graduates, of a dozen seniors who received classical degrees, completed extra courses in "natural science and agriculture": Charles Rogan, W. A. F. Trenckmann, and A. Cunningham.[18] During commencement unrest among the faculty boiled over, with a disagreement between President Gathright and mathematics professor Alexander Hogg (no relation to future Governor James Hogg). Hogg had recently published a booklet entitled "Industrial Education," describing how an A&M college should be organized and managed. Hogg irritated Gathright by mailing a copy to the A&M board members and Governor Roberts—with the implied message that he knew better how to manage the college, and undoubtedly expressing his interest in someday becoming president. The clash between the two educators occurred in what should have been a routine meeting to approve the upcoming promotion of Corps of Cadets officers for the 1879–1880 term, from names submitted by the Corps commandant, Captain George T. Olmstead.

Hogg, taking advantage of a number of longstanding and festering disputes among the nine-member faculty, which included Gathright, orchestrated a rejection of the approval of Cadet John C. Crisp as the senior captain of the Corps and ranking cadet (today known as the Cadet Corps commander). The vote was 5–4. Professors L. M. Lewis, Alexander Hogg, William Banks, Port Smythe, and Robert Morris voted to disapprove the promotion, and Gathright, Olmstead, Louis

McInnis, and John Hand supported Crisp. Cadet Crisp was reduced from captain to private, with "the evil effect of the unsettled controversy . . . at the bottom of this trouble." Cadet Crisp was an exceptional student with no demerits and an excellent conduct and leadership record. No clear reason was given for the majority's disapproval, and the faculty meeting adjourned with both sides hostile to the decision—and Crisp at a loss over the unprecedented action.[19]

During the summer A&M Board member Anderson J. Peeler made the governor aware of the situation and expected it to be resolved by the faculty prior to the next board meeting in August and the opening of the 1879 fall term. Crisp, with Gathright's permission, remained on campus to study, taking the opportunity to write asking cadets and friends to send testimonials to the board of his good standing. Hogg, away from the campus for most of summer, returned in time for the August 25 board meeting to refute charges and the formal petition by Crisp that Hogg be dismissed for cause. Hogg, during his testimony to the board, conveyed his irritation once he learned that "Crisp wrote on postal card to cadets about me, saying, 'Hogg is trying to get me out; will you see a fellow student thus treated!' These postal cards are stuck up in show-cases [all] over the state."[20]

While not tied to the postponed hearing on the Crisp affair, the board in August, following the governor's guideline for "economy," cut the president's salary from $3,000 to $2,000 and professors' pay from $2,000 to $1,500. Then the board allocated the recent $7,500 appropriation for farm implements, development of a library, and acquisition of laboratory equipment, and medical supplies. Peeler intervened to advise Crisp to not appear before the board and to let the faculty resolve the problem. During the wait, Crisp gathered the many testimonials and filed a formal written statement to Governor Roberts and the board. The board adjourned with the news that Hogg was demanding that Crisp be immediately dismissed from the college. The feud spread to the college staff, merchants in Bryan, the Grange, and politicians in Austin. Professor Martin and board members Anderson Peeler and Senator George Pfeuffer—who received confidential behind the scenes information on all the parties involved in the dispute from the steward of the college, General Hamilton P. Bee —visited Governor Roberts in Austin to convey complaints and the impasse involving Hogg and Gathright. General Bee, fifty-seven years of age, was the most experienced member of the A&M staff. Bee, the former speaker of the Texas House, had known Oran Roberts since the mid-1840s, and in addition to crossing paths during the Civil War they had been engaged in the political affairs of East Texas for decades. It was clear to the governor after the briefing from Bee, the stalemate in the August board meeting, and the disruption in the weeks prior to the start of the fall term on October 20th, as Dethloff concluded, that "The imbroglio passed the point of reconciliation."[21]

Following a petition from two-third of the cadets, who by late October were fully engaged in the feud, requesting (with no direct reference to Cadet Crisp) that President Gathright be supported and vindicated against the harsh attack from Hogg and his cohort. Roberts expressed concern about the image of the college. He wrote to tell Gathright that "from different sources, from all of which I learn that there is a strong feeling of antagonism arising up between members of your faculty and it is spreading like a partisan struggle, broadcast over the country [Texas], to great injury of the institution under your charges." Within days, Roberts as the president of the A&M Board convened and personally chaired an emergency board session at the Academy of Music Building in Bryan beginning on November 18, 1879. Joining Roberts in the court of inquiry were Lt. Governor Joseph Sayers, and Speaker of the House John H. Cochran (both ex-officio board members), Anderson Peeler of Austin, Senator Pfeuffer, J. K. Dixon of Hillsboro, Edward Picket of Liberty, W. H. Lyday of Bonham, and J. W. Durant of Centerville. Few at Texas A&M or among the public had had a chance to witness in person the former chief justice of the Texas Supreme Court—and current governor—in action as he began what would be a massive, front-page-reported investigation of every facet of the campus disruption—and by extension, a critique of all aspects of Texas A&M and its president since the college opened in October 1876. Roberts was no stranger to conflict and politically sensitive proceedings before the court of public opinion. These proceedings involved the oldest public institution of higher education in Texas, which had not only state but also federal implications, given the annual funding (amounting to about $14,000) and covenants of the Morrill Act that the state had agreed to follow and implement.[22]

Governor Roberts's command of the investigation involved four intensive days of testimony from a cross section of faculty, students, and staff on campus and from vocal citizens about the unwinding of decorum and civility at the college. The calm and resolute approach by the seasoned former chief justice made it very clear to the standing-room-only gathering that "the rattle of crowd will not influence these proceedings." Following an extensive opening morning session to review and read "a large bundle of papers" presented by Governor Roberts—made up of petitions, letters, reports, and newspaper accounts—Lt. Governor Sayers proposed that the proceedings follow this agenda: "an investigation of the present condition of the college (including the finances) and especially into dissensions among the faculty, with a view to ascertain, in the first instance, whether the interests of the college require a change in its organization; second, if necessary, after consideration of matters above referred to, the board will proceed to consider the charges made against members of the faculty; then proceed to consider the appeal of Crisp." Wasting no time after the earlier presentations, a motion was passed to amend the proposal, and "to take up [only] the case of Prof. Hogg as the substance of all the trouble." The Sayers agenda was approved. President Gathright briefly appeared the first day to say he was not on speaking terms with any of the faculty, whereupon the governor, noting that any student or staff member who felt aggrieved by any decision or action of the faculty would have the right of appeal to the board, charged Prof. Martin with the duty of summoning the faculty when it was their time to testify.[23]

The proceedings opened in late November to a packed audience. Almost all of the faculty and staff, a large number of local citizens, and cadets as well as reporters were present, resulting in R. A. Bradley being retained as the sergeant-at-arms at $4 per day. Gathright did not attend the opening day, instead sending a letter. Captain Olmstead and McInnis were left in charge of the college for the duration of the hearings. On the second day the board traveled on the H&TC train south to the college, and they were greeted at the railroad station with a thirteen-gun salute and then escorted up the cinder path to the chapel to visit with cadets and staff. Roberts and the board members addressed the cadets and "referred directly to the present trouble and appealed to the cadets to stand to the college as the pride of their state, and to confide in the board as the guardian of their welfare."[24] The board returned to Bryan and one by one the faculty were questioned. A sample of the banter is indicated by the colorful testimony of Professor Banks:

Banks—I have heard that the students have been harangued. The discipline of college is not wholesome. There is want of faithful inspection of quarters. Boys have suppers in their quarters. We can't keep chickens at our house [on campus].
Peeler—You have lost chickens, then?
Banks—I have sir. Last Christmas cadets left drunk on a train. There was full proof on one boy, but his fellows were snakes and they got off.
Sayers—What do you mean by snakes?
Banks—Sons of influential men. By permission of the president a glass of egg-nog was put at every cadet's plate last Christmas. Never done before. Once there was a personal difference between Hogg and Gathright in the faculty. Another between Morris and Gathright. That was in 1877. There was another difficulty between Martin and Gathright.
The Governor—What, with old man Martin? (laughter)
Banks—Yes, with old man Martin and all these difficulties were between the president and some one of the faculty.[25]

During the final two days of the hearing each of the faculty, staff, and cadets appeared before the board. Captain Olmstead, an employee of the U.S. Army on assignment at the college, when asked his opinion by Roberts, noted that the petty faculty differences were "ridiculous." The climax of the hearings was highlighted with the concluding testimony of Gathright, Hogg, and Crisp. Conflicts dating back to the fall of 1876 when the college was opened were reviewed, with Gathright and Hogg venting accusations and counter-accusations on events surrounding the faculty, on Gathright's explosive temper, Hogg's meddling in the management of the college, financial concerns, and the deportment of the cadets. Dethloff concludes, "If Gathright was intemperate, most of the faculty must have been hot headed." The incident that caused the investigation, approval of Cadet Crisp as first captain, was nearly overlooked in the waning hours of the hearing. When called upon, Crisp under examination proved to be eloquent and ably represented himself and the Corps of Cadets. He dismissed rumors that Gathright had encouraged him to bring charges against Hogg—this he did on his own. The directors, after a long week of testimony, were impressed with Crisp, and the past events and faculty dissent were in no way his fault. On the issue of the promotion of Crisp, the board considered promotion a college procedural item, and that the faculty had full authority of approval. Roberts and the board next addressed the management and staffing of the college.[26]

During the final days of the hearing Governor Roberts had been contacted either by mail or with a personal visit to Bryan, after hours in the evening following the hearings, by General George F. Alford (formerly adjutant general under the command of General Bee during the war), representing the leadership of the Democratic Party, by local Bryan attorneys, and by representatives of the Grange, all expressing grave concern regarding the future of the college. General Bee was not directly involved in the altercation among the faculty; however, he was able to provide an update to Senator Pfeuffer noting his concern with the "*esprit of corps*" of the cadets. Bee's conclusion in his confidential letter was: "I tell you that the inadaptability [sic] and incompetency of Gathright is the matter, he is wayward, partial, envious, and mean . . . he is not fit for this place." There was general condemnation in the newspapers of ongoing complaints made by the Grange and the atrocious affairs of the faculty. However, none had a greater impact than the behind the scenes advice and indictment by Rufus L. Burleson that "They [faculty and Gathright] are guilty of petty wrangling and unprofessional bickerings," and Burleson's advising the governor to "go to the bottom and sweep away the rubbish."[27]

Resignations of the entire faculty were requested on Saturday morning, November 22, 1879. Gathright and the faculty were relieved of duty as of December 1. Sensational reporting and rumors on the situation at the A&M College soon followed, with the *New York Times* reprinting a story from the *St. Louis Republican* saying: "This institution is nearly ruined by petty jealousies. It is believed by leading men in the State to be almost a failure, and they advise its sale and the distribution of the proceeds to the general school fund. Nearly all the old faculty have gone, as have all the students."[28] The local Bryan newspaper, the *Pilot,* was equally derogatory about the proceedings, noting, "The late troubles in the college do not evince a very conciliatory spirit," given the "discourteous intimation of Gov. Roberts during the meetings of the board," who criticized "the 'little village of Bryan' as having no interest in the college," concluding that "the politicians run the board." That was hardly surprising, since the three most powerful politicians in Texas served on the board! News coverage of events at A&M spilled over into early 1880, yet Roberts was little concerned about the media reports. The fate and future of the A&M College in transition was at stake. In an effort to placate protests from the powerful Texas Grange, whose worthy master W. W. Lang stated, "Nothing of practical agriculture has ever been attempted at the institution," Governor Roberts made clear to the incoming president and faculty that the purpose of the A&M College was to train and educate farmers.[29] The private student secretary to Gathright, P. L. Downs, recalled years later: "As far as Governor Roberts' position in the matter was concerned, he did not know or care for any of the higher courses, classical or scientific. He simply believed in the sentiment that 'Civilization begins and ends with the plow.' He had been born on a farm, and he believed that the cadets ought to be taught to farm, to do practical farming, to raise agricultural products and to learn all about farm management. He knew nothing about scientific farming and cared less about it."[30]

Roberts and the board were swift to act to restaff the college. The Sunday *Galveston Daily News* published a feature article on the new president, Colonel John G. James, a graduate of the Virginia Military Institute, a veteran of the Army of Northern Virginia, and the superintendent of the Texas Military Institute in Austin at the time he was contacted and advised that he had been unanimously elected president by the A&M board. The governor instructed Colonel James to fill all the open faculty positions, settle down the Corps of Cadets, and draft a reorganization plan for academics at the college focusing on agriculture and engineering. Since 1875 James had been a member of the Board of Visitors at the U.S. Naval Academy, and he was a close friend of Lt. Governor Sayers, who nominated him for the presidency. By the first week of December the new faculty were on campus, yet cadet and local resentment persisted on the rapidly unfolding events. Hogg went to work with the H&TC Railroad in Houston, Morris departed to law school in Minnesota, Hand taught school in Brenham, Lewis became the president of Marion College in Waxahachie, and Banks opened a private school in Austin. Gathright moved to East Texas in hopes of opening a school but died in May 1880. Cadet Crisp never received his expected appointment in the Corps and departed the college without completing a degree, later becoming a successful journalist and manager of the Uvalde Publishing Company. Only Capt. Olmstead, Dr. Smythe, and McInnis remained at A&M since there was no cause to fire them.[31]

After issuing a press release stating that "the directors found the institution in an excellent condition, except as certain unhappy dissensions existing in the faculty," Governor Roberts and the board completed their meeting on Monday, November 24th, and departed to Prairie View A&M to reconvene deliberations of the board of directors.[32]

The governor was pleased to read on the front page of the often hostile *Statesman* about the A&M College: "There are 193 'cadets' at the Agricultural and Mechanical College. They ought to be designated otherwise, for the institution is beginning to assume its legitimate purpose." Ironically, offering military training was stipulated by the Morrill Act, a fact most Texans overlooked.[33]

Prairie View: "Can we afford to let it drop"

Governor Roberts was no stranger to Prairie View. Historian George Ruble Woolfolk at Prairie View A&M College captured the essence and direction of higher education in Texas: "The sentiment of the old South had dictated that the races could not be educated together, but then rough democracy of the new West said that they should have an equal chance. This constitutional provision, quite exceptional at the time, is a monument to the public conscience of Texas."[34] Shortly after the A&M College for white students was opened there was a clamor by African American leaders in Texas to address the needs of Black students and honor the provision in the Texas Constitution of 1876 for the creation of a college for "colored youths when deemed practical." Representative William H. Holland, a former slave, was assisted by Fort Bend senator Walter M. Burton (also Black) to sponsor and pass an enabling bill for the establishment of the "Agricultural and Mechanical College for the Benefit of Colored Youth" on August 14, 1876. It was not clear if this met the constitutional mandate or was intended to be an unrelated school. A formal committee chaired by Ashbel Smith was named by the governor to locate a suitable site. The commissioners purchased a large tract of land that encompassed the Alta Vista Plantation in Waller County near the small farming community of Hempstead, north of Houston. The state named the new public college the Alta Vista Agricultural College, and it was placed under the management of the A&M College Board of Directors. President Thomas Gathright as the chief executive of the A&M College was also named the CEO of Prairie View. In his absence, a "principal" on campus would run the day-to-day operations at Alta Vista. After over a year to prepare the new campus, Gathright was given the authority to recruit and hire the new principal. Harking back to his days in Mississippi, he contacted

Lawrence W. Minor, an honor graduate in the class of 1850 from Oberlin College. Minor had had vast experience in business and in teaching ancient languages at Alcorn University in Mississippi before going to work for the secretary of state in Jackson—all of which roles were instructive for the challenges facing him in Hempstead.[35]

Minor arrived in Texas to find a dilapidated former cotton plantation, with a poor water supply, and the old Kirby family home being the only major structure to house all the functions of the new college. Eager to start classes, Minor posted advertisements in newspapers for the opening on March 1, 1878. Eight students appeared the first day, only to be underwhelmed by the facilities and the focus on agricultural education. Students soon began to drop out. "The primary reason," according to Dethloff, was "that the Negro youths did not want to go to college to learn to be sharecroppers or dirt farmers." The high expectations by Minor, Gathright and the A&M Board were quickly dashed. Detractors in the Grange and vocal white opponents of any advancement for Blacks demanded that the college be closed. However, Minor re-posted the advertisement to reopen in October 1878. Despite low enrollment, meager support in Austin, and a dwindling budget, classes continued through the end of 1878. Gathright reported to the A&M Board in late 1878, "There is no demand for higher education among blacks" in Texas—an assessment he later regretted and retracted.[36]

Following Governor Roberts's inauguration in January 1879 he made only a brief mention of the need to support public higher education and the normal schools. White residents of Waller County demanded that the college, which they called a "sham," be closed. The prospects for Prairie View seemed bleak, its situation seemingly terminal, with the board advising Principal Minor that "his engagement [would] be terminated" on February 13, 1879. However, learning of the plight of Prairie View, A. H. Belo, the editor of the leading newspaper in Texas, the *Galveston Daily News* noted in an editorial, "We can not afford to let that institution drop . . . instead of 'disbanding' the colored college, and declaring it a failure, let us, on the contrary, reorganize it on a better plan."[37]

Gathright contacted Roberts and stressed that closing the only public state-supported Black institution was not acceptable. Gathright and Roberts, both rabid southern segregationists and white supremacists, could easily have heeded detractors and closed the college. Instead, they agreed to find a solution. Minor ignored the termination notice and worked with Gathright to submit a plan to Roberts. There were three options: first, stress a classical curriculum and ignore agricultural courses; second, use the "training in military tactics" clause of the Morrill Act and establish a uniformed corps of cadets; or third, given the state's shortage of Black teachers, establish a normal school to produce teachers, modeled after the Hampton Normal and Agricultural Institute in Virginia. Minor and Gathright submitted the third option to Roberts with a plan for the legislature to reopen and rename Alta Vista College as the Prairie View Normal Institute for Blacks—a teachers' college. The Minor-Gathright plan gained approval and additional funding on April 19, 1879, in the midst of Roberts's budget cuts. In a significant contribution, Dr. Barnes Sears, general agent for the Peabody Endowment Fund, provided an additional stipend of $6,000 for teacher training, and an equal amount was sent to Sam Houston State Normal College.[38]

The funding from the Peabody Educational Foundation in Boston had a tremendous impact on the formative years of education in Texas. In addition to providing annual stipends to Sam Houston Normal, Prairie View Normal, and Texas A&M, Roberts was in the final stages of adding two more normal schools, one in the "southwest and one in northern Texas." A detailed proposal was submitted to Dr. Sears and the Peabody Board. Unfortunately Sears, the champion of educational funding in Texas, died, and the trustees apparently took no action. Writing to the foundation, Roberts lamented the death of Sears and noted his detailed plans for expanding education. Prairie View historian George Woolfolk confirmed that "schools to train teachers for the masses" would "have favorably been approved had he lived." The foundation's donations sent to Texas after Sears's death were managed by O. N. Hollingsworth, secretary of the Texas Board of Education.[39]

Meeting on the Prairie View Normal campus in late November 1879, following the Crisp-Hogg affair hearings at Texas A&M, the board was convened by Governor Roberts and five members for an inspection and received an update from the staff on the progress at the college. It was reported that forty-two "scholars" were in attendance, thirty-two on state scholarships and ten as paying students. The governor noted that unlike the disruption in College Station, "Harmony and concert of purpose of president [principal] Minor and his assistant teachers were evident in their discipline and the course of the studies arranged for the pupils . . . and the school is being conducted on the most economic principles." As Prairie View began to receive publicity due to the reorganization efforts of Principal Minor, Black leaders, also reading about the tentative plans for a "white" University of Texas, began to lobby to follow through with the 1876 Texas constitutional mandate to establish a separate "colored branch of the State University." Roberts and the A&M board members returned to Prairie View in June 1880 to enthusiastic commencement exercises to celebrate the progress of the college under Minor's direction.[40]

The progress at the struggling college was noticeable, However, shortly after the A&M College Board meeting at Prairie View, Minor died on November 5, 1880. Ernest H. Anderson, a graduate of Fisk University, thirty-four years old, and a seasoned teacher with unknown administrative experience, was named the interim principal on November 13, until Roberts could convene the entire board for official approval. Roberts advised Lt. Governor Sayers of his decision that this was "the best man that I could get as a colored teacher," and wrote to a confidant in Hempstead, "I thought best to try him, temporarily at least." Roberts took an active hands-on approach in management of Prairie View and was in constant contact with Anderson. Following a minor crisis over student enrollment and school financing, the governor was firm in his view on the role of the school: "This is a normal school to make teachers for common schools, and not to make collegiate graduates. And therefore there are two leading objects to be attained, to wit; first to learn them as thoroughly as you can the rudiments of a good common English education. The more thorough by reviewing and re-reviewing the better, and second to learn them how to teach, by having the most apt and most advanced to practice teaching others, and the supervision of the teachers. This is to be borne in mind all the time." A growing concern among Blacks in Texas included the need for Austin to address the constitutionally mandated "colored state university." Wright Cuney and Principal Anderson at Prairie View encouraged the Colored Teachers' State Association to demand action from the legislature and governor.[41]

Student enrollment at Prairie View continued to grow through the fall of 1881, when the comptroller, W. W. Brown, refused to release funding to sustain the school until the next legislature met in early 1882. At issue was the source of the funding being provided to the school from what was deemed a reserve for the yet to be opened white state university—and presumably the yet to be opened constitutionally mandated Black university. Roberts was immediately critical of Brown demanding that any action be delayed until the next legislative session. The dispute over funding of Prairie View erupted in statewide news coverage with Roberts backed by Attorney General McLeary noting that the "imbroglio" was within the authority of the state constitution.[42] The governor first contacted President John James at Texas A&M, who could also be impacted by the decision for clarification of the situation and requested any assistance possible. In the midst of this crisis, George Pickett, president of the A&M Board, who might have taken immediate action, died. With no quick fix in sight, Roberts sent the *Galveston News* a detailed review of the situation and a condemnation of Brown, stating that Prairie View had his full support. Roberts provided a copy to each Texas A&M board member. Under no condition was Roberts going to allow Prairie View to flounder. He directed board members George Pfeuffer, James Garrison, Thomas Scott, and Charles Wiggins to canvass potential supporters and use their influence to get supplies and interim funding to bridge the temporary financial gap. He told the members, "I am trying to have the Prairie View school held up until you meet," at the next board meeting in

February and pending a called session in Austin. The reaction was immediate, with Roberts encouraging Principal Anderson "to hold it together as we find some means." Merchants in Galveston and Houston provided both groceries and credit in the short term. Cash donations of $600 per month came from James Burroughs of Galveston, Frank Hamilton of Austin, and James Raymond of Houston, two private businessmen, to assist with "necessary expenses."[43] Roberts wrote to Wiggins, "I am determined that Prairie View School shall not now be crushed down, if I can prevent it." Additionally, newly appointed A&M Board chairman John Thomas advanced $2,200 (most likely with the endorsement of Roberts) from the congressional Morrill Act funding at A&M to pay teachers and staff. The use of Morrill funds to support a Black college (prior to 1890) was unusual. When questioned later by the legislature on the use of the A&M funds, Roberts, having bridged the crisis, noted that it was "an act of simple justice to the colored race, in giving them a small share of the benefit from the special fund donated by the federal government." These events only created more attention for the disposition and status of the constitutional pledge for the "university for colored youths of the state."[44]

Following the 1882 Colored Men's State Convention in Waco, leaders in the Black community including John N. Johnson, Hightower Kealing, William Holland, E. H. Anderson, Edward Blackshear, and Bishop Abraham Grant of the A. M. E. Church, formed a strategic alliance to bring their request for the "colored university" to the attention of the governor and legislature. At first the white-controlled Democratic legislature ignored calls to address the provisions of the constitution, with many deflecting the debate on the grounds that Prairie View was the substitute for the "colored university" and that should suffice. But that conclusion did not meet the letter or spirit of the law. In spite of state budget pressures, both self-imposed and from the legislature, Roberts saw cause to support the fledgling 'normal' school: "Why cripple them [at Prairie View] in their progress in the ineffectual effort to establish and maintain something higher. It would seem to be far more practical to hold on to what has been attained and gradually build up the higher departments as it may be found practicable."[45]

University of Texas

Calls for action on the "colored university" were ignored and all attention in Austin was directed toward the "white" university. Governor Roberts was comfortably in his second term in office and already was receiving inquiries about standing for a third term. Throughout 1881–82 he worked behind the scenes to open the white state university, following the Seventeenth Legislature's approval on March 30, 1881, to proceed. The first meeting of the board of regents chaired by Colonel Ashbel Smith was not held until mid-November 1881. In August prior to the regents' meeting, the former professor of math at the A&M College, Alexander Hogg, fired during the 1879 Crisp affair and later chief of engineers at the Houston and Central Railroad, made detailed remarks for the State Teachers' Association at Corsicana. This detailed outline was published as a feature article in the *Austin Statesman* giving his views on how to organize the proposed University of Texas. The extensive presentation was surely seen by Roberts, Smith, and Terrell, given that the events and organization that followed adhered to much of his proposal, which was based on the historical rise of other universities. For example, the directors would be designated "regents"; even before the vote on the location, Austin should be the location of the main campus; the faculty with the approval of the board should select their own president or chairman of the faculty; both a law school and medical school should come under the umbrella of the university; and a series of "normal" schools should be established for the purpose providing "didactics or the science of teaching," an educational system that, as Hogg noted, "dated back to the days of Socrates, Plato, and Aristotle."[46]

To garner broad statewide support for the university among educators, Roberts once again secured the endorsement of the State Teachers' Association. The approval of the university was a major victory for Roberts, who had often recalled prior efforts to inaugurate the university dating back to 1839. At the urging of Republic of Texas President Mirabeau Lamar, the newly formed congress had passed an act on January 26, 1839, to create two universities, setting aside 50 leagues, 221,420 acres, of land for their establishment, of which 47 had been surveyed by 1841. John Marshall's *State Gazette* on November 3, 1855, provided a detailed article on the legislation as well as the need to follow the example of other states such as Virginia and South Carolina to open the state institute. The plan to open two universities was different than the 1858 Texas Constitution, which provided for a sum of $100,000 in U.S. bonds to be set aside for development of a university, or the Texas Constitution of 1876, which specifically provided that a "university of the first class" be established. The unknown writer of the article, possibly read by Oran Roberts in Austin as he worked on the 1855 campaign, was identified only as "E. F." and was clear in stating: "The immediate necessity for these Universities is so obvious that no argument is necessary to impress upon the mind of any Statesman the importance of their speedy establishment."[47] Only time would tell.

The grand public educational plan outlined in 1839 was to establish two universities—one for boys and one for girls, marking this as the earliest mention of higher education for women in Texas. The writer noted: "Happily for us we live in an age, fully awakened to the necessity of the culture of the female mind. . . . Texas alone has the power to advance our daughters." As early as 1855 there was a debate as to where these two universities would be. The first option was to locate one in East Texas and the other in West Texas, but this plan was short-lived when it was determined that it would be best to locate both new universities "at the Seat of government"—so noted when Austin had been selected as the capital on January 14, 1839, and land had been specifically set aside as a site of the future university. Two countervailing reasons for the East-West universities were that it might give future credence to dividing Texas into two states, whereby Texas would surrender the grand size of the state, yet gain two additional U.S. senators. This idea of two separate sites was quickly abandoned. After further assessment, "E.F." concluded, "In one University with two departments, let our sons and daughters be trained up for the service of the State as enlightened patriots."[48]

In over a quarter of a century there were failed attempts to establish the university by Governor Pease in 1858, possibly based on the argument in the Austin *State Gazette* by Minister Clayton C. Gillespie that private religious universities and teachers' "normal" colleges would be a better use of state funding. This was followed by the outright veto of the idea to establish the state university by Governor Sam Houston in 1860 on the eve of the war. The university was further stalled in 1871, when the Texas legislature focused on the post-war education agreement and funding under the Morrill Grant Act of 1862 to establish the Agricultural and Mechanical College of Texas. What followed was the Texas Constitution of 1876, which provided for the white university with the A&M College as a "branch" and with a provision outlined to create a "colored university." By law, an election a decade later on September 6, 1881, determined the site of the white university to be in Austin, which Roberts strongly supported after his college days at the University of Alabama in Tuscaloosa, and simultaneously with the medical branch to be located in Galveston.[49]

In a presentation to the Eurosophic Society on a return visit to the University of Alabama in May 1892, Roberts reflected on his days as a student in the capital city of Tuscaloosa: "It fastened on me the lasting impression, that the University of the state ought to be located at the Capital of the state, in order to give students, coming from all parts of the country, the greatest advantages attainable in attending such an institution. And I have fortunately lived to be able to actively participate in producing that result in the state—Texas–of my adoption."[50]

What Roberts and the solid white Democrats did not expect to encounter was the insistence by the African American community to open the colored university. The burning of the old state capital building on November 9, 1881, seemed to have little impact on the debate and political wrangling over public universities, given the fact that the constitutional provisions had already been made to build a new capitol building. In May 1882 the legislature approved a measure to call for the statewide election to vote on the location of the proposed "colored" institution. Over a dozen Texas cities lobbied, with the greatest interest in Austin, Houston, and Prairie View at Hempstead. At the June 1882 commencement ceremonies at Prairie View, Governor Roberts publicly backed the location of the colored branch of the proposed university at Prairie View. The election date was set for November 7, 1882. Austin won the canvas with 28,329 votes, followed by Houston with 14,000 votes, and Prairie View with 13,160. The executive office of the governor paid for and was reimbursed by the legislature both for the special election for the location of the colored university and for repayment of funds advanced to Prairie View from the University Fund. Thus the Austin site was formally certified by the chief election officer (a Democrat) and Secretary of State T. H. Bowman—"as the location of the State University for the instruction of colored youth"— resulting in panic in the white Democratic ranks concerning the "white" university.[51]

As plans were accelerated to open the white university, notice was given by representatives from the legislature that no tax could be levied or funds appropriated to establish a Black university, although a site had been officially selected and verified. The initial conclusion was that the fifty leagues of land in West Texas set aside for public higher education were thus a manipulation of both the letter and spirit of the law and the means of prejudicial educational funding for the white university only. The Republican Party in Texas, while weak, responded with a resolution declaring that to comply with the constitutional requirement of 1876, they favored not only "the early completion of the University of Texas [for whites]," but also the establishment of "its colored branch."[52]

Governor Roberts's long-held dream of the state university for Texas to be established in the capital became reality as he worked behind the scenes with Ashbel Smith, Richard Hubbard, and Alex Terrell to determine the initial composition of the university staffing and facilities as well as to set plans to organize a board of regents. The capstone action by the governor was the official proclamation in

October 1881 to convene the regents. The foundational document stated the following:

Proclamation

By the Governor of the State of Texas convening the Board of regents of the University of Texas.
Whereas the official returns of the election held Sept. 6th 1881, which said returns are now on file in the office of the Secretary of State, show that Austin has been selected by the people as the location of the University of Texas with the medical branch at Galveston.
Now therefore I O. M. Roberts, Governor of Texas by virtue of the authority vested in me by the laws of this State do hereby call the Board of Regents of the University of Texas to convene in the city of Austin on Tuesday the fifteenth day of November 1881 to effect the permanent organization of the Board and to take such action as the law requires for the establishment and organization of the university.
In testimony whereof I hereto sign my name and cause the Seal of the State to be affixed at the city of Austin this 11th day of October A. D. 1881.
O. M. Roberts Governor

Governor Roberts solidified exclusive control of all the so-called "University of Texas Lands" and any income received to the Permanent University Funds. After securing an initial appropriation of $140,000 for buildings, Roberts further ordered the immediate laying of the cornerstone for the first Main Building on "College Hill" in Austin only a few blocks from the capital on November 17, 1882—ten days after the voters of Texas had also selected Austin as the site for the "colored university."[53]

Transition

The adjournment of the special session of the Seventeenth Legislature on May 2, 1882, brought to a close Roberts's direct gubernatorial influence over legislative and fiscal affairs in Texas. The pay-as-you-go program had shown the results it was intended to produce and corrected over three decades of misguided fiscal policies and deficits. The economic growth and in-migration of the growing population resulted in an increase of taxable property from $280,000,000 in 1877 to $410,000,000 in 1882. Interest expense on the public debt dropped by 35 percent, and the state's credit rating vastly improved. State revenue increased even as *ad valorem* taxes were reduced from fifty to thirty cents on one hundred dollars in property valuation. While he was encouraged to stand for re-election for a third term, at sixty-seven he had other plans in mind for the years after the governorship. The July 1882 Democratic Convention met in Galveston, Roberts's favorite city for dining and entertainment. Noting that the "convention was without special excitement or interest," Roberts's old comrades-in-arms, staunch political and personal friends, provided the nomination of an able slate. Rumors circulated in the summer preceding the convention that Roberts might seek a third term, but they had no foundation. John Ireland of Guadalupe County was nominated for governor and Marion Marin of Navarro for lieutenant governor. Unlike the splintered party factions in the preceding two gubernatorial elections, Roberts observed that in the "ensuing campaign all elements of the Democracy support the nominees." The 1882 Democratic platform reflected the major issues of the past few years, noting the endorsement of coinage of gold and silver, opposing the protective tariff, and encouraging reform of the civil service as well as opposing monopolies, favoring of the endowment of the University of Texas out of the unappropriated lands, being in favor of the "fullest education practicable for the scholastic population," and declaring that railroad and other corporations doing business in Texas were "subject to the political power of the State." Opposition at the ballot box in the fall of 1882 was marginal, with the Independent Greenback Party marshaling most of the fringe and disaffected and opposing factions in support of George Washington "Wash" Jones of Bastrop. The upstart Prohibition-Union-Labor ticket candidate was General J. B.

Robertson. Ireland captured 60 percent of the statewide vote cast in 169 organized counties.[54]

The Empire State

Texas by 1882 was returning to a solid economic footing driven by population growth, increases in agricultural production, Gulf Coast seaport activity, and expansion of the railroad network that connected most of East Texas in the area east of where Interstate 35 lies today. The two largest cities in population were Galveston and San Antonio, each with about 30,000 residents in 1882, followed by Houston with 27,000 inhabitants. However there was a vast gap in capital investment, with the Galveston assessed value of taxable property nearly twice the amount of either San Antonio in Bexar County, or Houston in Harris County. The economic driver of the Galveston economy and investments was the export-import trade, hallmarked primarily by cotton exports that totaled some 1.3 million bales in 1881. In 1882 two landmark publications on Texas were released that provided an excellent snapshot of the state during the period of the Oran Roberts administration. The first was a report by A. W. Spaight, Commissioner of Insurance, Statistics, and History, on *The Resources, Soil, and Climate of Texas.* This published data on 170 of the organized counties, the first of its kind on Texas, covered the economic trends, transportation improvements, demographics, agricultural output, and general growth over the past decade. The second volume was a retrospective look at Texas by Governor Roberts, *A Description of Texas: Its Advantages and Resources with Some Account of their Development, Past, Present and Future.* The book has a wealth of stories on the activities in East Texas and provides a vivid image of how the woodlands of the region appeared to the settlers who pioneered the area. It is lacking in similar details for western and northern Texas and generally has nothing about the immigrant populations of Germans and Mexicans, and it provides at best a biased view of African Americans. A review in the *Galveston Daily News* commenting on how Roberts collected material "for this great work" indicated that "he attributes it mostly to his having traveled about a great deal on horseback with other lawyers, attending the courts when a young practitioner at the bar," noting one observation that the "wonderful tar oil near San Augustine can be used as tar in greasing wagons and also as a remedy for the toothache." Not everyone enjoyed the book. The Clarksville *Standard,* for example, considered the volume "dull and stupid . . . the style is prosy and tiresome in the extreme"; and the often obstinate *Galveston Daily News* pointedly concluded: "Roberts's Texas is a very thin affair . . . the Old Alcalde as a book-maker is not a success."[55] Nevertheless, Roberts's roots in traditional deep East Texas are reflected in the dedication:

> This little work is respectfully dedicated to the Texas farmer, upon whose labors, rightly directed, the material prosperity of Texas must largely depend, and whose intelligence and integrity in public affairs must be relied on to sustain good government capable of republican, local *self-government begins and ends with the plow.*

GOVERNOR ORAN ROBERTS, who "had a settler's eye for countryside and a lawyer's dream of empire," proudly noted that by 1882 the economic viability of Texas, while not as anti-business as some believed, would be "accommodated" by railroads in all parts of the state. The days of the ox cart were soon to be over. With the growth and diversification in agricultural production and the demands by farmers, the Grange, and the Farmers Alliance for better freight rates and safer transportation, the Texas legislature a decade before a formal railroad commission prescribed a maximum intrastate rate of fifty cents per hundred pounds per hundred miles. For bulk products like cotton and lumber, the Houston & Texas Central established a mileage-postage rate—for example, based on mileage with a maximum of $4.50 per bale. Prior to 1883, the majority of cattle, approximately 284,000 head annually, were driven overland to market. In 1880 the price of cattle in Texas averaged $9.24, and they sold at between $34 and $40 in Chicago and New York. While cotton remained king, Texas faced rapid change.[56]

A better understanding of the cost of doing business, the beginning of mechanized agriculture, and the ever expanding markets beyond Texas' borders would usher in a new generation of Texans. The overriding engine of the growth in Texas would be determined, according to Oran Roberts, "by the level of educational attainment and expertise of its citizens to meet the transition of Texas" during the late nineteenth century from a frontier society to a more diversified global economy.

CHAPTER 6

LAW PROFESSOR 1883–1893

The people will take no educational starveling, no institution big in name but meager in performance. They demand a university to be now organized in a manner and on a basis soon to be developed into an institution on the high level of the foremost institutions of knowledge in the entire world, a university whose instruction, absolutely free, shall offer to every child in the state, poor or rich, that knowledge which is power to the individual, and, in the aggregate, power inherent and indefeasible to the magnificent, imperial state of Texas.

— ASHBEL SMITH PRESIDENT OF THE BOARD OF REGENTS JANUARY 8, 1883

Amidst all the evils of government, if there was one benefit that was conferred upon the mass of the Texas people, it was in teaching them the glorious blessing of living in a well regulated civil government of their own choice and creation.

— ORAN M. ROBERTS, A LECTURE UNIVERSITY OF TEXAS 1892

At high noon on Wednesday, January 24, 1883, Oran M. Roberts entered onto the floor of the Texas Legislature as governor of the state of Texas for the last time. The standing-room-only chamber was packed as Roberts "received enthusiastic cheers." Turning away from a possible campaign for a third term, in one of his shortest speeches, he simply noted, "In leaving the office of governor with which the people have honored me, I desire to return my sincere thanks . . . to my fellow-citizens throughout the length and breadth of this great state, for their favorable appreciation and confidence." The venerable "Old Alcalde," who by this time had held sway over four decades of political intrigue from perspectives ranging from that of a local East Texas judge, and the designer of the secessionists' revolution on the Colorado River in 1861, to the vocal unreconstructed senator-elect holding court on the Potomac River to espouse his stance and views against the post-war Radical U.S. Congress. It must have been a sight as Roberts stood alone at the close of his valedictory address, and "amid complete stillness," the oath of office was administered to the next governor of Texas—"Ox-cart" John Ireland.[1]

Oran Roberts had been nominated for governor under rather unusual circumstances in the hot summer of 1878 and accepted the honor. His fellow Democrats and the Greenback opposition underestimated his ability to campaign aggressively. His East Texas knowledge of farm issues, his concern with an increasing rural tax burden, as well as his message about the need for an effective albeit limited government were well received. One of the oldest men to enter the Texas governor's office, the sometimes eccentric old man always dressed for comfort in his well-worn Prince Albert coat. He was a man of few words, only saying what was necessary. Yet he was still energetic. A visiting reporter from the Cincinnati *Enquirer* described the Old Alcalde as he stepped from the governor's mansion for the last time: "A lean, simple, wiseish, skinny faced old man of sixty odd [actually 67], with one tooth ever trying to make connection with a wagging under-lip, on which is a sheet of white beard. He has a pair of grayish eyes, full of transparent light and self-appreciation, reminding you of their feeble confidence." To his fellow Texans, friend and foe, he demonstrated no signs of "feebleness."[2]

Roberts's energy and demands for a conservative pay-as-you-go budget strategy were painful during his early years in office but allowed him to leave the state in 1882 in the best fiscal shape it had ever known. One observer concluded, "The Roberts administration paid all the expenses of government, reduced the public debt $1,000,000, and left a half million dollars on hand." The permanent school fund had been increased from $1.6 to $5.4 million by the sale of public land. Some anti-Roberts newspapers charged that his toying with a third term was only a ploy and stepping-stone for a run for the U.S. Senate. Roberts, during informal conversations with reporters in Bryan after the A&M College board meeting in the summer of 1882 had sent mixed signals about his future, with the Brenham *Daily Banner* noting: "He repeated that he was not a candidate, *but that men who were not candidates were sometimes nominated for office and occasionally accepted.*" While he was reflecting on his first hasty nomination for governor in the fall of 1878, this brief comment was repeated in newspapers across the state and created some confusion; however, his future focus was elsewhere. An habitual smoker of a corncob pipe and connoisseur of fine whiskey, he quickly turned his full attention for the next decade to the University of Texas.[3]

Governor Roberts carried the vision of the establishment of the University of Texas for nearly a decade. From the time of his first executive message to the legislature, notwithstanding the lingering state debt, budget crunch, and poor revenue stream, he made it clear that one of his key objectives was to ensure that the new state university was opened. Roberts was fond of reviewing the historical underpinnings of the broad support of public schools dating back to the earliest leaders of colonial Coahuila and Texas in their Constitution of 1829, calling for suitable public schools, followed by equal attention from representatives of the Republic of Texas and then the state.[4] But both state and local governments failed to provide funding, thus these were empty promises. While Sam Houston was doubtful about the need for institutions of higher learning, favoring instead more rural common schools, Mirabeau Lamar as early as 1838 advocated planning for "the establishment of a university where the highest branches of science may be taught." An endowment of fifty leagues, 211,400 acres, was set aside. Progress languished for years, and Roberts's retort to all who raised objections about moving forward with the university was: if not now, then when? Assisted by Dr. Rufus C. Burleson of Waco University, Roberts for four years as governor garnered support primarily from the Texas State Teachers' Association—especially as they were dealing with local school budget cuts during his first administration. Both Roberts and Burleson realized that educational reform was needed and insisted that public education at all levels should be expanded. Secondly, the governor received key endorsements from the state's newspaper editors. The Austin *Weekly Statesman* provided a clear endorsement: "A university is wanted in Texas now or never, we want it as the foundation for a great . . . school of education." Roberts's role and contribution to enabling the opening of the university has not been fully appreciated. As he exited the governor's mansion he left nothing to chance. To ensure he was near to the day-to-day planning for the university, during the last days in office he acquired a small farm northwest of Austin in order to stay in close contact.[5]

The two major components for moving forward with the establishment of the university were legislative approval and the selection of a site. The constitutions of the early republic and the state in 1845, and those that followed through 1876, included exact language for higher education in Texas. The primary basis for this support of the university involved the more than two million acres set aside from the public domain to establish the "permanent university fund" (PUF)—the land pledged by the legislature. From the PUF the available fund of expendable revenue was created. Many delays slowed the university's final approval, with the last question being whether it opened as an all-male institution. Roberts expressed support for coeducation, since coeds attended state-supported colleges in other states. Senator Alex Terrell, an alumnus of the co-educational University of Missouri, lobbied to have the enabling legislation amended to be open "to male and female on equal terms." Those opposed agreed to support the new bill in return for the stipulation that the management be vested in a chairman of the faculty and not in a university president—thus initially placing all the power and operations in the hands of the chairman of the Board of Regents and its members. The reason for the concern over the title and role of chief faculty member designation was based on the fear by some legislators that Roberts might possibly be named the university's first president. There was also concern that Senator Terrell, who had only a partial role in establishing coeducation at the university, was, according to biographer Lewis Gould, "a life-long opportunist" who later in life claimed to be the "father" of the University of Texas. The university had many fathers, the least of whom was Terrell. Roberts never made a public claim or took credit, and noted, "The merit of its [the university's] establishment is not due to any one man, nor even to any one hundred . . . but to the citizens of Texas [who] contributed their efforts." However, the on the eve of the opening of the university, the Austin *Weekly Statesman* singled out Roberts for a lion's share of the credit: "The university had its most recent origins with Governor Roberts. Every law passed in regard to the university was adopted under his advice, and often by his direction were measures incorporated in the university laws." However, in 1881 much still needed to be done to ensure the opening by the fall of 1883.[6]

Governor Roberts determined that the legislative session in 1881 was opportune "to initiate the establishment of the university." At the request of the governor, Burleson assisted the Teachers' Association in the preparation of a "memorial" endorsing that action be taken. The petition addressed to the governor and legislature encouraged and recommended three key objectives: "one university, and only one, should be organized"; "no religious qualification should be prescribed," and a statewide election should be held as soon as possible for the site location.[7] The committee members assembled in Austin to lobby the lawmakers and "outline their" support. At long last, the Texas Legislative Act of March 30, 1881, fulfilled the mandate to establish and open the University of Texas. From this date forward, and for the next six to seven years, Roberts made a majority of the major decisions concerning the school, often with the aid and advice of Ashbel Smith, Alexander Terrell, Sul Ross, and Rufus Burleson. On October 11, 1881, the governor issued a proclamation confirming that the statewide election in early September had selected Austin as the site for the new university. Interestingly, ex-Governor Hubbard, possibly still irritated by Roberts "stealing" the governorship in 1879, "believed Austin was not legally elected [selected]"—yet this was little more than sour grapes. The procedural action in which voters selected Austin and a forty-acre site known as "College Hill" had been recognized as early as 1839. Roberts knew the location well; during the first months of his governorship he ordered four Texas Rangers to camp on the site to be close to the state treasury following rumors that bandits were threatening to rob it. Senator Alexander Terrell, in his 1898 commencement address at the University of Texas, recalled that he had listened to the first speech made on the hill north of the capitol to a gathering of Rangers and Texas veterans by Sam Houston in 1856 under the big oaks—long before the site was considered for the future location of the university. Furthermore, despite the positive vote for Austin, Roberts made it clear, reflecting back on his days at the University of Alabama in that state's capital, that the new school was predestined to be located in Austin. He then called for the inaugural Board of Regents to convene in the capital on November 15, 1881, to "effect the permanent organization of the board . . . and organization of the university."[8] In an emotional presentation to the Seventeenth Legislature, Roberts left no doubt of his support of the university and his vision for the institution's mission:

> The whole question about the establishment of a first-class University and its branches is shall Texas give her own native-born sons and daughters the faculties for fitting themselves to occupy those higher walks, so necessary in the proper direction of her future destiny . . . Every great state should rear its own men in every stature of manhood, of intelligence and of culture, according to their capabili-

ties, upon its own soil, and thereby engender and preserve an intense homogeneousness [sic] in the character of its population.[9]

In the fall of 1881 Roberts, in consultation with Ashbel Smith, selected the first members of the Board of Regents. Smith's life and accomplishments on behalf of Texas helped lead and establish the state's formative years. An undergraduate of Yale College, he received a medical degree in 1828. After practicing in North Carolina and taking further medical studies in Paris for a year, he was persuaded by fellow Carolinian James P. Henderson to come to the newly formed Republic of Texas in the spring of 1837. First appointed by Sam Houston as the surgeon general of the Army of the Republic, Ashbel was pivotal as an able negotiator and was sent in 1838 to meet with the Comanche Indians, and then dispatched to Europe in 1842 as the chargé d'affaires to ink a treaty of amity and commerce between England and Texas. Smith served three terms in the state legislature and took an active part in the organization of the state Democratic Party. During the Civil War he was commander of Company C, Second Texas Infantry, and was severely wounded at Shiloh in April 1862. Recovering from his wounds he returned to active duty for the duration of the war—and in his final assignment was sent by Governor Pendleton Murrah to negotiate peace for Texas with Union officials. In the post-war period he dedicated much of his time to the cause of education in a number of capacities. including as one of the three-member commission in 1876 to establish the site for the "Agricultural College for the Benefit of Colored Youths" in Waller County —known today as Prairie View A&M University.[10]

Like the Roberts court appointed by Governor Coke in 1874, the state university's first Board of Regents members were veterans or had been closely tied to the Confederacy during war. The regents, in compliance with the law, were selected from different parts of the state. The first meeting was held in the board room of the Supreme Court. Colonel Smith was selected as board president, and Roberts named to the board former governor James Throckmorton;, Thomas J. Devine of San Antonio; former governor Richard Hubbard of Tyler;

James H. Starr; A. N. Edwards, president of the Grange from Sulphur Springs; and Smith Ragsdale of Weatherford. After the initial meeting, Throckmorton and Starr resigned and were replaced by T. M. Harwood of Gonzales and Thomas D. Wooten of Austin. By the time of the first regents' meeting in 1883, board membership had again changed, with Roberts presiding, and Smith as president, joined by Ragsdale, Wooten, and Harwood, with the addition of M. L Crawford, W. E. Jones, E. S. Simpkins, and T. E. McKinny. Roberts attended the board meeting as a "visitor" and made a number of "suggestions" on future operations and recruiting, advising the board to take care in hiring and to get the best professors and "compensate with good salaries, so as to have superior teaching in comparison with that of all other schools in the state." In addition to reviewing plans for facilities, the regents set the date for opening of classes as September 15, 1883.[11]

Many opposed the creation of the institution, charging that universities were "for rich men's sons" and were "hot beds of immorality, profligacy, and licentiousness." Opposition notwithstanding, prior to leaving the governor's office, Roberts personally selected the Board of Regents as well as hand-picking and approving the first faculty. As early as August 1882 the *Galveston Daily* News referred to the Old Alcalde as "Professor Roberts." This was the same board that hired him—arguably the first university employee—and his close friend former Supreme Court Justice Robert Gould as the first two law professors. The board also set his projected future annual salary at $3,000. This was all confirmed in late November 1882, after the gubernatorial election and nearly two months before Roberts left office. One scholar notes that a number of potential professors at other law schools had been considered for the opening of the Texas Law School Department, and if they had accepted "there would have been no room for Roberts." This assumption is a bit misleading, given that the jurists they considered were not from the South or Texas, they did not want to move their families, and were in the latter years of their careers. Thus it was unlikely that they wanted to transfer to a start-up the program in Austin. Nevertheless, the hiring of Roberts into the law school in the last days of his governorship became a "political football" for the next decade as opponents questioned the validity of such action.[12]

There was no doubt that Judge Roberts was determined to be the first law professor at Texas.

Furthermore, the governor, prior to leaving office met with Senator Ross, chairman of the Finance Committee, State Treasurer Frank R. Lubbock, and Land Commissioner William C. Walsh to confirm that as estimated, $140,000 remained available for the initial expenses of the university. A *Seguin Times* editorial noted, "The university is a hobby of Governor Roberts and he has dropped into a lifetime professorship. The *Times* approves the old alcalde's appointment . . . for, without doubt, he possesses preeminent legal ability, but the hurry to organize a full corps of professors before there is any university building seems little out of place." Moreover, the editor of the Clarksville *Standard,* Charles DeMorse, who had opposed Roberts over his public land policy, published a continuing series of articles questioning the viability of the new university. , Learning of Roberts's rich new university salary, DeMorse attacked him for "milking" the taxpayers by living off the state. It appears Roberts ignored the criticisms and proceeded with his plans for the university. Following the board meeting in January 1883, professors also received an additional $500 per annum for "house rent," thus, all the professors' salaries, including those of Roberts and Gould, were raised to $3,500 per year, and $4,000 for the chairman of the faculty. Professors at Texas A&M had been assigned campus housing since the school opened in 1876, there being no nearby housing to rent.[13]

As early as November 1882, just prior to the laying of the cornerstone presided over by the Grand Master of the Grand Lodge of Masons, the Odd Fellows, and the Knights of Pythias, with a time-capsule of memorabilia in a lead box embedded in the stone—including a picture of the Queen of England donated by a man confined in the Travis County jail—Roberts and Smith hand-picked and interviewed the first faculty. Smith, at his own expense, traveled throughout the South in the summer of 1882 to obtain information and recruit "first class educators." Newspaper editors around the state expressed a great deal of interest that the faculty be "men with first-class talent and experience" and that "wire-pullers"—as political manipulators of the era were termed—be avoided. Selection of the first professors immediately became controversial as many questioned whether Texans should have preference over outsiders.[14] As chronicled in the *Alcalde Alumni Magazine,* the "gentlemen to be professors" were all white, all male, and all veterans of the late Confederate Army. All held degrees, with proven extensive experience, and agreed to come to Austin as early as the summer of 1883. As noted, Roberts was the first faculty member hired, accompanied by Judge Gould—both graduates of the University of Alabama—in the newly created Department of Constitutional, International, Common and Statute Law. Other faculty were Leslie Waggener, LL.D., in English Language and Literature and History—an infantryman wounded at Shiloh and Chickamauga; J. W. Mallet, F.R.S, LL.D., in Physics and Chemistry—general superintendent of Confederate ordinance; J. Leroy Brown, LL.D., in Pure and Applied Mathematics—colonel in the ordinance department; Milton W. Humphreys, LL. D, Ph. D., in Latin and Greek Languages and Literature—captain, 13th Virginia Light Artillery; and Robert L. Dabney, M. A., professor in Mental and Moral Philosophy—chief of staff for General Stonewall Jackson. The sole faculty member who was neither a southerner nor veteran was Professor Henry Tallichet from France. He first arrived in the country in 1869 and was recruited by Colonel Smith while he was visiting the University of the South at Sewanee, Tennessee, to teach modern languages. The aggregate of the salaries of this first group of professors amounted to $23,000 annually.[15]

In the months prior to the opening of classes, Professor J. W. Mallet was named the chairman of the faculty, with the duties to oversee class schedules, allocate resources, and represent the faculty to the regents. In advance of classes Mallet, aware of the start-up dynamics of a new educational institute—as experienced by the A&M College in its early years between 1876 and 1880—expressed his concerns to President Smith:

It is impossible to overstate the importance of the University of Texas making a good beginning of actual teaching work. If at the outset the impression be made upon its first students and the public that the institution is not prepared to do thorough work within the scope as it professes to occupy; that its efficiency is among the possibilities of the future, but not among the realities of the present, long years may, and probably will pass before this evil representation can be shaken off, and the confidence of the people of Texas secured. For example, without the equipment and the materials, and other appliances as advertised, the university would in vain expect or hope to present a faculty which would meet just public expectations.[16]

Upon learning the details of the Roberts and Smith plan to open the university in September 1883, Governor Ireland expressed concern about a "premature opening," saying that Roberts and the regents were moving too fast and, possibly, at added expense to the state. Ireland had backed the university bill. While he questioned Roberts's land policies and his reduced support of public common schools, Ireland fully understood the priority of the opening. Roberts created some excitement among legislators and university staff by advising non-resident student applicants who wrote him about the law school, to "Come to Texas, our university is now free to the world." By law the fee of admission could, in the early years, never exceed $30—a policy the regents had not considered for non-Texans, so all were welcomed in the first few years. In addition to concerns about land policy, Ireland favored additional regulation of the railroads and a slowing of state construction subsidies, hence the nickname, "Ox-cart John." Bids on the construction of what came to be known as "old main" on the new campus were opened in mid-July 1882. Judge Roberts assured Ireland that planning had been in process for over a year and the general design for buildings had been completed by architect Frederick Ernst Ruffini. Construction of the west wing of the Old Main Building, according to Ashbel Smith, "wholly avoiding mere ornamentation," began in late 1882. And Oran Roberts was on the "hill" with Ruffini and the site crew to assist in "selecting and laying off the ground" and the orientation of the first building.[17]

During the summer of 1883 Roberts and Smith continued to make arrangements for the university, monitor the construction, review last-minute additions to the staff, and stay in contact with key groups around the state. In June they attended the annual meeting of the State Teachers' Association in Galveston as special guests, to thank the gathering for their legislative outreach and endorsements. Both made presentations to outline the challenges ahead to prepare qualified students to attend the university. While both men were in Galveston reporters for the *Galveston Daily News* questioned them, insisting on knowing when the medical college would be opened on the island. Colonel Smith was candid, noting that given the high construction cost in Austin and salaries, insufficient funds were left for Galveston. One suggestion was to encourage the city to provide a site and financial aid to help defray expenses. The shortage of funding delayed opening the medical branch for three years.[18] After a lengthy illness, Frances Wickliffe Roberts died of pneumonia in Austin on November 27, 1883. The funeral was "one of the most impressive ever held in Austin," with the entire law class at the university acting as an honorary escort, marching on either side of the hearse" en route to Oaklawn Cemetery.[19]

While construction continued on the main building, arrangements were made to hold classes temporarily in the capitol and adjoining buildings until January 1884. On the eve of the dedication, the state comptroller, after an update due to adding accumulated interest, advised Roberts and Smith that the available funds on hand amounted to $156,673. That would only be enough to start the first phase of the main building until more funds were transferred to the university account. This did not delay opening ceremonies set for September 15, 1883. A reported 119 students matriculated. At the opening ceremonies Dr. Smith presided, and Professor Mattel spoke on behalf of the faculty, followed by Governor Ireland. Then Ashbel Smith presented the sculptor Elisabet Ney, who was introduced as the granddaughter of "Marshal Ney of the Army of Napoleon," to present the university with a life-size bust of ex-governor Roberts in white marble. Roberts, seated in the front row, was exceedingly proud of the opening of the university, reminding the audience, "In years to come doubtless costly statues and rare works of art will grace these halls, and adoring eyes will gaze on many sculptured forms, but among them all I believe no face will more surely invoke a sincere recognition of honest worth and earnest patriotism as this of the old Alcalde." Ironically, Governor Roberts's marble bust is now on display in the reading room of the Briscoe Center for American History in Austin, looking through the glass doors of the entrance at the bigger than life-size statue of Jefferson Davis in the lobby, which was removed from campus display in 2015 following student protests.[20]

Other than an interest in studying law, admission qualifications for the legal program were lax: a fair command of English, some background in "classical studies," and being familiar with the history of the United States and England. Later, applicants had to be at least eighteen years of age and complete a two-page essay to "exhibit a fair degree of culture and mental training." The university had no formal curriculum or law library, no laboratories, no dormitories or dining facilities, and little furniture in the temporary classrooms spread in and around the capitol building. Students continued to arrive and enroll, with a final total in May 1884 of 218 students. The university requirement for a law degree was only two years of study, and the purely academic program was four years. All religious denominations were represented among the students. Two groups that were absent from the Texas Department of Law were women and African Americans. The university, eager to celebrate, held its first commencement of first-year students in June 1884, with Governor Ireland introducing the keynote speaker, Governor Roberts, as "your distinguished and worthy professor." Among the thirteen members of the first class was Albert Sidney Burleson, a former student of Texas A&M, who was destined to be postmaster general in the Woodrow Wilson cabinet in 1913, followed a year later by fellow Texas law graduate Thomas W. Gregory, who became U.S. attorney general. Once law students finished their studies and received a diploma they could remain for one more year of study or, given that there were no formal academic prerequisites, and with a two-year diploma in hand, they were relieved of the requirement of examination for bar admission to practice in law Texas.[21]

Student Enrollment: 1883 through 1890

	University of Texas			Texas A&M College
Session	Academic	Law Dept	Total	Total
1883–84	166	52	218	122
1884–85	151	55	206	153
1885–86	138	60	198	181
1886–87	170	73	243	186
1887–88	176	73	249	231
1888–89	187	91	278	226
1889–90	230	78	308	293

Source: J. J. Lane, *History of the University of Texas*, p. 274; Adams, *Keepers of the Spirit*, p. 16.

Politics was never far from Roberts, and he remained in the news media—often referred to as the "Old Alcalde with the cob pipe and cash balance"—with the incoming Ireland administration constantly compared to the previous years and programs. Ireland and the legislature scrapped Roberts's land policy. The minority Republican Party posed little problem, and when E. J. Davis died in 1883, he was replaced by Waller County mulatto and Galveston dock workers' organizer Norris Wright Cuney to lead the party. Economic development growth across the state continued, indicated by the population reaching more than two million by 1885 and the increase in completed railroad track miles from 1,650 in 1875 to over 5,000 miles in 1885. While cash flow was tight, the El Paso *Daily Times* reported the vast domain of Texas was "land poor," even though "Only four years ago Texas stood third in wealth among the Southern States, today she stands first, having an assessed property valuation of $250,000,000." Thus, the challenge facing the legislature was where to set tax rates. The *Statesman* noted, "We do not know who is right, but the popular plan is to 'pay-as-you-go.' The people have had enough of deficiencies. They want the current expenses met promptly, and if this is not done they will begin to make inquiry about the whereabouts of one Oran M. Roberts."[22]

In the meantime, Roberts and Gould were able to split the classes in the Law Department, given that there were generally never over sixty students enrolled in law. One observer noted that it was customary in the early years of the law school to address all the professors as "Judge"—the "one exception to the rule: Oran Roberts, the senior professor, was invariably called 'Governor' and was known colloquially as the Old Alcalde."[23] The new institution had neither a general library nor a law library. The course curriculum and classes for the law school were designed by Roberts to prepare each graduate with the needed legal instruction for them to practice before the Texas Supreme Court—following the outline of the tried and true prerequisites drafted by Roberts in his capacity as state chief justice in 1877. The curriculum further called for a robust inclusion of the moot court in the first year of attendance—with Roberts and Gould serving as judge, jury, and teacher. During the early January 1885 recess of classes, Roberts organized a small group of law students to travel via Galveston to New Orleans to attend sessions of the U.S. Court of Appeals for the Fifth Circuit.[24]

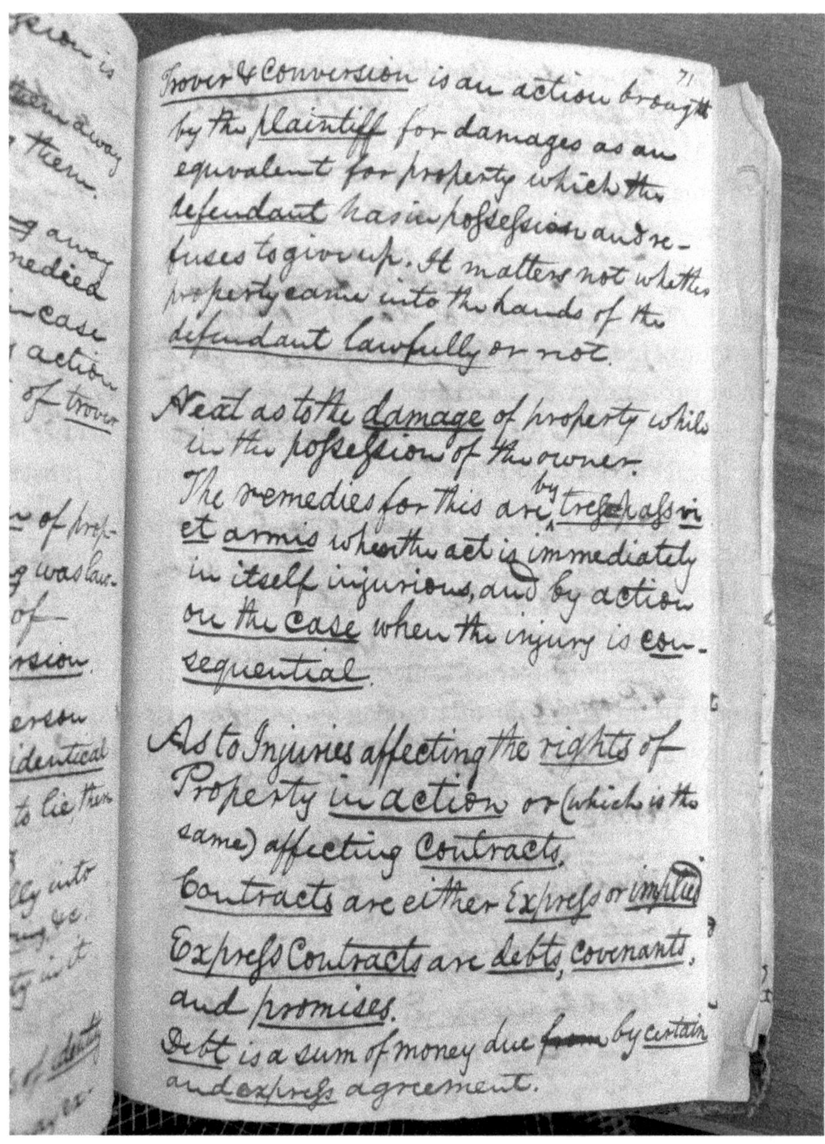

Trover & Conversion is an action brought by the plaintiff for damages as an equivalent for property which the defendant has in possession and refuses to give up. It matters not whether property came into the hands of the defendant lawfully or not.

Next as to the damage of property while in the possession of the owner. The remedies for this are by trespass vi et armis when the act is immediately in itself injurious, and by action on the case when the injury is consequential.

As to Injuries affecting the rights of Property in action or (which is the same) affecting Contracts. Contracts are either Express or implied. Express Contracts are debts, covenants, and promises. Debt is a sum of money due ~~from~~ by certain and express agreement.

Roberts was focused on cases and court precedents in Texas law. In 1883, there were no law books or journals, so he developed his one-of-a-kind notebook of case law for law students. (Roberts Papers, Biscoe Center for American History, Austin)

THE TWO FORMER justices during the law school's first decade maintained a firm hand over all aspects of instruction and neither took, nor welcomed, any advice from the faculty committee. Roberts tolerated no attacks on Texas, its history, or the university, as is reflected in the reprimand and eventual firing of Professor Joseph Baldwin for disparaging remarks against the South. Former law professor Hans Baade noted that with his independent "mercurial temper," Roberts had little regard for the faculty at large. By 1888 Roberts had donated the bulk of his personal law library to the school. Soon to be seventy years of age, he remained popular among Texans, often strolling after classes down Congress Avenue, greeting acquaintances and stopping for an occasional drink. He never again actively sought office, although he was often mentioned as a promising candidate to run again. While the Democrats had a new group of rising leaders and aspirants eager for political office, the old governor was constantly urged to stay active in state politics.[25]

The stories and anecdotes on the Old Alcalde continued to entertain Texans, many flowing from the law school:

> He stood before his class one day, in the extreme throes of a cold, and in a croaking tone, he said, "Please excuse me a minute." He returned to his office and closed the door. Several minutes passed, and then he reentered the room with vigorous tread, and his voice rang as he began the lecture.
>
> A student broke in: "Governor, I'd like to ask a question."
>
> "Very well sir."
>
> "Governor, don't you think a better remedy could be found for coughs and cold than whisky?"
>
> "Young man," exclaimed Roberts, "who in the hell would want a better remedy?"[26]

Where Is the Old Alcalde?

Beginning in mid-1884 many Texans wondered why Roberts could not run for governor again.

Texas, with a population that grew from 1.6 million in 1880 to nearly two million in 1885 with increasing numbers of European immigrants, was in the throes of major social change and economic expansion. Complaints about the railroads notwithstanding, Texas was being rapidly connected statewide, facilitating farmers moving produce to market and making consumer goods more widely available. As cotton boomed in Central and East Texas, the West was being rapidly opened to cattle ranchers, and with the expansion came a rise of unchecked lawlessness. Squabbles over free range land, herd law, barbed wire (and fence cutters), and water rights ushered in a completely new set of complexities to settlement west of the 100th meridian. In the process land defaults driven by speculators increased invalid or fraudulent transactions, land prices dropped, and in the process the school fund during the late 1880s lost eight to twelve million dollars. The newspapers, many of which had not liked Roberts, soon turned anti-Ireland, claiming his administration was prospering on the back of Roberts's reforms as well as a growing population and larger tax revenue base.[27]

One particularly powerful group arose with the re-emergence of the State Grange. The *Statesman* seemed surprised at the growth of the organization, which often claimed it was nonpolitical, but in fact it advocated on several political issues, such as better prices (and profits) for crops and an improved quality of life for farmers and ranchers, who in 1885 accounted for some 75 percent of the state's economy. An editorial noted, "The convention at Galveston shows one thing, if nothing else. It is that the Grange not only still lives in Texas, but is enjoying a degree of prosperity hardly anticipated for it by its most sanguine friends half a dozen years ago." Furthermore, the paper added, they "seem not to have lost confidence in their present power or its future destiny."[28] Roberts was on generally good terms with the Grange under the leadership Texas Grand Master Archibald J. Rose of Salado, even after the 1880 election, and they shared a common interest in education. While Roberts championed the "state university," he was also supportive of the other Texas public institutions of higher education, as was demonstrated while he was governor. He noted "The Constitution also designated the available fund to be appropriated for the creation and support of the University, and the A. and M. College was recognized as a branch of it. There was a further provision for the maintenance of a branch University, when practicable, for the colored youths of the state . . . and in the establishment of Sam Houston Normal School."[29]

In 1886 Roberts was once again drawn into the debate over who should be the next governor. The reaction to call on him resulted in part from the lackluster administration of Governor Ireland. However, those quick to endorse Roberts overlooked the steady campaign and popularity of Senator Sul Ross. Roberts and Ross were close friends and had worked together on key issues: to balance the state budget, the founding of the University of Texas, and cooperative support to launch construction of the new state capitol building. Roberts, concerned with funding from the legislature and the use of the permanent university fund, again called for all public higher education in Texas to be under one board—the University of Texas Regents, to include Texas A&M. The local catalyst for Roberts considering getting back into state politics first surfaced in Democratic Party county meetings, where people remembered the former governor's "steady hand, cool judgment and executive ability."[30] While both county party members and statewide leaders debated the 1886 nomination for governor, by late June the Old Alcalde had "declared in favor of General Ross." Much of the speculation and intrigue surfaced in the news media: "The alcalde will not reject the nomination . . . no one conversant with the methods of political wire-pullers supposes that the instruction of a county convention for the alcalde is a spontaneous premeditated indorsement [sic]."[31] The two old comrades-in-arms decided this was not going to lead to any personal or political conflict. General Ross, who was clearly the frontrunner, had earlier asked former governor Roberts if he intended to run again, saying, "I will withdraw in your favor and bring to your support as loyal and gallant a crowd as you commanded in the days of your 'Rebel' experience." By July 1, 1886, the Austin *Weekly Statesman* reported that the "dark horse" excitement by Roberts had ended and "the waters have calmed and the waves subsided . . . and [it was] no longer in doubt [that] . . . Governor Roberts will be for Ross."[32]

The Democratic Convention that followed nominated Sul Ross by acclamation on the first ballot. He was overwhelmingly elected in November, polling the largest majority of popular votes up to that time—78 percent—. At the inauguration reception that followed at the Driscoll Hotel on Congress Avenue, Governor Roberts was greeted as a special guest and friend. Governor Ross, one of the most popular Texans of the nineteenth century, adopted many of the conservative fiscal policies founded in the Texas Democrats' philosophy, which was grounded in the Jacksonian fondness for limited government, balanced budgets, and low taxation. These included the budget oversight polices started by Roberts, as well as support for public education, the indigent "lunatic" asylum, the veterans' home facilities, and an expanded land policy to open up West Texas, driven by the expansion of agricultural production to address the demand for cotton for northeastern mills and beef for the midwestern urban markets. Furthermore, to support the expenses of the new capitol and the expanding public universities, Ross learned from Roberts that financing by use of the large public domain could minimize any tax increases on rural residents. Limited government had been the mantra of the Old Alcalde's pay-as-you-go programs, and Ross agreed: "A plain, simple government, with severe limitations upon delegated powers, honestly and frugally administered is the noblest and truest outgrowth of the wisdom taught by its founders."[33]

While Judge Roberts continued his active role as an adviser to the university regents, the delay in finishing Old Main and adding new classrooms created unrest, as did a shortage of laboratory equipment and the lack of a library. Oddly enough, this mirrored earlier problems encountered during the formative years at Texas A&M. While Roberts was accustomed to exercising authority, concern with the growth and staffing of the university as well as his involvement with the day-by-day faculty activities became less intense as he aged. Roberts was revered by the students, who often challenged his temperament. His lectures often turned into free-wheeling debates and reflections on a half-century of Texas history or on one of his many famous supreme court opinions. However, his focus was always on working to ensure that the university received an adequate appropriation to expand programs. The primary challenge, notwithstanding any fiscally conservative policies from the legislature and governor's office, was that the university constantly needed and requested more general revenue funding above and beyond the tight budget constraints. Similar funding problems plagued Texas' other institutions of public higher education. Land held in trust for the Permanent University Fund and yielding only income from agricultural rent (long before the discovery of oil) could not be converted (sold) to provide available funding fast enough to address the budget needs. Roberts was the foremost expert on Texas public-land law, having issued the foundational opinion decades earlier on the status of the public domain dating back to Mexican land titles. He reminded the regents and legislature that the land was not federal but purely Texan. The *Statesman* lobbied for immediate attention, noting, "The university does not stand today where she should," and thus, "let the legislature pay the state's honest debt." Any direct legislative appropriation was not at the time constitutional. Only the west wing of the main building had been completed when architect Frederick Ruffini died in November 1885, yet construction plans remained in motion. In mid-December 1887, Oran married Catherine E. Borden of New Braunfels (widow of his friend Colonel John P. Borden), and the couple "left on a tour for Philadelphia."[34]

Governors Roberts and Ross remained staunch friends, and they supported education until their deaths and were active supporters of the university. The elder statesman continued his law lectures and was constantly solicited for advice and political observations. In the spring of 1887, after a couple of years of debate, the Texas legislature authorized a referendum on prohibition. Both Roberts and Ross made it very clear that they opposed any prohibition measures, primarily on the grounds it these were a violation of personal liberty. The exception was "local option," whereby communities, with a vote of the local citizens, could impose some limited restrictions on use of alcohol. The "anti-wets" measure was put forward by a small minority of prohibitionists hoping to gain a political foothold to advance other "progressive" issues. Given the growing traditional tastes and opposition by a coalition of the German population, African Americans, and Mexican Americans, the spirits ban by the "drys" was roundly defeated by the "wets" with a two to one margin. This would be a smearing hot-button issue, debated for the next four decades. Following Ross's re-election, the excitement in Austin centered around the dedication of the new state capitol on May 16, 1888. Judge Roberts was the center of attention, surrounded on the reviewing stand by master-of-ceremonies Governor Ross, Colonel Santos Benavides representing President Diaz of Mexico, Senator Alex Terrell, Colonel Abner Taylor, the capitol site contractor, and Sam Houston's youngest son Temple Houston. The week-long festivities and parades were attended by over 10,000 citizens.[35]

The completion and dedication of the massive new capitol ushered in a renewed optimism. As one writer noted, "No section of country and no people in the world have made such rapid strides in material prosperity, increasing industrial pursuits and general welfare as has been the case with the South and her people since the war."[36] As Ross rode this era of good feelings into his second term as governor, many editors across Texas kept Roberts in the news, as demonstrated by the *San Antonio Express* in the fall of 1889, ten years after he was first elected governor:

It has been rather the fashion to poke fun at Oran M. Roberts mainly, we presume, because he is white-haired, smokes a cob pipe, and left a neat cash balance in the treasury. White hairs come with age, and should excite veneration, not ridicule. Every smoker knows that the cob pipe is the cleanest and sweetest of all pipes. By using it the alcalde demonstrated his clear judgment. The man who objects to a cash balance in his favor, or can see anything ludicrous in it, is a singular man indeed. The Express has always felt a sincere respect for Governor Roberts. It has appreciated his hard common sense and absolute refusal to hearken to the demagogic yowls of the hour. There is no office within the gift of the people of Texas too exalted for his steady patriotic and inflexible honesty."[37]

First Texas Farmers Institute

Oran Roberts maintained an active schedule outside his duties at the law school. The advancement of agriculture in Texas was a main focus, and while never an active agriculturist, he was fully engaged with concerns of farmers and ranchers. His activity in promoting education across the state, and especially the advancement of public higher education, was reflected in his support of the Texas A&M-sponsored Texas Farmers Institutes. The institute was A&M's first extensive effort to expand agricultural extension programs, previously confined to campus classes and summer courses, to hold farmers' conferences around the state. Judge Roberts was selected as the keynote speaker at the inaugural event in Austin in early February 1889 on the subject of "Taxation and Its Bearing on Farmers." The three-day agenda was dominated with presentations by professors from the college and state officials, joined by local farmers and ranchers, to update attendees on the most current production, efficiency methods, and marketing information. One objective—to launch the A&M-sponsored Institute program organized by the Texas A&M Extension Service directed by Clarence N. Ousley in cooperation with the staff of the Dallas-based *Texas Farm and Ranch Journal* —was in part to take advantage of the new federal funding under the Hatch Act, which mandated the expansion of "research and experiment" under the Morrill Land Grand Act of 1862 that had established Texas A&M. When the state was notified in early 1888 of new federal funding under Hatch, there were questionable efforts by politicians in Austin to challenge the letter of the law allowing all the new federal funding to go to A&M. Both Roberts and sitting Governor Ross were drawn into the debate, but in the end Ross made sure the funding went only to Texas A&M. Roberts was unequivocal in support of Texas agriculture: "Agriculture is, and will long continue to be, the great interest in Texas . . . the production of Texas may be largely increased, if not doubled, by the same amount of labor and capital if practical scientific knowledge in agriculture and the mechanic arts could be impacted generally throughout the country to those who do and will follow those pursuits through life."[38]

Texas Railroad Commission

The old white-haired statesman was not quiet for long. Roberts became publicly involved in debate over the merits of the proposed state commission to regulate the railroads when a former law student brought to the attention of a number of legislators an incisive lecture presented by the judge in 1887 as a university lecture, titled "On the Violations of the Right of Private Property by American Governments, and Their Consequences." A heated issue for advocates of regulation, one writer noted, was the looming question: "Shall the great railroad octopus be shorn of its talons, so long, grappling the flesh of the defenseless farmer and rancher?" There was general consensus among most Texans that some form of regulation was needed; the question was how best to proceed. After the surfacing of Roberts's lecture, Senator Alexander Terrell, who was shepherding the railroad commission bill through the legislature, protested the use of Roberts's lecture by the opposition to question the legality of creating a commission. Previous attempts to pass an extensive railroad commission bill had failed. Hence a number of members of the Twenty-First Texas House strongly requested, in a notice in the Austin *Statesman*, a reply and clarification of Roberts's views. The Old Alcalde agreed by responding, "Though not designed to influence action, I had no objection to the use of the views [in the 1887 lecture] therein presented by any one who might think them worthy of adoption." It is unknown if Terrell asked the House members to place the request for Roberts's reply. The old judge replied in what amounted to a detailed legal brief, entitled: "The Commission."[39]

The reply gave the legislature and public much to consider as the railroad commission legislation was being debated. In no way were Roberts's concerns about the propriety of creating such an entity or his views intended to support the railroad. There is no indication that he did support it, beyond encouraging the expansion of transportation across the state to link farmers with markets. His reservations concerned the legislative bill's language and intent, and the resulting appointive and regulatory powers of such a commission to levy monetary rates and binding regulations that might impinge on the property rights and freedom of Texans. "My lecture," Roberts reviewed, "while not directly on the railroads, must have noticed that a commission was only incidentally referred to in the discourse, without any extended argument upon the subject." However, "there was enough said to show my opinion that the legislature had no power under the [Texas] Constitution to create a commission and delegate to it the power to prescribe rates and fare for the control of railroads." Debate on the need for some form of railroad regulation dated back to the private Texas Traffic Association in 1879, which tried to control rates and limit competition. Opposition to these monopolistic concerns resulted in the first major attempt to pass a commission bill in 1881, during Roberts's first term as governor. That bill was easily defeated by the railroads on the grounds that it was unconstitutional. Furthermore, as railroad historian William Childs noted, "Only ten percent of all railway traffic in Texas was intrastate. Texas roads were not charging maximum rates, so what need was there for a commission." A decade later, by 1889, competition of new tracks and complaints against the railroad as well as rate wars had changed matters substantially.[40]

In Roberts's reply to the *Statesman*, and in effect to the legislature, he restated his 1887 assessment on the inability of the legislature under the state constitution to form a "commission." Roberts's judicial experience and excellent memory of past legal proceedings and legislative actions combined for him to state both the limiting factors and the solution, recapping: "It has been often held in our courts that when a power to do a particular thing in a specified way has been conferred on a body and that body is expressly required to perform it by its own action, it cannot constitutionally dispute the power to do it to another body created to act for them." That is, the legislature could not grant its power to regulate to an independent body. In essence Terrell had tried to force the commission bill through the legislature, and each time it failed, he fully ignored that the legislature had no power under the constitution to create a commission and delegate power to it to control the railroads. Having already been advised that if passed, it would most likely be held unconstitutional, Terrell nonetheless persisted. Terrell's reputation was overshadowed by an undercurrent of suspicion about his integrity.

Historian Lewis Gould labeled Terrell as purely an "opportunist." In the process Terrell alienated many in the Texas House, as well as Ross and Roberts, and issued a public letter defending the right of the legislature to take action. Once again he failed. Recognized as the most eminent constitutional scholar of the late 1800s in Texas, the Old Alcalde quietly outlined the path to take that satisfied both the letter and spirit of the law—introduce a constitutional amendment for the establishment of a railroad commission for voter approval! In spite of Terrell, and with the backing of the Farmers' Alliance, the amendment passed by a margin of more than two to one. Roberts, who had been a confidential adviser to incoming Governor James Hogg, influenced the governor to overlook the bombastic Terrell, who expected a commission appointment. Hogg instead recalled Congressman John Reagan from Washington to chair the first Texas Railroad Commission.[41]

The idea of a railroad commission was greeted with lively debate in the legislature. The halls were filled with lobbyists both for and against it. The old ex-governor and law professor seemed to be the only expert source who understood both what was within the scope of the state constitution and what, once enacted, would survive a future challenge in the courts. One senator during the debate read a letter on the floor of the chamber from a railroad executive "complaining of discrimination by the railroads," noting, "He referred to the opinion of ex-Governor Roberts. He said seemingly it would be a public calamity if he should die, as it appears from the argument of the other side he is the only man in Texas who was capable of understanding or construing the Constitution." Furthermore, "all have a high opinion of the governor, but he did think that now after feeding for thirty years at the public crib, he should in his retirement upon the

University fund leave the decision to live questions to live men . . . in these days of dotage leave the questions alone." Alive and well, at 75 years of age, Roberts had to issue a stern denial, saying he was not seeking the nomination for governor in 1889. The Old Alcalde was still a force to command attention for his legal acumen and political savvy.[42]

The Old Alcalde was quick to express his full support of the political process and the role of the courts to review and interpret the covenants of the constitution and always to act accordingly, replying to the persistent *Galveston Daily News* in what amounted to a classic legal Roberts response, to dampen their obstinate attitude:

> It is a truism in jurisprudence that no court can suspend or abrogate a law of the state upon any ground whatever except in the one case that is being adjudicated; and a decision that holds a law inoperative in that one case does not imperatively bind the same court, or any other court, holding differently; nor does it bind authoritatively any other department of the government in reference to any other case than that particular one decided, even though another case should arise similar in facts to the one decided. Much less so the opinion and action of a single judge in a summary proceeding of habeas corpus. If, as it is assumed, the decision of a court of last resort declares a law in the statute book to be unconstitutional or repealed by implication, and by that decision the law is absolutely annulled and is henceforth nonexistent, the same as if it had never been enacted and put in the state book, no court could ever reverse that decision because there would be no law in existence upon which the subsequent court could act in reversing it. A reversal of such a decision presupposes the continued existence of the law that was held previously to have been inoperative by the first decision. In no other way could such a decision be reversed."[43]

Roberts's judicial advice was often sought during his days at the law school—and not limited to case work, disputes, and judgments in Texas. Following the appointment by President Grover Cleveland of former governor Richard Hubbard as minister plenipotentiary at the legation in Tokyo, Japan, in 1885 Roberts assisted his old friend in untangling a critical extra-territorial legal issue. The United States and Japan were in the delicate process of normalizing trade relations as the country emerged from centuries of feudalism. Hubbard, as the chief arbitrator, worked to streamline procedures to resolve legal disputes. In an effort to resolve a case before the United States Ministerial Court, Hubbard requested assistance from Roberts, given what he termed the "extraterritorial condition of Japan and the inharmonious character . . . in relation to all judicial enquiries [sic]." In question were the proper court "procedures" and the correct "application of the law" in cases involving international trade disputes. As chief justice, Roberts had indirectly had similar challenges and experience years earlier when he rewrote and codified the procedures and pleadings in Texas courts. Thus Roberts reviewed Hubbard's pending opinion in the case of the United States vs. John Kernan, with Hubbard responding that Roberts's assistance was timely, noting the importance, "for such an exposition of questions which deeply concern the interest of American citizens resident in all Oriental and non-Christian lands." Among the main beneficiaries of Roberts's ongoing active attention to legal questions were his law students, who received a real-time presentation on an international case that with which they would otherwise never been involved. Given the void in legal texts pertaining to Texas law, the Japan case became a part of Roberts's handwritten case studies booklet, highlighting over four decades of cases the Old Alcalde deemed pivotal for a background in Texas jurisprudence.[44]

The election and administration of Governor Hogg marked the first change in decades of the traditional, post-reconstruction way of doing business among the Democrats. Roberts, close friends with the Hogg family, had known the new governor since he was a young boy. Hogg was the first native-born governor of Texas. Within a short period, beginning in the mid-1890s, many of the old- guard active Redeemers passed into the history books. Claiming to be the champion of the Texas Railroad Commission, Hogg soon alienated the farmers. He promised the Farmers' Alliance that for their support in the election, he would name one of their representatives to the commission. He ignored his pledge. This action by Hogg helped fuel the simmering revolt by Texas farmers against the inaction by both major political parties. Expecting assistance from the government, farmers protested the high cost of production, the resulting low price for crops—that is, low profit, and the rising tenancy rates. From this deterioration in rural conditions and lifestyle, farmers across the South and in the Midwest organized the People's Party, also known as the Populist Party. Since the Civil War there had been a few upstart challenges from the Prohibitionists, and Greenbackers, yet this was seen as a major political threat at both the state and national level. The Populists' demands were seen as a call for radical changes, to include women's suffrage, public ownership of railroads, prohibition, more funding of rural education, and direct election of U.S. senators.[45]

Hogg and the Lily-white Republicans unwittingly played into the hands of the Populists by driving the African Americans, poor white tenant farmers, and Mexican Americans in South Texas to the alternative People's Party. Leaders like Black political activist John Rayner, a mulatto from Calvert, were quick to preach across the state the need for change and the need to vote, telling the *Southern Mercury:* "The greed, rottenness and incivism [sic] of the two old parties have divided the people into two belligerent forces viz: plebian [sic] and patrician . . . the plebians are unified and working in harmony . . . the patricians are divided into two old parties working secretly together."[46] Rayner mobilized Black voters and encouraged community organizations, while in public sarcastically calling the ambitious governor the "piney woods' parvenu." Hogg and the Democrats did not have an immediate answer for the grassroots challenge. In addition to supporting Alexander Terrell's ongoing punitive drive to institute poll taxes to limit Black voting, Hogg did little to aid Black or white rural schools, which were already sub-par. He supported segregated rail station waiting rooms and train passenger cars, supported limited access for Blacks to the judicial system, tolerated whitecapping, and failed to address the lax and unenforced anti-lynching laws. Thus, a mix of poor white and Black farmers and urban voters were drawn to the Populist movement by the promise that changes would be made, and they would at last have a voice and receive economic support. One observer noted that the upstart political movements "led to a racist backlash on the part of whites unparalleled since the darkest days of Reconstruction. The backlash convinced Rayner that participation in Populism, however noble its intentions or pregnant with democratic possibilities, had been a tragic mistake for Blacks." As historian Campbell concluded, "Populism soon disappeared—but it enlivened politics in Texas for a few years and provided impetus for reform that outlived the movement."[47]

As Hogg and the Democrats grappled with the Populists, Judge Roberts's focus remained on support of the university in particular and Texas public education in general. Working only a few blocks away from the capitol, he was called in February 1893 to a House committee hearing on the impact and importance of the public domain on funding higher education. Roberts was joined at the witness table by Edward Blackshear, principal of Prairie View A&M in Hempstead, and by longtime Texas A&M College board member William R. Cavitt of Bryan. Roberts testified first, offering a recap of the use of public lands dating back to 1858. While making statements to protect the so-called "university lands" and PUF, he suggested a means to fund the "black university," noting, "When it comes every session to asking for taxes to support the main university and the college and the medical branch, as you know it is agreed to establish the nigger college—I beg pardon, the colored college, as named in the constitution—I say, when it comes to taxing the people for these institutions or supporting them by endowment, the people will say they should be maintained by endowment. I am opposed to taxation when we can help it. How can we help it? By a liberal donation of land . . . the patriots of 1836 rescued them [the lands] from the Mexican foe." Another concern expressed by Roberts was a statement by Hogg that the university did not have as much claim to public lands as they represented, further confirming there was little doubt that land and public education were a "political football." One final critical item discussed was a suitable site in Austin for the "Black University," with the recommendation that the state purchase the property of the African American Tillotson Institute east of the state capitol for the new university as designated in the state constitution and voted on by the people. The excitement and lobbying died down and no action was taken. There is little doubt that Roberts retained his racial prejudices through his life, even when he advocated improvements to Black education in Texas.[48]

Judge Roberts had a front seat to the attempts of the Democrats to shore up the rank and file of the party as well as to reduce the growing strength and political appeal of the Populists to Texas voters. Recalling his head-on confrontation with the Know-Nothings in 1879–80, he urged caution in organizing party members as well as in recruiting and informing the thousands of new voters who had arrived in the state over the past few years. In June 1893, at age seventy-nine and after a decade at the University of Texas Law School, Roberts retired and moved to Marble Falls, fifty miles west of Austin. Other than his little home in Marble Falls and 200 acres, Roberts in his later years was of modest means and had accumulated little wealth. There was no university or state pension or medical insurance. Surrounded by family, a new accumulation of law books, and constant visitation by friends, lawyers, and neighbors seeking legal advice, the Roberts settled into retirement.[49]

A New Political Force

In retirement Roberts remained an active observer of political events across the state. Prior to the 1892 State Democratic Convention in Houston an informal "inquiry" (poll) was conducted on "who is the most honorable and beloved Democrat in Texas?" The answer "unhesitatingly" was, first, Oran Roberts, and second, Richard Coke. Governor Hogg would win a second term, yet the unrest and party divisions created uncertainty months before the next gubernatorial election. Debate was spirited in the news media, with the *Waco Evening News* admonishing the party: "The state is feverish with wild fancies perplexed with the subtle vagaries of enthusiastic Populists with insidious and dangerous suggestions. . . . If necessary, Reagan, Dave Culberson, Oran Roberts, Tom Brown, Crane, Hogg, Bailey, Sayers, Lanham, Coke, and other leaders, should be called into conference and the plan of the next campaign arranged."[50] Confusion among the state party leadership as well as local organizations and citizens continued for over a year. Clarence Ousley, editor of the Galveston *Tribune*, penned an editorial that captured the scene: "That political conditions and political sentiment in Texas have undergone a vast change within the recent past is beyond controversy. Old time political ties have been sundered, party attachments have been weakened or wholly obliterated." Speculating on the cause, he noted that "conditions in the South are not as they were a few years ago, when the 'bloody shirt' of rank sectionalism in the north and the fear of negro supremacy in the South were strong inducements to unbroken solidarity." The 1890s ushered in a new era of bitterly waged campaigns and also efforts to limit the Black and poor white vote by the Democratic Party intent on establishing the poll tax and "white primaries" statewide. The result was that by early 1896 thousands of true and staunch Democrats, now disgruntled, considered their political fortunes with the Populists—a further indication, that while generally in defeat, the People's Party made inroads in Texas. From his Marble Falls home and after a broad solicitation—and hearing of no plan to unify the party—eighty-year-old Oran Roberts sent a letter on May 6, 1896, to the Austin *Statesman* announcing the candidacy of the "Old Alcalde." He "has sounded the bugle call of a new campaign, of a new political force in Texas state politics . . . [he] consents to make the race for governor on the platform and slogan . . . "For Texas."[51]

Roberts's announcement caused both statewide surprise and immediate widespread endorsements, one supporter noting: "There is life in the old man yet." Another, concerned with the divided political environment, observed, "It is evident that we are in the 'wilderness.' Gov. Roberts believes himself capable and is willing to become the 'Moses.'" Soon it was announced that Roberts was a candidate for the independent "old-line" Democrat Party—a departure from the confusion of the last two years in the Democratic Party. Backers of the Roberts campaign, led by his close political ally John Reagan, looked to capitalize on the Democratic Party split over the silver question as well as what seemed a rising fusion challenge by Republicans and a lingering number of Populists. The Old Alcalde as an independent was possibly the best compromise, given the uncertainty. One sarcastic writer noted, "So far there are only three democratic parties in Texas—odd numbers are unlucky." The silver issue was strongly advocated by the Farmers' Alliance, who "demanded" a safe, sound, and flexible national currency with free and unlimited coinage of both silver and gold at a "legal" ration of 16 to 1.

Furthermore, the *Southern Mercury*, one of the leading publications with circulation statewide, confirmed the possibility of a fusion of disgruntled voters, noting that the number of those supporting the Populists in Texas had grown from 99,447 in 1892 to 168,812 in 1894. Furthermore, Texas in 1894 ranked as the number one state with Populist members, with twice the number of the state with the second highest, namely Minnesota with 87,931.[52]

May was generally a slow news month in Texas, being the time of the early spring rush by farmers to plant their cotton and corn crops, yet the Old Alcalde dominated the press and for the entire month filled pages of speculation on his true "political" intentions. The political excitement and rumors of Roberts's bolting the Democrats as a third party ended on May 24, 1896, with a letter from the judge to the *Statesman.* While Roberts's full intentions may never be known, it was clear that his main objective was a wake-up call to the rank-and-file Democrats not to forget their foundational principles. One analyst noted, "We confess that Governor Roberts candidacy embarrassed to some extent the Democrats of Texas." The "Old Roman" Reagan, a leading member since the founding the Texas Democratic Party, had emphasized as early as his thunderous speech to the deadlocked 1878 convention that the "party and its principles were far more important than the success of any one individual." Thus, decades later, Roberts in 1896 recognized sooner than others that the lingering possibility of the Republicans and the last elements of the Populists could upset

Democratic control unless they remain united. Answering his critics, Roberts denied "emphatically that he was being used by 'designing politicians'—he as always was his own man."[53]

Challenged on his intentions, Roberts made it clear that there were unwanted elements in the party who needed to be purged. A backcountry comment and story circulated by the hungry press was a quintessential Roberts tactic: "A gentleman just arrived from Marble Falls says that a neighbor of his overheard Governor Roberts's cook remark to another colored person that she heard the Alcalde tell his grandson to get out the old Choctaw rifle, as he intended to go down the country as soon as [he] could spare the time, and amuse himself by shooting some of the political skunks that he learns infest the granite state house he had built for gentlemen."[54]

During May there were few public comments from either Stephen Hogg or Charles Culberson. With political strategist Colonel Edward House working in the shadows to select the next governor, unlike in 1878, there was little chance that Oran Roberts would be a compromise candidate! Clarence Ousley of the *Tribune* concluded: "It will be observed that there is a string to the withdrawal, but it is not considered likely it will be pulled. The general opinion is that the Alcalde is on the shelf for good."[55]

By midsummer 1896 Judge Roberts had endorsed Culberson for governor. Thereafter, little was heard from the judge. Friends and well-wishers continued routinely visiting Marble Falls. Calm returned to political activities as Democrats maintained the dominant position at the polls. Months later, on the same day that Roberts endorsed the candidacy of Joe Sayers for governor, January 2, 1898, he learned of the death of Lawrence Sullivan Ross. Governor Roberts's last public appearance would be as pall bearer at Sul Ross's funeral in Waco, where the other bearers included governors Culberson, Ireland, and Sayers. Only a few months after the passing of General Ross, on the evening of May 19, 1898, Oran Roberts died at a family home in Austin. His body lay in state in the state capitol, followed by burial with full Masonic rites at Oakwood Cemetery. The passing of the Old Alcalde was noted statewide and across the South, with the *Memphis Commercial Appeal* delivering this tribute, "A conspicuous character, he was a man of simple habits who won the hearts of the masses."[56]

The bedrock of Roberts's support, as was the case for scores of Texas Democrats through the early 1890s, consisted of active and supportive Confederate veterans, and even some Union veterans, who routinely joined Texas veterans' activities, camp meetings, and rallies. The annual Confederate reunions gained momentum during Roberts's administration in the early 1880s. Even with the steady influx of new immigrants and, as the years passed, the gradual dwindling in the number of veterans, the former men in gray remained a major source of support in towns and rural areas across the state, with some gatherings attracting over 4,000 people. While many of the former Confederate leaders—Ross, Coke, Hubbard, Reagan, Lubbock, and Culberson—were called upon to address these reunions, Roberts was always a popular speaker and much in demand. Into his eighties by 1895, he attended a camp meeting, even in the heat of summer. While delivering the annual address on a hot July afternoon in Burnet County to the United Confederate Veterans reunion, he fainted. He quickly recovered, and when he arose to the cheers of the veterans and their families, he said, "Well, boys, I faltered during the speech, but did not falter while on duty."[57]

Prolific Author

Unlike most Texas politicians of his era, Roberts lived a long and purposeful life, leaving a cornucopia of writings that chronicled both the history of the period and his ardent and uncompromising beliefs and prejudices. During his nearly six decades in Texas, from 1840 to 1898, he basically knew almost every major historical figure, scores of their families, and hundreds of everyday Texans across the state. Interestingly his embrace of John C. Calhoun's centric political philosophy and beliefs based on "states' rights,", a strict interpretation of the U.S. Constitution, and white supremacists' views on the place and role of African Americans changed little over his lifetime. True to his unreconstructed lifelong beliefs, the governor's widely read accounts and views on Texas history and political dynamics were biased, a direct reflection on his life, and highly influential on generations of white Texans. Oran Roberts's writings fall into the following general categories: first, the dozens of court decisions he authored on the Texas Supreme Court and in legal monographs; second, documents and proclamations surrounding the disunion and secession of Texas in 1860–1861; third, a contribution of his version of the Civil War, "Texas," in the *Confederate Military History*, published by editor Clement A. Evans; fourth, his published interviews and writings related to his term as governor; fifth, publication by the University of Texas of a series of detailed lectures he presented while a law professor in the late 1880s and early 1890s, as well as a number of articles in the *Southwestern Historical Quarterly*; and finally, sixth, at the request of close friend and Dallas lawyer Dudley G. Wooten, a compilation of his observations on "The Political, Legislative, and Judicial History of Texas for Its Fifty Years of Statehood, 1845–1895." This publication was in one of the first detailed, two-volume presentations on Texas—*A Comprehensive History of Texas,* edited by Wooten and released at the time of Roberts's death in 1898. This was long considered a standard history of the period; only decades later did historians began to push back at Roberts's conclusions.[58]

Roberts's monograph *A Description of Texas,* mentioned in the preceding chapter, is an enchiridion on his experiences and observations of East Texas. He completed this work in 1881 at the height of his gubernatorial term. It can only be viewed as a nostalgic labor of love, an extra-curricular reprieve from his hectic years in the governor's mansion. A fuller assessment of his rulings on the Texas Supreme Court and his copious law school notes and lectures will be left to others.

However, what can be said is that he quickly grasped and understood the letter of Texas law and was astute in his ability to analyze and resolve many of the most difficult questions placed before the court in its earliest days. His book *The Elements of Texas Pleadings* (1890) was the standard law text for decades. Furthermore, in an ongoing effort to improve jurisprudence in Texas, he made tremendous contributions in both court protocol and proceedings that are embedded in many of the court traditions to this day. In Roberts's honor, the campus Students' Association named the student newspaper the *Alcalde,* first published in December 1895, and later to become the formal publication of the Texas Ex-Students Association.[59]

The volume of documents, letters, and newspaper articles during the secession period in Texas remains one of the largest trove of material of any southern state. Oran Roberts was at the epicenter, both principal philosophical leader and publicly engaged with Texas rebels in fomenting secession and disunion. He organized the meetings, set the outline for the causes of secession, then wrote a lengthy justification—over the objection of his former friend Sam Houston—to plan, call, and manage the Texas Secession Convention as well as appoint committees, provide their working orders, and thus dictate much of the tenor and outcome of the convention proceedings. Little wonder, then that the northern Radical Republicans in Washington made sure in 1866 he would never have any role or seat in the U.S. Senate. And even in his abrupt vitriolic rejection, Roberts penned what other southern statesmen were reluctant to broach in his detailed "letter" and damnation of the Congress and federal government and his views on why there should be more consideration—fully ignored—of bringing the southern states back into the union. He further contributed writings on the Civil War years about his time as a colonel in the 11th Texas Infantry, followed by his compilation "Texas" in the *Confederate Military History of Texas,* a general overview of events and Texans during the conflict. This publication includes a concise introductory assessment of what he perceived as the "unfavorable political conditions" on the eve of secession. It was published after he died in 1899.

During his later years, Roberts presented lectures and a

commencement address at the University of Texas that were published in the state-funded campus *Bulletin* in what amounted to a rehash of Texas' role in the disunion of the state and the South more generally as well as presenting his pointed political views—which had changed little since the rebellion. These dozen lectures, published in 1892 as *Our Federal Relations From a Southern View of Them,* were presented to a new and younger audience of students, faculty, and Austin citizens not just as a justification of past events but also as a review of his objectives, and those of his secessionist cohorts, during the crisis period of the late 1850s and early 1860s. The overriding theme of these lectures is found in the first presentation of "The Impending Crisis," wherein he staunchly felt and argued that the "contract" with the federal Constitution had been breached: "The South would no longer be bound to observe the contract. A bargain broken on one side is broken on all sides." In an example of Roberts's concern about federal intervention in the states' affairs, even given his strong support for public education, the San Marcos *Free Press* noted that the Old Alcalde "most strenuously opposed the Congressional Blair Bill, supported by a resolution by the Texas State Teachers' Association, that proposed giving federal funds to each state. The funding would come with strings attached that threatened "the interference on the part of the National Government in the management of the schools of the several States." Thus, the TSTA was for funding, yet wanted the Texas representatives in Congress "to vote for a bill that will give Federal aid to education and not encroach upon the prerogatives of the State government" to manage its own educational system.[60]

Texas History

Given his keen interest in Texas history, Roberts was among the earliest to advocate the formation of a formal state historical association. His efforts dated back to 1874 while he served as chief justice, when he, Rip Ford, Guy Bryan, and John Reagan considered formation of the Historical and Statistical Association of Texas, but they failed to follow through on it. In April 1883 Roberts and Ford organized a second group in Austin to form the "Texas branch" of the Southern Historical Society, and this effort also foundered. Other attempts at forming a historical association were led by Clarence Ousley, editor of the *Galveston Tribune*, but that group was active for only a couple of years. At last in early 1897 a small group of "history cranks" at the University of Texas convened the Texas State Historical Association, with an organizational meeting at the capitol office of Archibald J. Rose on March 2, 1897. After the approval of a constitution and by-laws, Governor Roberts, eighty-two years old, was unanimously elected its first president. Roberts gave the first presidential address in June 1897, and papers were presented during the gathering and subsequently published in the *The Texas Magazine.* Thereafter articles were published in the inaugural issue of the *Quarterly of the Texas State Historical Association*—today known as the *Southwestern Historical Quarterly.* The new association highlighted an article by Governor Roberts in the August 1897 issue.[61]

CHAPTER 7

EPILOGUE

No man can be justly measured or judged amid the heat and passion of political conflict. His virtues are ignored, and his faults magnified, but when the fury of the political storm has passed, and men think normaly [sic] and calmly, they are just in their judgments.

— NORMAN G. KITTRELL *GOVERNORS WHO HAVE BEEN*, 1921

A CENTURY and three-score years after Oran M. Roberts orchestrated the 1860 drive for Texas to secede from the union, many hold the Old Alcalde in contempt for his actions during his lifetime. His early cultural background, economic and social environment, and education were shaped by southern ideals of the period. While his political views on secession and slavery ran counter to mainstream social and political thought, which severely criticized the dastardly peculiar institution, an old friend recalled that Roberts "belonged to that school of old-fashioned democrats who believed devoutly in the value of personal and private initiative and enterprise, rather than in the paternal philanthropy of government ownership and management."[1]

Notwithstanding his staunch segregationist views, Roberts, as a Supreme Court judge both before and after the secession and Civil War, was in favor of the African American right to be recognized as a person and the right to a fair trial. While rejecting other rights, he confounded many of his white Democratic contemporaries, who at the time opposed higher education for Blacks. As governor he went to extraordinary lengths to ensure the viability and survival of Prairie View Normal School. At the same time, Roberts opposed any efforts to support civil rights for African Americans. It must be noted that a sizable minority of white southerners opposed slavery. Roberts surely knew of these arguments but chose to reject them.

The death of Oran Milo Roberts in 1898 marked the end of a frantic and tumultuous era in the political and social events of late nineteenth-century Texas. Roberts was indeed an opinionated and impactful leader of his time. As the new century dawned, historian James Haley noted, a host of Civil War-Reconstruction era stalwart Confederates, secessionists, and the vanguard of the Texas Redeemers, "lined up at the pearly gates to claim their rewards." James Throckmorton died in 1894, Ox-Cart John Ireland in 1896; John "Rip" Ford and Richard Coke in 1897, and Sul Ross in 1898—followed shortly by Richard Hubbard in 1901. The old guard of those reared in the states' rights era of antebellum Texas yielded to the next generation.

Oran Roberts lived and died convinced of the righteousness of and responsibility to perpetuate the cause of states' rights, the preservation of the peculiar institution of slavery, and protection of the foundations of southern social culture and traditions. A loyal son-of-the-South, he held a devotion to what he felt was an unyielding defense of Texas and the South. Due to these regional social and political ties, he remained devoted to the cause of white supremacy to a fault. The southern cotton culture was the root of southern white supremacists' views and actions. Roberts never doubted the pre- war efficacy of slavery. In this regard, he was among the last of the discredited lineage that had been swept away by a wave of southern-first cotton nationalism.

Within a decade of moving to Texas from Alabama Roberts emerged as a recognized jurist, district judge, and leader in East Texas by 1850. A strict traditional constitutionalist, he supported the letter and spirit of the law and first agreed with Sam Houston that the federal Union Texas had joined was a just cause to support and defend. In these early days, he made it clear that he did not espouse a course to secession. The indestructability of the Union by those who were strict constitutionalists was gradually eroded in the minds of a rising element in the late 1850s in Texas. This group viewed northern agitators, who advocated for the freedom of colored people and the extension of civil rights to African Americans, as being a force attempting to upend the very foundations of the southern way of life.

One aspect of Roberts's lingering legacy is the extensive suite of publications and documents he left behind—which most assuredly reflect his vivid southern perspective dating from the pre-war era. Twentieth-century scholars have noted that in particular, his detailed history of Texas published by Dudley Wooten in 1898 was the first extensive attempt to write a history of Lone Star events, personalities, and politics during the later part of the nineteenth century. It is a classic example and statement of his strong views on the period. Historians continue to review this text as one perspective of the period. However, more balanced research and reassessments have been made on such topics as slavery and Roberts's vitriolic attack on Edmund Davis and Republican rule during Reconstruction in Texas.

Roberts supported segregation in all aspect of southern life, including public education.

However, in the realm of public higher education, he played a pivotal role in supporting the founding and expansion of the state's first four public institutions of higher learning—including a major role to ensure the opening viability of Prairie View A&M College—"for colored students." After leaving the governor's office in 1883, he appointed himself a law professor in the inaugural phase of the University of Texas. Over the next fifteen years he labored as a professor and a mentor to students—influencing a generation of lawyers, politicians, and judges. He also remained a major advisor to the Democratic Party and a rising generation of new state leaders. In addition to a volume of history on the Confederate Army in Texas, Roberts gave lectures on government oversight, property rights and regulations and subsequently had them published by the university, at state expense, on his long-held views on states' rights, slavery, and an ongoing concern with the need for a weak federal government. While most today identify and consider these texts as a means to justify his and other secessionists' actions, white audiences in the 1890s, with some objections, accepted his racist overtones and presentations at face value.

Close friend and biographical chronicler Norman Kittrell, during the last years of Roberts's life, left open the question of a final judgment, while others were also of strong opinion. "The story of Judge Roberts' life," noted DeShields, "is essentially the story of Texas' first fifty years of statehood. His public services were most unique. No man, save Sam Houston, was ever better known in Texas and no one ever had a longer and more varied and successful career." Nevertheless it is essential to understand leaders such as Roberts, if only for insight into how problematic beliefs became accepted by the electorate.

In spite of Roberts' long-held radical white supremacy views, he best captured his own vision and destiny for the future of Texas in his first inaugural address in 1879: "The future looms up grandly and glorious before us, and we should act in the living present as becomes men who would not only enjoy the confidence and esteem of those whom they represent, but would also achieve that immortality which is born of the grateful appreciations of generations yet to come."

THE SS ORAN M. ROBERTS

The SS Oran M. Roberts, *a U.S. Liberty cargo ship, provided supplies to Europe from 1943 to 1950. In 1974, the ship was sunk was part of an artificial reef program off the coast of Alabama, Roberts's home state.*

NOTES

CHAPTER 1

1. James L. Abrahamson, *The Men of Secession and Civil War 1859–1861,* Wilmington: Scholarly Resources, 2000, pp. 46–47; Eric H. Walther, *The Fire-Eaters,* Baton Rouge: LSU Press, 1992; ; Richard Lowe, *Walker's Texas Division C.S.A.: Greyhounds of the Trans-Mississippi.* Baton Rouge: LSU Press, 2004, 259 [quote].

   Note: A statement on the definition and use of the term "states' rights" is in order. The term has received much debate and interpretation. Yet the term "states' rights" is a misnomer. The U.S. Constitution did not convey rights to the states in the same fashion it grants rights to individuals. There is no states' rights clause in the Constitution, and proponents in the early and mid-1800s took the opportunity on a perception of state sovereignty to equate states' rights with an assumption of being pro-slavery. State power only exists where federal power ends. For the purpose of this study the opportunistic term is employed in the context used in the period concerned and by those who espoused its mistaken validity. See also Justin Collings, "What 'Rights' Do States Really Have Under the Constitution?" *Deseret News,* September 18, 2021.
2. "Volcanic Phenomenon," *Literary and Philosophical Intelligence,* August 1816, p. 167; Alan Robock, "Volcanic Eruptions and Climate," *Reviews of Geophysics,* May 2000, pp. 191–219.
3. Oran Milo Roberts, Memoirs of Early Years, Oran Milo Roberts Papers, 1815–1898, Austin: Briscoe Center for American History (hereafter cited as Roberts Memoirs); Llerena B. Friend, *Sam Houston the Great Designer,* Austin: University of Texas Press, 1954, pp. 6–7; Harry Toulmin, *Digest of the Laws of the State of Alabama,* Cahawba: Ginn & Curtis, 1823, pp. 88–89. Note: St. Clair County is one of two counties in Alabama (and 33 counties in the United States) with two separate county seats—Ashville and Pell City.
4. Inventory of the Estate of Oba Roberts, February 2, 1828, Alabama Archives and Museum, Ashville; James D. Lynch, *The Bench and Bar of Texas,* St. Louis: Nixon Jones Printing Company, 1885, p. 273; Thomas P. Abernethy, *The Formative Period in Alabama, 1815—1828,* Montgomery: Brown Printing Company, 1922, pp. 24–25, 52–53, 56, 164.
5. Inventory of the Estate of Oba Roberts; Abernethy, *The Formative Years,* p. 89. See also Alfred H. Stone, "The Cotton Factorage System in Southern States," *American Historical Review,* XX, pp. 557–65. Note: The Robertses' greatest assets or "property" were their slaves, with George, Prince, and Nick valued at $500 each; Alick $450; a girl, Beck, $400; and Isabel and the children $650. Other assets included a "road wagon," $70; horse, $90; hack, $70; and feather bed and furniture, $35. Total value of the livestock (2 horses, 6 hogs, and 18 cows) was about $90. See also Monica Dobbins, "Rogers, Shinn, and Smith: A History of Universalism in Alabama in Three Vignettes," *Journal of Universal History,* pp. 65–81.

6. Abernethy, *The Formative Years,* p. 138. See also Randolph B. Campbell, *Gone to Texas,* New York: Oxford University Press, 2003, pp. 214–15.
7. Roberts Memoirs; unpublished draft of Roberts's biography by R. S. Walker, n.d., Roberts Papers, BCAH.
8. "O. M. Roberts Education etc.," n.d., Roberts Papers, Briscoe Center for American History, Austin (hereafter BCAH); Oran M. Roberts, Reminiscences of the History of the University of Alabama, During Four Sessions as a Student, February 1883 to December 1836, May 30, 1892, p. 1, Roberts Papers, University of Alabama Archives (hereafter cited as Roberts Reminiscences).
9. Randolph B. Campbell, *An Empire for Slavery: The Peculiar Institution in Texas, 1821–1865,* Baton Rouge: LSU Press, 1989, pp. 82–83, 88; Leila Bailey, "Life and Public Career of O. M. Roberts, 1815–1883," PhD diss., University of Texas, 1932, pp. 10–11, 16; Robert W. Fogel and Stanley L. Engerman, *Time on the Cross: The Economics of American Negro Slavery,* New York: W. W. Norton & Company, 1974, pp. 54–57. See also: *McLemore v. McClellan,* 17 Tex. 122 (1856). and *Townsend v. Hill,* 18 Tex. 422 (1857).
10. Roberts Reminiscences, p. 2.
11. Ibid., p. 7.
12. Ibid., pp. 18–20. See also "O. M. Roberts Education etc.," Roberts Papers, BCAH.
13. Ibid., p. 20. Note: Van Buren won with 51 percent of the popular vote, with Harrison second, 37 percent, and White a distant third at 10 percent.
14. "O. M. Roberts Education etc.," Roberts Papers, BCAH.
15. Roberts, Reminiscences, p. 23; Letter, Roberts to Miller, October 21, 1837, Washington D. Miller Papers, Texas State Archives; Lynch, *Bench and Bar of Texas,* p. 274.
16. "Governor O. M. Roberts' Courtship," *Daily Texan,* February 4, 1904.
17. Barnes F. Lathrop, *Migration into East Texas 1835–1860,* Austin: Texas State Historical Association, 1949, pp. 69, 74, 75; Herbert E. Bolton, *Texas in the Middle Eighteenth Century,* Austin: University of Texas Press, 1970 [reprint], pp. 131, 142, 332; D. W. Meinig, *Imperial Texas,* Austin: University of Texas Press, 1969, pp 34–35. "Houston Prices Current," Houston *Musquito,* February 14, 1841. See also "Sketches of Texas," *San Luis Advocate,* April 20–21, 1841; and G. L. Crocket, "The Old Town of San Augustine," El Paso *Morning Times,* July 12, 1912.
18. James L. Haley, *The Texas Supreme Court,* Austin: University of Texas Press, 2013, p. 74, notes as an example of the conflicting laws across Texas, "Oran Roberts in one case declined to choose between whether a coastal land grant extended down to mean high tide, as under the common law, or only to the highest high tide, as under Spanish law. In *City of Galveston v. Menard* [1859], he extended the 'grant down to the water wherever it was, because the clear purpose of the grant was for the construction of a port.'"
19. Margaret S. Henson and Deolece Parmelee, *The Cartwrights of San Augustine,* Austin: Texas State Historical Association, 1993, pp. 119–20; H. P. N. Gammel, *The Laws of Texas,* 1822–1897, 10 vols., Austin: Gammel Book Company, 1898–1902, vol. II, pp. 177–80.
20. "Description of Texas Law License," Roberts Papers; "Texas," Houston *Telegraph and Texas Register,* January 12, 1842; George L. Crocket, *Two Centuries in East Texas: A History of San Augustine County and Surrounding Territory from 1685 to the Present Time,* 1932; reprint Austin: Hart Graphics, 1982, p. 115; Meinig, *Imperial Texas,* pp. 42–46; Haley, *Texas Supreme Court,* pp. 16, 29, 44.

21. "Professional Notices," San Augustine *Red-Lander,* May 19, 1842; "The District Court," San Augustine *Red-Lander,,* October 7, 1843; Haley, *Texas Supreme Court,* pp. 28–30; Campbell, *An Empire for Slavery,* p. 57.
22. John S. Ford, *Rip Ford's Texas,* Austin: University of Texas Press, 1963, pp. xix, 21; "O. M. Robert Law Office," *Red-Lander,* May 19, 1842; "Dr. John S. Ford," *Red-Lander,* May 26, 1842; State of Texas, *The Resources, Soil, and Climate of Texas,* Report of A. W. Spaight, Galveston: A. H. Belo & Company Printers, 1882, p. 274. Note: The *San Augustine Journal and Advertiser* was renamed the *Red-Lander* in May 1841.
23. Bill of Sale, Oran M. Roberts to Abner Parther, December 27, 1842, George L. Crocket Papers, East Texas Research Center, Nacogdoches, Texas.
24. "Whiskey and Slaves Were the Medium of Exchange in Days of Texas Republic," *Bartlett Tribune and News,* September 17, 1937; Meinig, *Imperial Texas,* p. 35; Letter, C P. Alexander to O. M. Roberts, June 10, 1849, Roberts Papers, BCAH. Note: The story is based on a document found in the San Augustine County Clerk's Office.
25. O. M. Roberts, "A History of the Establishment of the University of the State of Texas," *Southwestern Historical Quarterly,* April 1898, p. 238; Harriet Smither, ed., *Journals of the Sixth Congress of the Republic of Texas 1841–1842,* vol. II, Austin Texas State Library, 1944, p. 389; Roberts, "Criticism Upon the Presumption of M. A. Montrose," draft article for San Augustine *Red-lander,* 1943, Roberts Papers, BCAH; Oran M. Roberts, "The Political, Legislative, and Judicial History of Texas for Its Fifty Years of Statehood, 1845–1895," in Dudley G. Wooten, *A Comprehensive History of Texas,* Dallas: William G. Scarff, 1898, pp. 7–13 (hereafter Roberts, "Fifty Years"), p. 463.
26. "Gov. Roberts and Infidelity," *Jasper News-Boy,* August 19, 1881; "Correspondent of the *Christian Advocate,*" seen in Austin *Weekly Democratic Statesman,* January 8, 1880; O. M. Roberts to Rev. J. E. Carnes, January 14, 1861, in Galveston *Texas Christian Advocate,* reprinted in *Dallas Morning News,* November 14, 1886.
27. "University of San Augustine," *Red-Lander,* October 7, 1843; "Nacogdoches University," *Red-Lander,* October 2, 1845; "O. M. Roberts, President, University of San Augustine," *Red-Lander,* December 4, 1845; "Mr. President of the Board of Trustees," *Red-Lander,* February 12, 1846; Roberts, "Fifty Years," pp. 463–64; James Partin et al." *Nacogdoches: The History of Texas' Oldest City,* Lufkin: Best of East Texas Publishers, 1995, pp. 87–88; "Col. O. M. Roberts," Washington-on-the-Brazos, Texas, *Texas National Register,* August 21, 1846; Roberts, "Masonic Address: Dec. 1848 San Augustine," Roberts Papers, BCAH; William R. Hogan, *The Texas Republic: A Social and Economic History,* Norman: University of Oklahoma Press, 1946, pp. 149–58; G. L. Crocket, *Two Centuries in East Texas,* pp. 306–10; Campbell, *Gone to Texas,* pp. 229–30; Roberts to Miller, August 23, 1864, Washington D. Miller Papers, Texas State Archives.
28. William Kennedy, *Texas: The Rise, Progress, and Prospects of the Republic of Texas,* London: R. Hastings, 1841, vol. II, pp. 365–72; Roberts to Miller, September 14, 1843, Washington D. Miller Papers, Texas State Archives; Sam Houston to Roberts, March 19, 1844, Roberts Papers; Sam Houston, Senate Judicial Appointments, Executive Department, Washington (on-the-Brazos), February 5, 1844, in Williams and Barker, eds., *The Writings of Sam Houston, 1813–1863,* Austin: Jenkins Publishing Company, 1970, vol. IV, p. 245; "Government of Texas [1845 pay scale]," *Texas National Register,* August 21, 1845; "Law Notice: O. M. Roberts & H. W. Sublett," *Red-Lander,* October 23, 1845; "The Tariff," *Red-Lander,* October 7, 1843; Llerena B.

Friend, *Sam Houston the Great Designer,* Austin: University of Texas Press, 1954, p. 112; A Farmer of Lamar, "Tariff, No.2," *Northern Standard,* January 21, 1843. Note: Counties in the 1844 Fifth District: Anderson, Rusk, Houston, Kaufman, Sabine, Jasper, Shelby, San Augustine, Nacogdoches, Angelina, Cherokee, Henderson, and Newton.

29. Roberts, "Scrap of a Journal Commented by Me," July 9, 1845, Roberts Papers, BCAH. Note: Underlining by Roberts in original document.
30. Roberts, "Scrap of a Journal," July 31, 1845.
31. "Editorial Jaunt," Clarksville *Northern Standard,* July 10, 1847; J. B. Davenport, *The History of the Supreme Court of Texas,* Austin: Southern Law Book Publishers, 1917, pp. 52–53; Lynch, *Bench and Bar in Texas,* pp. 275–76.
32. Kennedy, *Texas,* vol. II, pp. 365–72; "Circular to the Independent Voters of San Augustine County," *Red-Lander,* July 7, 1842; "Speech of O. M. Roberts to the Jury while District Attorney 5th Jud'l. Dist–Texas: Upon the Obligation of the Citizens to Pay Duties," 1845, Roberts Papers, BCAH.
33. Message by Sam Houston to the Texas House of Representatives, December 30, 1841, *Journals of the Sixth Congress of the Republic of Texas,* vol. II, pp. 237–38; Kenneth E. Hendrickson, *The Chief Executives of Texas,* College Station: Texas A&M University Press, 1995, p. 31.
34. O. M. Roberts, "Anniversary of Texian Independence," March 8, 1843, copy of unknown newspaper, seen at East Texas Research Center.
35. Kennedy, *Texas,* vol. II, p. 369; "Public Meeting," *Red-Lander,* October 7, 1843; Letter, O. M. Robert, Dist. Atty, 5th Dist. to Wm. B. Ochiltree, Secy Treasury, Decr. 18th, 1844, *Texas Treasury Papers,* Austin: Texas State Library, 1955, vol. III, pp. 1064–67; "Protection of Home Industry," ibid., January 14, 1847; Asa K. Christian, "The Tariff History of the Republic of Texas," *Southwestern Historical Quarterly,* July 1917, pp. 1–7. Note: political foe Edmund Davis was also a deputy customs collector during his early career in Laredo.
36. Anson Jones, *Memoranda and Official Correspondence Relating to the Republic of Texas, Its History and Annexation,* New York: A. Appleton and Company, 1859, p. 267. (hereafter cited as *Memoranda*).
37. "The Tariff," *Red-Lander,* October 7, 1843; "Address of Mr. Calhoun," *Red-Lander,* December 18, 1845; "Annexation of Texas," Clarksville *Northern Standard,* February 10, 1844; Ford, *Rip Ford's Texas,* p. xx; Miguel A. González-Quiroga, *War and Peace on the Rio Grande Frontier, 1830–880,* Norman: University of Oklahoma Press, 2020, pp. 89–90; Andreas V. Reichstein, *Rise of the Lone Star,* College Station: Texas A&M University Press, 1989, pp. 172–77.
38. *Congressional Globe,* 28th Cong., 1st sess., vol. 13, p. 606, and 31st Cong., 1st sess., vol. 19, p. 165; U.S. *House Journal,* 28th Cong., 2nd ss., 1844–45, p. 191; U.S. *Statues at Large,* Boston: Little, Brown and Company, 1856, vol. V., pp. 797–98; Charles Edward Lester, *The Life of Sam Houston,* New York: J. C. Derby, 1855, pp. 231–50; Roberts, "Speech on the Texas-New Mexico Boundary Dispute," *Red-Land Herald,* July 27, 1850. See also Ronald N. Gray, "The Abortive State of West Texas," MA thesis, Texas Tech University, May 1969; Ernest Wallace, *The Howling of the Coyotes: Reconstruction Efforts to Divide Texas,* Collage Station: Texas A&M University Press, 1979. See also Mark J. Stegmaier, *Texas, New Mexico and the Compromise of 1850,* Lubbock: Texas Tech University Press, 2012.

39. Letters, Charles Elliot to My Lord [The Earl of Aberdeen, K. T.] from Galveston, November 2, 1842, and Elliot to Aberdeen, February 8, 1845, in Ephraim D. Adams, ed., *British Diplomatic Correspondence Concerning the Republic of Texas, 1838–1846,* Austin: Texas State Historical Association, ca. 1918, pp. 121–24, 442–45; "Memorandum of a Conference held at the State Department at Washington, on the Brazos," March 29, 1845, in Jones, *Memoranda,* pp. 473–75; Friend, *Sam Houston,* pp. 136–39. See also Letters, Governor George T. Wood to Geo. W. Crawford, Secretary of War, December 14, 1849, and January 19, 1850; *Message from the President of the United States to the Two Houses of Congress,* 31st Cong., 2nd sess., Ex. Do. no. 1, December 2, 1850, Washington: GPO, 1850, pp. 11–19; Friend, *Sam Houston,* pp. 145–47.
40. "Galveston: The Annexation of Cuba," *Galveston Weekly News,* November 15, 1845; "The Santa Fe Trade," *Red-Lander,* October 7, 1843; "Claims of British Subjects to Lands in Texas," *Red-Lander,* October 7, 1843; "The Position of Mexico—The Policy of the United States," *Red-Lander,* October 30, 1845, *Picayune* quote; Joel H. Silbey, *Storm Over Texas: The Annexation Controversy and the Road to Civil War,* New York: Oxford University Press, 2005, pp. 36–41; Ephraim D. Adams, *Great Britain and the American Civil War,* New York: Russell and Russell, 1924, pp. 12–15. Note: The *Galveston Weekly news* was first published on March 25, 1842, and soon changed to the *Galveston Daily News*; it is the oldest continuously published newspaper in Texas.
41. O. M. Roberts, "The Causes of the War Between the States," in Roberts, *Our Federal Relations,* Austin: Eugene Von Boeckmann Printer, 1892, pp. 12–13; Samuel J. Watson, *Peacekeepers and Conquerors: The Army Officer Corps on the American Frontier, 1821–1846,* Lawrence: University Press of Kansas, 2013, pp. 368–77.
42. Roberts, "Annexation Resolution Adopted in Favor of It Drawn," summer 1845, Roberts Papers, BCAH; State of Texas, *Journals of the Convention Assembled at the City of Austin in July 1845,* Austin: Miner & Cruger, Printers,1845, p. ii; "Colonization Contracts," Washington *Texas National Register,* August 21, 1845; Oran M. Roberts, "The Political, Legislative, and Judicial History of Texas for Its Fifty Years of Statehood, 1845–1895," in Dudley G. Wooten, *A Comprehensive History of Texas,* Dallas: William G. Scarff, 1898, pp. 7–13 (hereafter Roberts, "Fifty Years").
43. "Government of the State of Texas," Austin *Texas Democrat,* October 21, 1846; Letter, R. T. Wheeler to O. M. Roberts, February 23, 1847, Roberts Papers, BCAH. See also Chris Klemme, "Jacksonian Justice: The Evolution of the Elective Judiciary in Texas, 1836–1850." *Southwestern Historical Quarterly,* January 2002, pp. 428–50.
44. "Gen. J. P. Henderson for Governor; for the U.S. Senate Gen. Thomas J. Rusk; Gen. Sam Houston," *Red-Lander,* December 4, 1845; Henry W. Sublett to Roberts, April 1, 1846, Roberts Papers, BCAH; Lynch, *Bench and Bar in Texas,* p. 277; Haley, *Texas Supreme Court,* pp. 21, 53–55; William J. Chriss, *Six Constitutions Over Texas: Texas' Political Identity, 1830–1900.* College Station: Texas A&M University Press, 2024, pp. 45–54: Lance A. Cooper, "An Historical Overview of Judicial Selection in Texas," *Texas Wesleyan Law Review,* vol. 2, 1995, pp. 317–33. See also Roberts, "Fifty Years," pp. 10–13, 17; and A. E. Keir Nash, "The Texas Supreme Court and Trial Rights of Blacks, 1845–1860," *Journal of American History,* December 1971, p. 622. Note: Since gaining independence from Mexico, Texas has ratified six constitutions; four provided for judges by appointment, and two provided judges by election.

45. "Honorary Testimonial," *Northern Standard,* June 17, 1848; "The Huntsville Banner —Judge Roberts," *Northern Standard,* June 23, 1849; Roberts, "Fifty Years," pp. 23–24; Jacob De Cordova, *Texas: Her Resources and Her Public Men,* Philadelphia: J. B. Lippincott & Co., 1958, p. 190. Note: A joint resolution of the Republic of Texas legislature was passed to grant a leave and authority for Governor Henderson to command troops in Mexico. The Republic Constitution of 1836 gave Congress the power to grant such leave. The new Constitution of the State of Texas in 1845 did not grant any such provision for the chief executive.
46. San Augustine County Tax Roll, 1846, p. 12; Randolph Campbell, "Texas and the Nashville Convention of 1850," *Southwestern Historical Quarterly,* July 1972, p. 1; Seventh Census of the United States, 1850, Schedule 1, p. 351, and Schedule 2, September 1850, San Augustine County, Slave Schedule of Inhabitants, p. 10; "Europe, Mexico and the U. States," Houston *Democratic Telegraph and Texas Register,* April 1, 1846.
47. Robert G. Winchester, *James Pinckney Henderson: Texas' First Governor,* San Antonio: Naylor Company 1971; Maxwell Bloomfield, "The Texas Bar in the Nineteenth Century," *Vanderbilt Law Review,* vol. 32, 1979, p. 263.
48. San Augustine *Red-Land Herald,* March 8 and 15, 1851.
49. "The Discussion Was Opened," San Augustine *Red-Land Herald,* June 21, 1851; "Hon. W. B. Ochiltree," *Red-Land Herald,* July 5, 1851.
50. "A Card," Clarksville *Northern Standard,* April 12, 1851; "Judge Roberts' Speech," *Northern Standard,* May 24, 1851; "Eastern Texas: A Card," Austin *Texas State Gazette,* April 5, 1851.
51. "The Candidates for Congress," *Northern Standard,* May 31, 1851; Letter, O. M. Roberts to R. S. Hunt, editor of the *Bonham Advertiser,* published in ibid., May 31, 1851; Roberts, "The Causes of the War Between the States," in Roberts, *Our Federal Relations: From a Southern View of Them,* Austin: Eugene Von Boeckmann Printer, 1892, p. 18. Note: The resolutions comprising the "Compromise of 1850" include the abolition of the slave trade in the District of Columbia and the constitutional right of citizens "to be protected in their slave property in the territories"; however, there was "dubious language" on how the territory would be made states—free or slave.
52. "The Eastern Canvas," Galveston *Weekly Journal,* May 27, 1851, and "Meeting at Durst's Bridge," ibid., May 13, 1851; "Milam Account of Judge Ochlitree," *Red-Land Herald,* June 21, 1851; "Shelbyville on Saturday," ibid., June 21, 1851; "Mr. Burton Nominated Roberts," Clarksville *Northern Standard,* July 5, 1851; Roberts, "Fifty Years," pp. 29–30; Randolph B. Campbell, "The Whig Party of Texas in the Elections of 1848 and 1852," *Southwestern Historical Quarterly,* July 1969, pp. 17–34.
53. Letter, P. H. Bell to Roberts, December 6, 1849, *Northern Standard* Roberts Papers, BCAH. Note: The copy of the Bell letter in Roberts Papers has no notation of when it was received or if Roberts responded.
54. "P. Hansbrough Bell," Galveston *Weekly News,* May 6, 1851; Roberts, "Notes on Tender of Appointment as Attorney General," Peter Bell to Roberts, December 6, 1849, Roberts Papers, BCAH; "Government of Texas," *Texas State Gazette,* June 1, 1850.
55. Dallas T. Herndorn, *The Nashville Convention of 1850,* Montgomery: Alabama Historical Society, 1905, pp. 223–24; David M. Potter, *The Impending Crisis, 1848–*

1861, New York: Harper and Row, 1976, pp. 104–5, 461–62; Campbell, "Texas and the Nashville Convention of 1850," pp. 1–14.

56. "Correspondence on the Southern Question," and "Col. L. T. Wigfall Eulogy for John C. Calhoun," Marshall *The Texas Republican,* April 18, 1850; Campbell, "Texas and the Nashville Convention of 1850," p. 13.
57. Potter, *Impending Crisis,* pp. 59–60, 99–100. See also Roberts, "Fifty Years," p. 35; and Irving H. Bartlett, *John C. Calhoun,* New York: W. W. Norton & Company, 1993, pp. 339–46.
58. San Augustine, *Red-Land Herald,* July 27, 1850.
59. Roberts, "Fifty Years," p. 35.
60. Letter, Roberts to Governor Bell, March 14, 1851, Roberts Papers, BCAH; "The Candidates for Congress," Clarksville *Northern Standard,* May 31, 1851.

CHAPTER 2

1. Dudley G. Wooten, "The President's Annual Address: The Life and Services of Oran M. Roberts," *Quarterly Journal of the Texas State Historical Association,* July 1898, p. 7; Carl H. Moneyhon, *Edmund J. Davis of Texas: Civil War General, Republican Leader, Reconstruction Governor.* Fort Worth: TCU Press, 2010, p. 25.
2. John Marshall, "The Mass Meeting—Our Party United," Austin *Texas State Gazette,* June 23, 1855; Dale Baum, *The Shattering of Texas Unionism,* Baton Rouge: LSU Press, 1998, pp. 13, 31; Ben H. Procter, *Not Without Honor: The Life of John H. Reagan.* Austin: University of Texas Press, 1962, pp. 9–3.
3. Roberts, "Fifty Years," pp. 36–37; John H. Reagan, *Memoirs,* New York: Neale Publishing Company, 1906, pp. 64–65; Jones, *Memoranda,* pp. 536–41; Walter L. Buenger, "Texas and the Riddle of Secession," *Southwestern Historical Quarterly,* October 1983, pp.161–64; John Higham, *Strangers in the Land,* New York: Atheneum, 1972, pp. 12–14; Randolph B. Campbell, *A Southern Community in Crisis,* Austin: Texas State Historical Association, 2016, pp. 167–72.
4. "Know Nothings Going Armed," Washington, *Texas Ranger,* August 18, 1855; Roberts, "Fifty Years," p. 37; Walter L. Buenger, *Secession and the Union in Texas,* Austin: University of Texas Press, 1984, pp. 28–29; Ralph A. Wooster, "An Analysis of the Texas Know Nothings," *Southwestern Historical Quarterly,* January 1967, pp. 414–23.
5. "Great Meeting of the Unterrified Democracy at the Old Capital," *Texas State Gazette,* June 23, 1855; "Gen. Houston on the Kansas Bill [reprint of Houston's speech in the Senate, February 15, 1854]," La Grange *The True Issue,* June 19, 1857; Hendrickson, *Chief Executives of Texas,* pp. 64–65. See also Ernest W. Winkler, ed. *Platforms of Political Parties in Texas,* Austin: University of Texas, 1916, p. 37. Note: One delegate, T. S. Anderson, compared the Know-Nothingism "to the hundred-footed worm that drags its poisonous length across the body by midnight."
6. "The Election," Austin *Texas State Times,* August 18, 1855; "Table Will Exhibit the Vote," Washington, *Texas Ranger,* August 25, 1855; "Mammoth Barbecue, and Mass Meeting of the Democracy," Austin *Texas State Gazette,* October 8, 1855.
7. "More Idle Threats," San Antonio *Ledger,* August 25, 1855; "Improvement of Rivers and Bays," *Galveston Weekly News,* August 12, 1856; "Harbor Defense," *Indianola*

Bulletin, August 31, 1855; Charles A. Culberson, U.S. Senator, "General Sam Houston and Secession," *Scribner's Magazine,* May 1906, pp. 584–86.

8. "General Houston of Texas," *Montgomery Advertiser* (Alabama), n.d., seen in Austin *Texas State Gazette,* September 8, 1855.
9. Alvy L. King, *Louis T. Wigfall: Southern Fire-Eater,* Baton Rouge: LSU Press, 1970, pp. 58–61; James T. DeShields, *They Sat in High Places: The Presidents and Governors of Texas,* San Antonio: Naylor Company, 1940, p. 198; Friend, *Sam Houston,* pp. 239–42; Gregg Cantrell, "Sam Houston and the Know-Nothings: A Reappraisal," *Southwestern Historical Quarterly,* January, 1993, pp. 327–43.
10. Letter, Thomas J. Rusk to Roberts, October 1, 1855, Roberts Papers, BCAH; Frank H. Smyrl, "Unionism in Texas, 1856–1861," *Southwestern Historical Quarterly,* October 1964, pp. 172–95.
11. xiLetter, Lincoln to Joshua Speed, August 24, 1855, in Roy P. Basler, ed., *The Collected Works of Abraham Lincoln,* New Brunswick, 1953, vol. II, pp. 32–23, seen in Potter, *Impending Crisis,* p. 253; "A Slave State in Texas," San Antonio *Texan,* January 15, 1857; Waymon L. McClellan, "The Know-Nothing Party and the Growth of Sectionalism in East Texas," *East Texas Historical Journal,* vol. 14, 1976, pp. 26–36.
12. Smyrl, "Unionism in Texas, 1856–1861," pp. 178–81; Donald E. Reynolds, *Editors Make War: Southern Newspapers in the Secession Crisis,* Carbondale: Southern Illinois University Press, 2006, pp. 10, 205–6.
13. "Know-Nothingism," *San Antonio Ledger,* August 25, 1855; "Sam Around," *San Antonio Texas,* August 30, 1855; "The Know-Nothings Mortified," Washington, *Texas Ranger,* August 18, 1855; Buenger, *Secession and Union in Texas,* p. 30–32; Baum, *The Shattering of Texas Unionism, pp. 31–32.*
14. "The Isms," *San Antonio Ledger,* September 22, 1855; Jones, "Invisible New Ism," *in Memoranda,* p. 536.
15. Roberts, "Fifty Years," p. 40; Haley, *Texas Supreme Court,* pp. 54, 59–60; Letter, Wheeler to Roberts, December 13, 1856, and O. M. Roberts, "Notes on My Election to the Supreme Court," Roberts Papers, BCAH; Letter, O. M. Roberts to Gentlemen, *San Antonio Ledger,* January 10, 1857; "The Judgeship," *Southern Intelligencer,* February 4, 1857; "Judge of the Supreme Court," *State Gazette,* April 4, 1857. Note: Roberts won by 346 votes and Jennings in third place had 1,867 votes, followed by Franklin, 1,298, and Taylor, 239. Roberts in his memoirs states that he won by only 100 votes. An example of Roberts's concern on voter turnout: when the first 32 counties' returns were reported, it was Gray 2,384 and Roberts 1,483; a few days later with 42 counties reporting, it had narrowed to Gray 2,584 and Roberts, 2,264, and as returns slowly arrived, he would eventually win; see "The Election," *Galveston Daily News,* February 24, 1857.
16. "Decision in the Dred Scott Case," Austin *State Gazette,* April 4, 1857. See also Edward R. McClellend, *Chorus of the Union,* New York: Pegasus, 2024, pp. 6–90. Note: The case might have been reported in earlier Texas newspapers after March 6, 1857, but with the details provided in this edition of the *State Gazette.*
17. "The Dred Scott Case," *Galveston News,* March 10, 1857.
18. Roberts, "Fifty Years," pp. 43–44; "Texas Supreme Court," Austin *Southern Intelligencer,* October 28, 1857.
19. Roberts, "Fifty Years," pp. 48–50; "Department of Texas," and "Transportation of Army Supplies," *State Gazette,* April 4, 1857; "Walker's Victories Confirmed," *Galve-*

ston Weekly News, April 14, 1857; "Glorious News from Nicaragua," *State Gazette,* April 11, 1857; "Nicaragua and Walker," Marshall *Texas Republican,* January 23, 1858; and "Message of the President," ibid., January 30, 1858. See also William O. Scroggs, *Filibusterers and Financiers,* New York: Macmillan, 1916; and Robert E. May *The Southern Dream of a Caribbean Empire, 1854–1861.* Baton Rouge: LSU Press, 1973. See also Robert M. Utley, *Frontier Regulars: The United States Army and the Indian 1866–1890,* New York: Macmillan, 1973.

20. Letter, Wheeler to Roberts, March 12, 1857, Roberts Papers, BCAH; Cain v. The State, 20 *Texas Reports,* p. 366; "The Old Alcalde: 1896 Letter from O. M. Roberts," *Dallas Morning News,* November 10, 1933. Note: Both during the Civil War and later, Confederate veterans called Roberts "Old Gray."
21. Haley, *Texas Supreme Court,* p. 65; Nash, "The Texas Supreme Court and Trial Rights of Blacks, 1845–1860," p. 622.
22. State v. Stephenson, 20, *Texas Reports,* 152 (Tex. 1857), pp. 152–53; Haley, *Texas Supreme Court,* p. 64; Nash, "The Texas Supreme Court and Trial Rights of Blacks, 1845–1860," p. 627; Campbell, *An Empire for Slavery,* p. 112. Note: A. E. Keir Nash noted, "It is intriguing that the state bothered to pursue the matter to the higher court following a lower court finding for the white defendant."
23. Sean Kelley, "'Mexico in His Head': Slavery and the Texas-Mexico Border," *Journal of Social History,* Spring 2004, pp. 709–23; Robert S. Shelton, "On Empire's Shore: Free and Unfree Workers in Galveston, Texas, 1840–1860," *Journal of Social History,* Spring 2007, p. 720; John C. Gassner, "African American Fugitive Slaves and Freemen in Matamoros, Tamaulipas," MA, thesis, University of Texas–Pan American, December 2003; Harris E. Bell, "Slavery and Industry in the Antebellum South: The Texas Experience, 1850–1860," MA thesis, Prairie View A&M University, August 1979, pp. 9, 42, 56. See also Vera L. Dugas, "Texas Industry, 1860–1880," *Southwestern Historical Quarterly,* October 1955, pp. 151–61.
24. Campbell, *An Empire for Slavery,* pp. 88, 112, 130–32; *Boulware v. Hendricks,* 23 Tex. 667 (1859); *Rawles v. The State,* 15 Tex. 581 (1855); *Anderson v. The State,* 20 Tex. 5 (1857); Fornell, *The Galveston Era: The Texas Crescent on the Eve of Secession,* Austin: University of Texas Press, 1961, pp. 118–22. See also A. E. Keir Nash, "The Texas Supreme Court and Trail Rights of Blacks, 1845–1860," *Journal of American History,* December 1971, pp. 622–42. See also Norman G. Kittrell, *Governors Who Have Been, and Other Public Men of Texas.* Houston: Dealy-Adey-Elgin Co., 1921, pp. 40–41.
25. *Calvin* (a Slave) *v. the State,* 25 Texas 789 (1860), 796; A. E. Keir Nash, "The Texas Supreme Court and the Rights of Blacks, 1845–1860," *Journal of American History,* December 1971, pp. 622–42; William C. Yancey, "The Old Alcalde: Oran Milo Roberts, Texas's Forgotten Fire-eater," PhD, diss., University of North Texas, May 2016, p. 99. See also Campbell, *Gone to Texas,* pp. 220–26.
26. *The State vs. Southern Pacific R.R. Co.* 24 Texas 80, seen in Roberts lecture notes, Roberts Papers, BCAH.
27. "Bank Cases," *Galveston Weekly News,* March 6, 1855; William R. Hogan, *The Texas Republic: A Social and Economic History,* Norman: University of Oklahoma Press, 1946, pp. 97–103.
28. Margaret S. Henson, *Samuel May Williams: Early Texas Entrepreneur,* College Station: Texas A&M University Press, 1976, pp. 156–60; Joe E. Ericson, *Banks and*

Bankers in Early Texas 1835–1975, New Orleans: Polyanthos, 1976, pp. 2–16; Fornell, *Galveston Era*, pp. 51–57; *Chambers vs. Fisk*, 22 Tex., 504, seen in Roberts lecture notes, Roberts Papers, BCAH. Note: Details in *Chambers* decision on early Texas history dating back to 1685 may possibly have been found in the article "Compendium of Early History of Texas," *The Texas Almanac for 1857*, Galveston: Richardson and Co. 1856, pp. 142–59 as well as documentation presented in "Colonization Law of 1823," in Mary Austin Holley, *Texas*, Lexington: J. Clarke & Co., 1836, pp. 195–221.

29. Henson, *Samuel May Williams*, pp. 160–64; *R. and D. G. Mills and Others v. The State of Texas*, 23 Texas 295 (1859); Ericson, *Banks and Bankers*, p. 24; Fornell, *Galveston Era*, pp. 56–57; Mills and others v. The State, 23 *Texas Reports*, 300.
30. Roberts, "Fifty Years," p. 46.
31. Ibid., 46; Roberts, speech notes, "Know-Nothingism," Roberts Papers, BCAH.
32. Barnes F. Lathrop, *Migration into East Texas 1835–1960*, Austin: Texas State Historical Association, 1949, pp. 34–58; Dwight L. Dumond, *The Secession Movement, 1860–1861*. New York: Octagon Books, 1963, pp. 209–10; Campbell, *An Empire for Slavery*, pp. 255–56. See also Rudolph L. Biesele, *History of German Settlements in Texas 1831–1860*, Austin, 1964 (reprint, New York: Eakin Press, 1998).
33. Culberson, "General Sam Houston and Secession," p. 585; Jacob De Cordova, *Texas: Her Resources and her Public Men*, Philadelphia: J. B. Lippincott & Co., 1858; Buenger, *Secession and the Union in Texas*, p. 33; Campbell, *Gone to Texas*, p. 211. Note: The "upper South" of Virginia, North Carolina, Tennessee, and Arkansas; and many include the "border South states in a list of upper South to include Maryland, Kentucky, Missouri, and Delaware."
34. "Hon. T. J. Rusk is Dead," San Augustine *The Eastern Texian*, August 1, 1857; Letter, Henderson to Roberts, September 28, 1857, Roberts Papers; Roberts, "Resolutions in Favor of Judge Wheeler as Chief Justice," seen in Roberts, "Fifty Years," pp. 41–2.
35. Roberts, "Fifty Years," pp. 41, 44–7, 52–3; "A Slave State in Texas," San Antonio *Texan*, January 15, 1857; "Population of Texas, *Texas Almanac for 1857*, pp. 70, 103; Friend, *Sam Houston*, pp. 298–301; Reagan, *Memoirs*, p. 70; Randolph B. Campbell, *Sam Houston and the American Southwest*, New York: Pearson, 1964, pp. 168–73. Note: The slave population in 1850 of about 57,000–58,000 increased to over 105,000 by 1856, most brought by their masters from the deep South.
36. Roberts, "Fifty Years," p. 55; "The Ticket," Marshall *Texas Republican*, June 3, 1859; Ben H. Procter, *Not Without Honor: The Life of John H. Reagan*, Austin: University of Texas Press, 1962, p. 119.
37. Lester, *Sam Houston*, pp. 292–304; "The Slave Trade," Galveston *Civilian and Gazette Weekly*, August 4, 1857; "Tergiversation," New York *Daily Tribune*, November 15, 1859; Culberson, "General Sam Houston and Secession," pp. 584–86; Campbell, *Sam Houston*, p. 171; Buenger, *Secession and the Union in Texas*, pp. 38–39.
38. Ralph A. Wooster, "Wealthy Texans, 1860," *Southwestern Historical Quarterly*, October 1967, pp. 163–80; Yancey, "The Old Alcalde," p. 104.
39. O. M. Roberts, "Speech of Judge Roberts," Austin *State Gazette*, December 8, 17, 22, 28, 1860; Anne I. Sandbo, "Beginnings of the Secession Movement in Texas," *Southwestern Historical Quarterly*, July 1914, pp. 58, 62–65; Buenger, "Texas and the Riddle of Secession," pp. 157–61; Chriss, *Six Constitutions Over Texas*, pp. 72–74. Note: Roberts three decades later in 1892 presented the 1860 secession speech to

his law classes at the University of Texas, followed by the entire series published under the new title "The Impending Crisis," in O. M. Roberts, *Our Federal Relations From a Southern View of Them,* Austin: Eugene Von Boeckmann Printer, 1892.

40. Roberts, "Fifty Years," p. 58; King, *Louis T. Wigfall,* pp. 66–68, 72–73. See also Billy D. Ledbetter, "Slavery, Fear, and Disunion in the Lone Star State: Texans' Attitudes Toward Secession and the Union, 1846–1861," PhD diss., North Texas State University, August 1972.
41. Amanda Foreman, *A World on Fire,* New York: Random House, 2010, p. 64.
42. Roberts, "Constitutional Exposition of the Right of Protection of Slave-property in the Territories of the United States [1859], Roberts Papers, BCAH. Note: Twenty-five years after it was first written, Roberts modified his essay on "property" for a law school lecture open to the public at the University of Texas in 1887, "On the Valuation of the Right of Private Property," published in Roberts, *Our Federal Relations,* 1892. See also McClelland, *Chorus of the Union,* New York: Pegasus, 2024.
43. Ibid. See also Buenger, "Texas and the Riddle of Secession," and Robert W. Merry, *Decade of Disunion: How Massachusetts and South Carolina Led the Way to Civil War, 1849–1861,* New York: Simon & Schuster, 2024.
44. Procter, *Not Without Honor,* pp. 115–16; Hinton Helper, *Impending Crisis;* John Henry Brown, *History of Texas 1685–1892,* St. Louis: L. E. Daniell, 1892, vol. II, pp. 380–86.
45. U.S. House, "Troubles of Texas Frontier," 36th Cong., 1st sess., Ex. Doc. no. 81, May 5, 1860; U.S. Senate, "Hostilities Existing in the Rio Grande," 36th Cong., 1st sess., Ex. Doc. no. 21, March 7, 1860; J. Fred Rippy, "Border Trouble Along the Rio Grande, 1848–1860," *Southwestern Historical Quarterly,* October 1919, pp. 91–111; Jerry Thompson, *Tejano Tiger: Jose de los Santos Benavides and the Texas-Mexico Borderland, 1823–1891,* Fort Worth: TCU Press, 2017, pp. 90–4, 224–28; Ford, *Rip Ford's Texas,* pp. 261–65, 369–79.
46. Campbell, *An Empire for Slavery,* pp. 224–25; "Negro Insurrections," Marshall *Texas Republican,* December 10, 1859; Ford, *Rip Ford's Texas,* pp. 260–78; Reagan, *Memoirs,* p. 149; Buenger, *Secession and the Union in Texas,* pp. 46–57; "True Account from Corpus Christi," New York *Daily Tribune,* November 15, 1859; Reynolds, *Editors Make War,* pp. 97–117. See also Edward Yanez, "The Mexican Robin Hood: Antebellum Texas Identity Politics," BA thesis, Wesleyan University, April 2021.
47. "Sam Houston and the Presidency," Chardon, Ohio *The Jeffersonian Democrat,* May 4, 1860; "Houston's Message in Relation to the Resolutions of South Carolina," *Galveston Weekly News,* March 13, 1860; Reynolds, *Editors Make War,* pp. 8–10, 72, 97–117; Crocket, *Two Centuries in East Texas,* pp. 234–35. See also Jon Grinspan, *Wide Awake,* New York: Bloomsbury, 2024.
48. "Spirit of the Texas Press," Austin *State Gazette,* November 17, 1860.
49. Roberts, "An Address Delivered before the Smith County Agricultural and Mechanical Society," Tyler, July 20, 1860; Joseph Schmitz, "Impressions of Texas in 1860," *Southwestern Historical Quarterly,* April 1939, pp. 334–50.
50. Merry, *Decade of Disunion.*
51. "Constitutional Union Convention," Marshall *Texas Republican,* May 12, 1860; Barnes F. Lathrop, *Migration into East Texas 1835–1860,* Austin: Texas State Historical Association, 1949, pp. 34–51; Buenger, *Secession and the Union in Texas,* pp. 37, 60; Buenger, "Texas and the Riddle of Secession," p. 151; Vera L. Dugas, "Texas

Industry, 1860–1880," *Southwestern Historical Quarterly*, October 1855, pp. 151–56; "From Ash Springs," *Texas Baptist*, March 8, 1860; "The Lone Star of Texas," *Tyler Reporter*, December 26, 1860. See also Lester, *Sam Houston*, pp. 330–38. Note: The Constitutional Union Party of Texas reconvened in Tyler on April 16, 1860, to select delegates to the national Conservative Convention in Brooklyn, New York, scheduled for May 1860.

52. Judge P. W. Gray, "What Shall Be Done?" *State Gazette*, November 24, 1860; "The Governor's [Houston] Policy Again," Galveston *Weekly News*, December 18, 1860; Procter, *Not Without Honor*, p. 119. See also "How Black Republicanism will Affect Southern Men of Limited Means," *State Gazette*, November 17, 1860, and "The Crisis," ibid., November 24, 1860, and December 1, 1860.
53. Ford, *Rip Ford's Texas*, pp. xxxv–xxxvii; Brown, *History of Texas*, vol. II, pp. 387–407; Dumond, *The Secession Movement*, pp. 97–119; C. A. Bridges, "The Knights of the Golden Circle: A Filibustering Fantasy," *Southwestern Historical Quarterly*, January 1941, pp. 287–302; Earl W. Fornell, "Texas and Filibusters in the 1850s," *Southwestern Historical Quarterly*, April 1956, pp. 411–28.
54. George R. Woolfolk, "Cotton Capitalism Slavery in Texas," *Southwestern Social Science Quarterly*, June 1956, pp. 43–52; Stefanie Hustoft, "An Inferno of Anxiety: How Narratives Surrounding the North Texas Fires of 1860 Ignited Paranoia and Distrust in Texas Prior to Secession," MA thesis, Texas Women's University, May 2023.
55. "Speech of Judge Roberts," Austin *State Gazette*, December 8, 15, 22, and 29, 1860; Ford, *Rip Ford's Texas*, pp. xxxv–xxxvi; Procter, *Not Without Honor*, pp. 124–25.
56. Guy M. Bryan, "Address to the People of the State of Texas," Clarksville *Standard*, December 22, 1860; Roberts, "How I Came to be Elected President of the Secession Convention in 1861," Roberts Papers, BCAH; "The Convention for Secession," Corpus Christi *The Ranchero*, February 9, 1861.
57. Ernest William Winkler, ed., *Journal of the Secession Convention of Texas 1861*, Austin Printing Company, 1912, pp.15–16 (hereafter: *Secession Convention 1861*); O. M. Roberts, President of the Convention, "To the People of Texas," *Galveston Weekly News*, February 19, 1861; Ford, *Rip Ford's Texas*, p. xxxvi; "Marriages," *Texas Christian Advocate*, January 31, 1861; Jefferson Davis, *The Rise and Fall of the Confederate Government*, New York: Appleton and Company, 1881, vol. 1, p. v.
58. Roberts, "Fifty Years," pp. 99–100. See also "Judge Wheeler's Views," *Dallas Herald*, January 16, 1861; and O. M. Roberts, President, "A Declaration of the Causes Which Impel the State of Texas to Secede from the Federal Union," February 2, 1861, Roberts Papers, BCAH.
59. O. M. Roberts, President, "An Ordinance," February 1, 1861, and "Names of the Members of the Convention," list, January 28, 1861, Roberts Papers, BCAH; *Secession Convention 1861*, pp. 15– 22; Reagan, *Memoirs*, p. 105; Procter, *Not Without Honor*, p. 125; Matthew K. Hamilton, "'To Preserve African Slavery': The Secession Commissioners to Texas, 1861," *Southwestern Historical Quarterly*, April 2011, pp. 355–76; Ralph A. Wooster, "An Analysis of the Membership of the Texas Secession Convention," *Southwestern Historical Quarterly*, January 1959, pp. 322–35; Jimmie Hicks, "Texas and Separate Independence, 1860–61," *East Texas Historical Journal*, vol. 4, 1966, pp. 94–96; Dwight L. Dumond, *The Secession Movement 1860–1861*, New York: Octagon Books, 1963, p. 35.

60. Roberts, "Fifty Years," pp. 103–17; *Secession Convention 1861*, pp. 48–49; "Order of the Golden Circle—Its Objects, Aim and Principals," *Dallas Herald*, February 20, 1861. See also David M. Potter, *The Impending Crisis 1848–1861*, New York: Harper and Row, 1963, pp. 496–99; and "Address to the South [from South Carolina]," Beaumont *Banner*, January 8, 1861; "Message of Sam Houston," Houston *Weekly Telegraph*, March 12, 1861.
61. Buenger, *Secession and Union in Texas*, p. 148. See also Marcus L. Arnold, "The Later Phases of the Secession Movement in Texas," MA thesis, University of Texas, June 1920.
62. "Military—U.S. Troops on Rio Grande," Galveston *Weekly News*, February 26, 1861; "The State Military Movement," ibid., February 26, 1861; Anne I. Sandbo, "The First Session of the Secession Convention of Texas," *Southwestern Historical Quarterly*, October 1914, p. 193; Ford, *Rip Ford's Texas*, pp. xxxvii, 331–33.
63. "The Commissioner from Louisiana," Galveston *Weekly News*, February 19, 1861; Brown, *History of Texas*, vol. II., pp. 402–7; Richard B. McCaslin, "Rip Ford: Confederate or Texan?" *Military History of the West*, vol. 42, 2012, pp. 30–31; Dumond, *The Secession Movement*, pp. 209–10; Buenger, *Secession and Union in Texas*, p. 146; Roberts, "Fifty Years," pp. 104–10.
64. Roberts, "To the People of Texas," *Galveston Weekly News*, February 19, 1861; Moneyhon, *Republicanism in Reconstruction Texas:* College Station: Texas A&M University Press, 1980, pp. 16–17; Buenger, "Texas and the Riddle of Secession," p. 180; Fornell, *Galveston Era*, pp. 292–94; Carl C. Rister, *Robert E. Lee in Texas*, Norman: University of Oklahoma Press, 2004, pp. 158–16; Dale Baum, "Pinpointing Apparent Fraud in the 1861 Texas Secession Referendum," *Journal of Interdisciplinary History*, Autumn 1991, pp. 202–21. Note: For example, Galveston voted 765 for secession with only 33 opposed.
65. Sam Houston, "Address to the People," March 19, 1861 seen in Roberts, "Fifty Years," pp. 129–30. See also "Governor Houston's Address," San Antonio *The Daily Ledger and Texan*, March 19, 1861.
66. Hicks, "Texas and Separate Independence," pp. 98–99; Reynolds, *Editors Make War*, pp. 101, 205; Friend, *Sam Houston*, p. 336; Letter, O. M. Roberts to John Ireland, April 29, 1861, seen in Austin *State Gazette*, June 8, 1861.
67. "Texas Military Preparations," Galveston *Weekly News*, December 18, 1860; "Major Charles Bickley [K. G. C.]," ibid., November 19, 1861; "The Smith County Cavalry," *Dallas Herald*, June 19, 1861; Marcus J. Wright and Harold B. Simpson, eds. *Texas in the War, 1861–1865*, Hillsboro: Hill Junior College Press, 1965, pp. 61–66; James G. Partin et al., *Nacogdoches: The History of Texas' Oldest City*, Lufkin: East Texas Publishers, 1995, pp. 103–6; Williamson Murray and Wayne Wei-Siang Hsieh, *A Savage War*, Princeton: Princeton University Press, 2016, p. 74. Note: President Jefferson Davis called to duty 100,000 volunteers.
68. "Galveston News and Gen. Wigfall," *Dallas Herald*, November 6, 1861; Roberts, "Fifty Years," p. 142; Alvy L. King, *Louis T. Wigfall*, Baton Rouge: LSU Press, 1970, p. 135.
69. O. M. Roberts, President of the Convention, "To the People of Texas," Galveston *Weekly News*, February 19, 1861; Roberts, "Fifty Years," p. 146.
70. "Galveston News and Wigfall," *Dallas Herald*, November 6, 1861; Letter, Roberts to Secretary of War of the Confederate State, November 17, 1861, and Letter,

Oldham to Roberts, December 23, 1861, and "Troops Wanted," Poster, January 13, 1861 in Roberts Letter Book, BCAH; "Call for Troops by Judge Roberts," *Galveston Tri-Weekly News*, January 28, 1862; Brown, *History of Texas*, vol. II, pp. 408–14; Richard Lowe, *Walker's Texas Division C.S.A.*, Baton Rouge: LSU Press, 2004, pp. 8–9. See also Stephen B. Oates, "Recruiting Confederate Cavalry in Texas," *Southwestern Historical Quarterly*, April 1961, pp. 466–76.

71. Letters, Oba E. Roberts to O. M. Roberts, January 18, 1862, and M. D. Graham to Roberts, April 8, 1852, and Roberts to Governor F. R. Lubbock, March 30, 1861, Roberts Papers, BCAH; Lowe, *Walker's Texas Division*, pp. 16–18; Wright and Simpson, eds., *Texas in the War*, p. 109; Reagan, *Memoirs*, p. 118; Pearl C. Jackson, *Texas Governors' Wives*, Austin: E. L. Steck, 1915, p. 91; David S. Stieghan, "The Pine Springs Training Camps: Confederate Activities at the Camp Ford Site Before the Union Prisoner of War Camp was Established," *East Texas Historical Journal*, vol. 42, 2004, pp. 38–44; Oran M. Roberts, "Texas," in Clement A. Evans, *Confederate Military History*, vol. XI, New York: 1962, pp. 114–17.
72. Lowe, *Walker's Texas Division*, p. 28. Note: For a detailed review of Colonel Roberts's appeal to clarify his date-of-rank and claim of the command position he should hold, see Yancey, "The Old Alcalde," pp. 144–48.
73. Lowe, *Walker's Texas Division*, pp. 112–15; Harry M. Henderson, *Texas in the Confederacy*, San Antonio: Naylor Company, 1955, pp. 56–57; Ford Dixon "Oran Milo Roberts," in W. C. Dunn, ed., *Ten More Texans in Gray*, Hillsboro: Hill Junior College Press, 1980, pp. 105–6.
74. Report of Brig. General Thomas Green, November 8, 1863, *War of the Rebellion: A Compilation of the Official Records of the Union and Confederate Armies*, Washington, D.C.: 1880–1901, series I, vol. XXVI, pt. 1, pp. 393–95 (hereafter cited as *War of the Rebellion*); Lowe, *Walker's Texas Division*, pp. 134–36; W. C. Dunn, ed., *Ten More Texans in Gray*, Hillsboro: Hill Junior College Press, 1880, pp. 19–23. Note: Thomas Green, after returning from the Mexican War, was a Texas Supreme Court clerk from 1849 to 1860 at a salary of $300, "Judiciary," Austin *Texas State Gazette*, September 29, 1849.
75. Colonel O. M. Roberts, Col. Comdg. 11th, 15th, 18th Texas Infantry to Lt. E. R. Wells A A Genl., Camp near Opelousas, La. Nov. 6th 1863, in Alwyn Barr, ed. "The Battle of Bayou Bourbeau, November 3, 1863: Colonel Oran M. Roberts' Report," *Louisiana Historical Association*, Winter 1965, pp. 83–91.
76. Report of Brig. General S. G. Burbridge, November 7, 1863, *War of the Rebellion*, series I, vol. XXVI, pt.1, pp. 359–61; Oran M. Roberts, *Confederate Military History of Texas*, 1899, p. 125, republished in Clement A. Evans, ed. "Texas," *Confederate Military History*, vol. XI, Atlanta: Confederate Publishing Company, 1899; Lowe, *Walker's Texas Division*, pp. 140–44; David D. Porter, *Incidents and Anecdotes of the Civil War*, New York: D. Appleton, 1885; Wright and Simpson, eds., *Texas in the War*, pp. 157–58.
77. Lowe, *Walker's Texas Division*, pp. 146–47; Bayou Bourbeau, November 3, 1863, *War of the Rebellion*, series I, vol. XXVI, pt. 1, p. 359; Harry M. Henderson, *Texas in the Confederacy*, San Antonio: Naylor Company, 1955, pp. 56–57, 94–95. Note: General Thomas Green was killed at Blair's Landing on the Red River in April 1864.
78. Letters, General Thomas Green to Roberts, November 19, 1863, and F. B. Sexton to Roberts, March 12, 1864, Roberts Papers, BCAH; Campbell, *Gone to Texas*, pp.

265–69; Carl H. Moneyhon, *Texas After the Civil War: The Struggle of Reconstruction,* College Station: Texas A&M University Press, 2004, pp. 38–41; Baum, *Shattering of Texas Unionism,* pp. 119–20. See also James R. Norvell, "The Supreme Court of Texas Under the Confederacy, 1861–1965," *Houston Law Review,* Spring 1966, pp. 46–61; and Donald L. Stelluto, "A State of Law and Order: Legal and Constitutional History in Civil War Texas," *Journal of the West,* Fall 2000, pp. 35–48.

79. Charles L. Robards, *Synopses of the Decisions of the Supreme Court of the State of Texas,* Austin: Brown & Foster, 1865; Albert B. Moore, *Conscription and Conflict in the Confederacy,* New York: Macmillan Company, 1924; Marcus J. Johnson, "Responding to the Exigencies of War: The Supreme Court of Texas During the Civil War," MA thesis, Baylor University, May 2001, pp. 73– 83.
80. Roberts, "Fifty Years," p. 145.
81. Wright and Simpson, eds., *Texas in the War,* pp. 59–61, plate no. 66–68; Hendrickson, *Chief Executives of Texas,* pp. 87–144; John A. Adams, Jr., *Sul Ross at Texas A&M,* College Station: Texas A&M University Press, 2022; Thompson, *Tejano Tiger,* pp. 204–78; A. Christian Klemme, "The Rise, Fall, and Redemption of Oran M. Roberts," MA thesis, University of North Texas, May 2004, pp. 93–95. Note: Colonel Simpson in *Texas at War* has one of the best lists of Texas Confederate veterans' service after the war; also see list of CSA officers in Brown, *History of Texas,* vol. II, pp. 437–43.

CHAPTER 3

1. iRoberts, "Fifty Years," p. 150; Charles H. Wesley, *The Collapse of the Confederacy,* Columbia: University of South Carolina Press, 2001, pp. xli, 48, 104, 170–71; Reagan, *Memoirs,* p. 271; Lloyd Uglow, *A Military History of Texas,* Fort Worth: TCU Press, 2022, pp. 240–44. Note: Governor Roberts recounted his memories of Texas at the end of war in a law school lecture in the late 1880s, published as "A Lecture: Upon the Close of the War and the Reconstruction," in O. M. Roberts, *Our Federal Relations,* Austin: Eugene Von Boeckmann Printer, 1892, pp. 69–80 (hereafter, Roberts, "Lecture," in *Our Federal Relations*).
2. Woodrow Wilson, "The Reconstruction of the Southern States," *Atlantic Monthly,* January, 1901, p. 6; Uglow, *A Military History of Texas,* pp. 243–44; A. Scott Berg, *Wilson,* New York: G. P. Putnam, 2013, pp. 134–35. Note: Shortly after Wilson's article, while with no direct connection to it, he was part of a faculty revolt at Princeton to dismiss sitting President Francis Patton (not related to Gen. George Patton), and the Board of Trustees named Wilson the thirteenth university president!
3. Roberts, "Fifty Years," pp. 151–53; Ford, *Rip Ford's Texas,* pp. 401–3; Randolph B. Campbell, *Grass-Roots Reconstruction in Texas, 1865–1880,* Baton Rouge: LSU Press, 1997, pp. 7–10. See also "Speech of the Hon. Richard Nelson on the Anniversary Celebration of Emancipation June 19, 1871," Galveston *Representative,* June 26, 1871.
4. Message of the President of the United States, "Present Condition of Mexico," 39th Cong., 2nd. Sess., House Ex. Doc. No. 76, p. 521; Carl C. Rister, "Carlota, A Confederate Colony in Mexico," *Journal of Southern History,* February 1945, pp. 41, 44.

5. Dale Baum, *The Shattering of Texas Unionism,* Baton Rouge: LSU Press, 1998, pp. 129–30. Baum noted, "Even when officials actually administered the oath, many newly sworn men declared afterwards that they regarded it as 'enforced & not binding'— enforced because they could not vote unless they took it and not binding because support for the United States Constitution now included what they believed amounted to the unlawful sanction of emancipation." For a list of Confederate exemptions see Chriss, *Six Constitutions Over Texas,* pp. 91–92.
6. "From the Convention," Houston *Tri-Weekly Telegraph,* February 14, 1866; Roberts, "Fifty Years," pp. 151–55; Certificate of Amnesty, Certificate #286, issued to O. M. Roberts, Smith County, September 15, 1865, and "List of Objections for 1866 Constitutional Convention," Roberts Papers, BCAH; Reagan, *Memoirs,* p. 240; Moneyhon, *Texas After the Civil War,* pp. 28–29, 39–41; Elizabeth Silverthorne, *Ashbel Smith of Texas: Pioneer, Patriot, Statesman, 1805–1886.* College Station: Texas A&M University Press, 1982, pp. 170–75; Campbell, *Gone to Texas,* pp. 270–73.
7. Texas, *Journal of the Texas State Convention, 1866,* Austin: Southern Intelligencer Office, 1866, pp. 5–7, 132–33 (hereafter *Texas State Convention, 1866*); Kenneth W. Howell, *Texas Confederate, Reconstruction Governor: James Webb Throckmorton,* College Station: Texas A&M University Press, 2008, pp. 84–85, 179–80.
8. *Texas State Convention, 1866,* p. 119.
9. Ibid., pp. 40, 219–20, 233–34; Roberts, "Lecture," in *Our Federal Relations,* p. 76; "An Ordinance Proving for the Election of State Officers," Galveston *Flake's Daily Bulletin,* April 3, 1866; "The Indian Committee," Houston *Tri-Weekly Telegraph,* March 19, 1866; "Indian Affairs Committee," Austin *Southern Intelligencer,* March 22, 1866; Chriss, *Six Constitutions Over Texas,* pp. 95–96; Haley, *Texas Supreme Court,* pp. 78–79; William L. Richter, *The Army in Texas During Reconstruction, 1865–1870,* College Station: Texas A&M University Press, 1987, pp. 60–75.
10. "Sec. 2. Mr. Roberts' Amendment," *Goliad Intelligencer,* March 17, 1866; "Texas Convention," Austin *Tri-Weekly State Gazette,* March 20, 1866.
11. Roberts, "Lecture," in *Our Federal Relations,* pp. 77, 79; "Latest Dispatches from Austin," *Flake's Daily Bulletin,* February 21, 1866: "Texas State Convention," ibid., February 28, 1866; Haley, *Texas Supreme Court,* p. 76. Note: Judge Roberts noted that the law defined persons of color "to be all those having one-eight or more of African blood."
12. Barry A. Crouch, "'All the Vile Passions': The Texas Black Code of 1866," *Southwestern Historical Quarterly,* July 1993, pp. 21–24.
13. Letter, O. M. Roberts to James Burroughs, June 20, 1868, Roberts Papers, BCAH. See also Robert W. Shook, "Federal Occupation and Administration of Texas, 1865–1870," PhD diss., North Texas State University, August 1970.
14. William L. Richter, *Overreached on All Sides: The Freedmen's Bureau Administrators in Texas, 1865–1868,* College Station: Texas A&M University Press, 1991, pp. 93–99; C. Vann Woodward, *The Strange Career of Jim Crow,* New York: Oxford University Press, 2002, pp. 7, 23–25. See also Barry A. Crouch, *The Freedmen's Bureau and Black Texans,* Austin: University of Texas Press, 1992.
15. Baum, *The Shattering of Texas Unionism,* quote at p. 132; Roberts, "Objects to Be Attained in the Convention of 1866," Roberts Papers. BCAH; *Texas State Convention, 1866,* pp. 119, 160; "Roberts Amendment on State Expenses," Austin *Southern Intelligencer,* March 22, 1866; "The Convention," Bellville *Texas Countryman,* March

23, 1866; "Proceedings of the State Convention [re: school funding]," *Goliad Intelligencer,* March 17, 1866; "Widow of Gen. Sam Houston," *Flake's Daily Bulletin,* April 3, 1866; Roberts, "Fifty Years," pp. 155–57; Chriss, *Six Constitutions Over Texas,* p. 102; Lawrence D. Rice, *The Negro in Texas 1874–1900,* Baton Rouge: LSU Press, 1971, p. 141.

16. Moneyhon, *Texas After the Civil War,* pp. 50–53; Baum, *The Shattering of Texas Unionism,* p. 234.
17. "The Texas Press: Burnet and Roberts," *Southern Intelligencer,* September 6, 1866.
18. O. M. Roberts, "The Experiences of an Unrecognized Senator," *Southwestern Historical Quarterly,* October 1908, p. 110 (hereafter, Roberts, "The Experiences"); Charles W. Ramsdell, "Presidential Reconstruction in Texas," *Quarterly of the Texas State Historical Association,* April 1908, pp. 277–332; Procter, *Not Without Honor,* p. 180.
19. Carl H. Moneyhon, *Republicanism in Reconstruction Texas,* College Station: Texas A&M University Press, 1980, p. 50.
20. Roberts, "Fifty Years," pp. 158–64; Roberts, "The Experiences," p. 89; Charles W. Ramsdell, "Presidential Reconstruction in Texas: III. The Restoration of State Government," *Quarterly of the Texas State Historical Association,* January 1909, pp. 204–230; Baum, *The Shattering of Texas Unionism,* pp. 147–49; Haley, *Texas Supreme Court,* pp. 78–79; Reagan, *Memoirs,* p. 301; Ramsdell, "Presidential Reconstruction in Texas," p. 210, 230. Note: General Sheridan quote on Texas seen in *Mobile Daily Times,* February 22, 1866; Memphis *Public Ledger,* March 30, 1866; and *Pittsburgh Gazette,* March 19, 1866.
21. Bailey, "Life and Public Career of O. M. Roberts," p. 162.
22. *New York Tribune,* October 12, 1866; Moneyhon, *Texas After the Civil War,* pp. 62–63. Note: Benjamin Epperson was exempt from Confederate military duty due to lameness in one leg.
23. "An Impressive Speech by Judge Roberts," Denison *Daily Herald,* September 12, 1878. See also Deuteronomy 32: 48–52 and Numbers 27: 12–14.
24. Ramsdell, "Presidential Reconstruction in Texas," p. 212; Procter, *Not Without Honor,* p. 180.
25. Roberts, "The Experiences," pp. 94, 97.
26. Henson and Parmelee, *The Cartwrights of San Augustine,* pp. 252–23.
27. O. M. Roberts, "An Address: To the Congress and People of the United States," Washington: January 1, 1867, pp. 81–93, in Roberts, *Our Federal Relations,* Austin: Eugene Von Boeckmann Printer, 1892, pp. 81–93 (hereafter: Roberts, "An Address 1867"); Roberts, "The Experiences," pp. 87–147; "To the Sovereign People," *Wilmington Journal* (NC), February 22, 1866; Ramsdell, "Presidential Reconstruction in Texas," pp. 219–23.
28. Roberts, "The Experiences," pp. 110–11; Ramsdell, "Presidential Reconstruction in Texas," p. 219. See also: O. M. Roberts, "The Congressional Reconstruction of the Southern States and Especially Its Revolutionary Change of the Federal Government, and Its Operations in Texas," in Roberts, *Our Federal Relations From a Southern View of Texas,* Austin: Eugene Von Boeckmann Printer, 1892, pp. 94–110.
29. Roberts, "The Experiences," pp. 94–95.
30. Roberts, "The Experiences," p. 11; William C. Griggs, *The Elusive Eden: Frank McMullan's Confederate Colony,* Austin: University of Texas Press, 1987.
31. An excellent account of Roberts's confrontation with Hamilton can be found in Chriss, *Six Constitutions Over Texas,* pp. xvii, 225–26. See also A. W. Terrell, "A

Memoriam: Proceedings Touching the Death of Hon. Oran M. Roberts, Late Chief Justice of the Supreme Court," *Texas Reports,* 92, 1898, pp. vii–viii; and Roberts, The Experiences," pp. 100–1.

32. "Hon. O. M. Roberts," *Galveston Daily News,* February 3, 1967.
33. Roberts, "Fifty Years," pp. 167–70; Charles W. Ramsdell, "Presidential Reconstruction in Texas: The Restoration of State Government," *Southwestern Historical Quarterly,* July 1909, pp. 204–9; Haley, *Texas Supreme Court,* p. 80; Moneyhon, *Republicanism in Reconstruction Texas,* pp. 68–70.
34. Moneyhon, *Texas After the Civil War,* pp. 70–72, 84; Roberts, "Fifty Years," pp. 169–70; Moneyhon, *Republicanism in Reconstruction Texas,* pp. 71–77. See also Randolph Campbell, "The District Judges of Texas in 1866–1867: An Episode in the Failure of Presidential Reconstruction," *Southwestern Historical Quarterly,* January 1990, pp. 368–70; and Barry A. Crouch, *The Freedmen's Bureau and Black Texans,* Austin: University of Texas Press, 1992.
35. Roberts, "Fifty Years," pp. 465–67; J. J. Lane, "The Educational System in Texas," in Dudley G. Wooten, ed., *A Comprehensive History of Texas,* Dallas: William G. Scarff, 1898, vol. II, pp. 465–67 (hereafter: Lane, "Education"); DeShields, *They Sat in High Places,* p. 313.
36. Morgan Looney, Circular Letter, November 20, 1867, Roberts Papers, BCAH; "Gilmer School," Marshall *Weekly Harrison Flag,* May 13, 1869.
37. Lane, "Education," pp. 466–67; Frank L. Owsley, *Plain Folk of the Old South,* Baton Rouge: LSU Press, 1982, pp. 148–49; Roberts, "Fifty Years," p. 467; "The Gilmer School," Marshall *Weekly Harrison Flag,* July 22, 1869.
38. "Gov. Roberts' Encounter With a Sow," *Dallas Herald,* n.d., seen in San Marcos *Free Press,* November 3, 1881.
39. Roberts, "Fifty Years," p. 169; Roberts, *Our Federal Relations,* pp. 119–21.
40. Roberts, "Fifty Years," p. 170. See also Campbell, *Gone to Texas,* p. 281; and "Gessler's Cap in New York," Galveston *Representative,* August 26, 1871. For an alternate view of Reconstruction reaction to the Klan, Black Codes, the judicial system, Freedmen's Bureau, and Radical rule, see Edgar P. Sneed, "A Historiography of Reconstruction in Texas: Some Myths and Problems," *Southwestern Historical Quarterly,* April 1969, pp. 435–48.
41. John W. Gorman, "The Crucible of Freedom: Reconstruction Violence in Texas, 1865–1868," PhD diss., Texas A&M University, August 2019; Rebecca A. Kosar, "Regression to Barbarism in Reconstruction Texas: An Analysis of White Violence Against African-Americans from the Texas Freedmen's Bureau Records, 1865–1868," MA thesis, Southwest Texas State University, August 1999.
42. Roberts, "Fifty Years," pp. 169–71; Roberts, *Our Federal Relations,* pp. 115–22; Gregg Cantrell, "Racial Violence and Reconstruction Politics in Texas, 1867–1868," *Southwestern Historical Quarterly,* January 1990, pp. 350–51; Crouch, *The Freedmen's Bureau and Black Texans,* pp. 117–27; A. Christian Klemme, "The Rise, Fall, and Redemption of Oran M. Roberts," MA thesis, University of North Texas, May 2004, p. 137, fn 23.
43. Bailey, "Life and Public Career of O. M. Roberts," p. 192; Richter, *The Army in Texas During Reconstruction,* p. 149.
44. Letter, F. B. Sexton to Roberts, August 6, 1869, Box 4M309, correspondence, vol. IV, 1861–1875, Roberts Papers, BCAH.

45. Roberts, "Speech Delivered by Judge Roberts Before the Military Commission," news clipping, unknown, October 24, 1869; and Letter, J. H. Rogers to Roberts, November 4, 1969, Roberts Papers, BCAH.
46. Winkler, ed., *Platforms of Political Parties in Texas,* p. 106; "Democratic Texas," Galveston *Representative,* May 4, 1872; Moneyhon, *Texas After the Civil War,* p. 172.
47. Moneyhon, *Texas After the Civil War,* pp. 150–52, 156, 159, 162–65; "Cotton," *Galveston Daily News,* February 3, 1867; Eric Foner, *Reconstruction: America's Unfinished Revolution, 1863–1877,* New York: History Book Club, 2005, p. 441; Campbell, *Gone to Texas,* pp. 283–84, 310–13; Alwyn Barr, *Reconstruction to Reform: Texas Politics, 1876–1906,* Dallas: SMU Press, 1971, pp. 28–32, 94–96. See also Ann P. Baenziger, "The Texas State Police During Reconstruction: A Reexamination," *Southwestern Historical Quarterly,* April, pp. 475–76; Dugas, "Texas Industry, 1860–1880," pp. 166–83.
48. "Governor Davis Interviewed: No Desire to Hold Office Longer [than April 1874]," *Galveston Daily News,* January 7, 1874; Roberts, "Fifty Years," pp. 197–99; Charles Ramsdell, *Reconstruction in Texas,* New York: Columbia University Press, 1910, p. 317; Carl H. Moneyhon, *Edmund J. Davis of Texas: Civil War General, Republican Leader, Reconstruction Governor,* Fort Worth: TCU Press, 2010, p. 2. See also Carl H. Moneyhon, "Edmund J. Davis in the Coke-Davis Election Dispute of 1874: A Reassessment of Character," *Southwestern Historical Quarterly,* July 1996, pp. 131–51.
49. "Relieve to Certain Persons from Restrictions Imposed by the Fourteenth Amendment," H. R. 2564, 42nd Cong, 2nd sess., April 26, 1872; James A. Rawley, "The General Amnesty of 1872: A Note," *Mississippi Valley Historical Review.*
50. Haley, *Texas Supreme Court,* pp. 82–87; George E. Shelley, "The Semicolon Court of Texas," *Southwestern Historical Quarterly,* April 1945, pp. 449–68; Louis J. Wortham, *A History of Texas,* Fort Worth: Wortham-Molyneaux Company, 1924, vol. 5, pp. 81–86.
51. "Spirit of the Press," Houston *Daily Mercury,* January 7, 1874; "Gov. Davis Opportunity," *Galveston Daily News,* January 7, 1874; Patrick G. Williams, *Beyond Redemption: Texas Democrats After Reconstruction.* College Station: Texas A&M University Press, 2007, pp. 33–35; Lance A. Cooper, "'A Slobbering Lame Thing?': The Semicolon Case Reconsidered," *Southwest Historical Quarterly,* January 1998, pp. 321–29; *Ex Parte Rodriquez,* 39 Tex. 705 (1874).
52. "Austin: Jan. 5," Richmond *The Four Counties,* January 8, 1874. See also Judge James R. Norvell, "Oran M. Roberts and the Semicolon Court," *Texas Law Review,* 37, 1959, pp. 279–302; and Jim Paulsen and James Hambleton, "Confederates and Carpetbaggers: The Precedential Value of Decisions from the Civil War and Reconstruction Era," *Texas Bar Journal,* October 1988, pp. 916–20.
53. "Federal Intervention Hoped for by Radicals," *Galveston Daily News,* January 7, 1874; "A Plain Statement and Protest," *Galveston Daily News,* January 9, 1874; "Governor Davis to the Front," Austin *Weekly Democratic Statesman,* January 15, 1874; T. B. Wheeler, "Reminiscences of Reconstruction in Texas, *Southwestern Historical Quarterly,* July 1907, pp. 56–63; Roberts, "Fifty Years," pp. 201–3; Haley, *Texas Supreme Court,* pp. 83–86.
54. Chief Justice Roberts, Supreme Court Clerkship, Austin Term, 1874, *Cases Argued and Decided in The Supreme Court of the State of Texas,* Austin: Democratic Statesman Book and Job Print, 1875, pp. 1–4; "The Personnel of the New Supreme Court,"

Houston Daily Mercury, January 29, 1874; Brown, *History of Texas*, vol. II, pp. 477–80; Kittrell, *Governors Who Have Been*, p. 38; Cantrell, *The People's Revolt*, p. 32; Edward King, *Texas: 1874*, Houston: Cordovan Press, 1974 (reprint). See also Campbell, *Gone to Texas*, pp. 288–89, 308, 321–22.

CHAPTER 4

1. Quoted from the *Marshall Herald* in "State Press," *Galveston Daily News*, July 27, 1878; Barr, ed., "The Battle of Bayou Bourbeau," *Louisiana History*, Winter 1965, pp. 83–91.
2. Moneyhon, *Texas After the Civil War*, pp. 198–203; Campbell, *Gone to Texas*, pp. 304–5; Chriss, *Six Constitutions Over Texas, pp.* 124–31; Williams, *Beyond Redemption*, pp. 52–60, 119–40.
3. Williams, *Beyond Redemption*, pp. 91–104; Lewis L. Gould, *Alexander Watkins Terrell*, Austin: University of Texas Press, 2004, pp. 62–65; Letter, Roberts to Col. Thos. N. Murray [Denison & Pacific Railway], May 19, 1879; H. D. Mirich to Roberts, December 2, 1879, Oran M. Roberts Papers, Texas State Archives.
4. John F. Dillon, "Power of the Judiciary to Control the Official Acts of Officers of the Executive Department of the Government," *Central Law Journal*, January 1875, pp. 20–31.
5. "Gov. Coke and the New Constitution," Austin *Weekly Statesman*, December 2, 1875; "Article V–Judicial Department, Sec. 2, 5, and 6," *Texas Constitution of 1876*, Austin: February 1876; Chriss, *Six Constitutions Over Texas*, pp. 127–47; Bailey, "The Life and Public Career of O. M. Roberts," pp. 238–40; Williams, *Beyond Redemption*, pp. 108–18; Barr, *Reconstruction to Reform*, pp. 24–27; Gould, *Alexander Watkins Terrell*, p. 65; Haley, *Texas Supreme Court*, pp. 91–92.
6. "Governor Coke," Austin *Weekly Democratic Statesman*, December 7, 1876; Barr, *Reconstruction to Reform*, pp. 28–31; Haley, *Texas Supreme Court*, pp. 88–94.
7. 48 *Texas Reports*, p. 604. See also "A Writer From Galveston," *Weekly State Gazette*, February 2, 1878. Note: For a good overview of Roberts's comments on the courts and judiciary see Roberts, "Judge Roberts on the Bar," *Galveston Daily News*, July 30, 1878; and "A Lecture by Judge Roberts," ibid., February 17, 1878.
8. "Chief Justice Roberts," *Weekly Democratic Statesman*, August 8, 1878.
9. "Col. Loughery of Marshall," Austin *Weekly State Gazette*, June 22, 1878; "Editorial Paragraphs," ibid., June 22, 1878; Reagan, *Memoirs*, p. 242; Kenneth E. Hendrickson, *The Chief Executives of Texas*, College Station: Texas A&M University Press, 1995, pp. 104–5; Alwyn Barr, *Reconstruction to Reform: Texas Politics, 1876–1906*, Dallas: SMU Press, 1971, pp. 38–40; Billy M. Jones, *The Search for Maturity* Austin: Steck-Vaughn Company, 1965, pp. 37–38.
10. "Danger Ahead," Austin *State Gazette*, July 13, 1878; Roscoe C. Martin, "The Grange as a Political Factor in Texas," *Southwestern Political and Social Science Quarterly*, March 1926, pp. 370–74.
11. "Faithful Stewards and a Poor Estate," *Galveston Daily News*, July 14, 1878; Robert L. Hunt, *A History of Farmer Movements in the Southwest*, College Station: A&M College Press, 1934, pp. 20–22; Oran M. Roberts, "The Political, Legislative, and Judicial History of Texas for Its Fifty Years of Statehood, 1845–1895," in Dudley G. Wooten, *A Comprehensive History of Texas*, Dallas: William G. Scarff, 1898, pp. 224–

27 (hereafter Roberts, "Fifty Years"); Jones, *The Search for Maturity*, p. 37. See also Roscoe C. Martin, "The Grange as a Political Factor in Texas," *Southwestern Social Science Quarterly*, March 1926, pp. 368–74.

12. "The Gubernatorial Canvass," *Galveston Daily News*, July 16, 1878; Louis J. Wortham, *A History of Texas*, Fort Worth: Wortham-Molyneaux, 1924, vol V, pp. 90–91.
13. "The Dead-Lock Still Continues," *Galveston Daily News*, July 17, 1878.
14. "The State Convention," *Galveston Daily News*, July 18 and 19, 1878; "Indications: Thermometer 102 in the Shade," ibid, July 23, 1878.
15. "The State Convention," ibid., July 21 and 23, 1878; "Austin and the Dying Cities," *Weekly Democratic Statesman*, September 5, 1878; Charles L. Martin, *A Sketch of Sam Bass, the Bandit*, Norman: University of Oklahoma Press, 1956, pp. 155–59. Note: Yellow fever, also known as "Yellow Jack," was spread by mosquitoes and enhanced by poor sanitary conditions. Cities like Austin, which had no knowledge on how to cure or stop the spread of the deadly fever, resorted to a city-wide quarantine—not letting anyone in or out of the city limits. Also Procter, *Not Without Honor*, notes that over five days there were at least twenty-seven ballots for a nominee.
16. "Roberts and Sayers," and "Hon. Joseph D. Sayers," *Galveston Daily News*, July 24, 1878; Procter, *Not Without Honor*, p. 229; Reagan, *Memoirs*, pp. 245–46. Note: Vote totals on each ballot vary as some members abstained.
17. Roberts, "Fifty Years," pp. 225–26; John H. Reagan, *Memoirs*, New York: Neale Publishing Company, 1906, pp. 245–46.
18. Roberts, "Fifty Years," p. 227; Billy M. Jones, *The Search for Maturity*, Austin: Steck-Vaughn Company, 1965, p. 39.
19. "Sam Bass and His Band," *Galveston Daily News*, July 24, 1878; "The Austin Convention Dark Horse," Jacksboro *The Frontier Echo*, July 26, 1878
20. Barr, *Reconstruction to Reform*, pp. 42–43; "Hon. O. M. Roberts," *Galveston Daily News*, July 24, 1878; Editorial, "The Recent State Convention and the Convention System," ibid., July 25, 1878; "Hasty and Unnecessary Conclusions," ibid., July 31, 1878; "State Press," ibid., July 27, 1878; "Supreme Court Vacancies," ibid., August 30, 1878; "The Agony Over," and "Hon. O. M. Roberts," Brenham *Weekly Banner*, July 6, 1878.
21. "O. M. Roberts," Graham *Leader*, August 3, 1878; "A Writer in the Galveston News," reprinted in *Weekly State Gazette*, February 2, 1878.. Note: Joel W. Robinson moved to Texas in 1831, and is noted as one of the party that captured Antonio López de Santa Anna following the Battle of San Jacinto.
22. "State Press," *Galveston Daily News*, August 7, 1878. Note: Other examples of letters and observations of Judge Roberts include: "Judge Roberts of the Bar," *Galveston Daily News*, July 30, 1878; "Adequate Means to the Proper Ends of Government," ibid., July 30, 1878; and "Hon. O. M. Roberts," Brenham *Weekly Banner*, July 26, 1878.
23. "Hon. O. M. Roberts Resigns His Seat on the Bench," Austin *Weekly Democratic Statesman*, August 15, 1878; "The Possible True Inwardness of the Demand for Judge Roberts's Resignation," *Galveston Weekly News*, August 10 and 12, 1878; Barr, *Reconstruction to Reform*, p. 49; "Tarrant County," cotton report in the Fort Worth *Post*, reprinted in the *Galveston Daily News*, August 31, 1878; "Cotton: Official Quotations," ibid, April 29, 1879.

24. "The Greenback Platform Adopted at Waco," Austin *Weekly Democratic Statesman,* August 15, 1878; "Greenbackers and Democrats—The Difference," ibid., August 22, 1878; "More Cotton: Fayette County," *Galveston Daily News,* July 27, 1878; "M'Lennan County: 200 Bales of New Cotton Per Day," ibid., August 30, 1878; "Greenback Canvas on State Issues," ibid., October 2, 1879; Roberts, "Fifty Years," pp. 230–32; Roscoe C. Martin, "The Greenback Party in Texas," *Southwestern Historical Quarterly,* January 1927, pp. 166–67.
25. "The Waco *Telephone,*" article reprinted in the *Brenham Weekly Banner,* March 22, 1878.
26. "The Waco Convention and Its Nominees," and "The Greenback Meeting," Austin *Weekly Statesman,* August 15, 1878; "Destruction of the Democratic Party," Austin *Weekly State Gazette,* August 24, 1878; "The Greenback Canvas: Speech of Gen. Hamman at Austin," *Galveston Daily News,* August 29, 1878; Barr, *Reconstruction to Reform,* pp. 43–50; Ernest W. Winkler, ed., *Platforms of the Political Parties in Texas,* University of Texas Bulletin no. 53, Austin, 1916, pp. 187–90.
27. "The Brenham *Volksbote,*" quoted in the *Galveston Daily News,* August 29, 1887. Note: The *Volksbote* had taken the same position as the San Antonio *Freie Presse,* stating: "We extend no right hand of fellowship to a coalition with the Greenbackers, but will cling to the old flag until the last glimmer of hope had faded away."
28. "All About Public Free Schools," and "Prepare to Weep, O, Fiats," *Austin Weekly Democratic Statesman,* September 5, 1878; "Texas—Facts and Fancies [Coke speech]," ibid., August 29, 1878; "Judge Roberts Speech at Bonham," ibid., October 3, 1878; "Governor Throckmorton Opened Campaign at McKinney," ibid., August 22, 1878; "Col. Culberson Speech at Marshall," ibid., August 15, 1878; "Hubbard at San Antonio," *Galveston Daily News,* October 29, 1878; Patrick G. Williams, *Beyond Redemption: Texas Democrats After Reconstruction,* College Station: Texas A&M University Press, 2007, pp. 146–48; Moneyhon, *Edmund J. Davis of Texas,* p. 26. Note: The partisan publisher and editor of the *Austin Statesman* modified the paper's name to the Austin *Democratic Statesman,* published in both weekly and daily issues.
29. "Hempstead: Waller County's First Bale," *Galveston Daily News,* July 31, 1878; "Bryan: Grand Democratic Barbecue—New Cotton," ibid, July 30, 1880; "Speaking at Sherman," *Galveston Daily News,* September 21, 1878; Norman G. Kittrell, *Governors Who have Been, and Other Public Men of Texas,* Houston: Dealy-Adey-Elgin Co., 1921, p. 39. See also "Canvassing the State: Judge Roberts and Senator Coke at Waco," *Galveston Daily News,* October 5, 1878; and Kyle G. Wilkison, *Yeoman, Sharecroppers, and Socialists: Plain Folk Protest in Texas, 1870–1914,* College Station: Texas A&M University Press, 2008, pp. 162–64.
30. "Governor E. J. Davis Affiliation with Greenbackers," Austin *Weekly Statesman,* August 22, 1878; "Judge Roberts at Bonham," ibid., October 3, 1878; "Waiting for Fiat Money," ibid., September 19, 1878; "Judge Roberts and Obligations of the US Government," ibid., September 5, 1878; "Hon. O. M. Roberts: Effect of Flooding Country with Greenbacks," ibid., September 5, 1878; "Corsicana *Observer" in Galveston Daily News,* August 6, 1878; "Gov. Hubbard's Address," ibid., October 30, 1878.
31. "The Approbation of Judge Roberts," *Galveston Daily News,* November 7, 1878.
32. "State Election," *Galveston Daily News,* November 7 and 8, 1878; "The Results in Texas," ibid., November 9, 1878; "The People Who Voted Against Hancock and Why They Did It," Austin *Weekly Democratic Statesman,* November 14, 1878; Barr, *Reconstruction to Reform,* pp. 51–54; O. M. Roberts, "Fifty Years," pp. 232–33; Greg

Cantrell, *The People's Revolt: Texas Populists and the Roots of American Liberalism,* New Haven: Yale University Press, 2020, pp. 32–33; Hunt, *History of Farmer Movements in the Southwest,* pp. 27–30.

33. Reagan, *Memoirs,* p. 49.
34. Roberts, "Fifty Years," pp. 235–36; "Platform of the Democratic Party as Adopted by the Austin Convention," Jacksboro *Frontier Echo,* August 2, 1878; Campbell, *A Southern Community in Crisis,* p. 354.
35. Roberts, "Fifty Years," p. 236; Program, "Inaugural Ball," January 21, 1879, Oran M. Roberts Papers, Texas State Archives; "Appointment of Governor Roberts Confirmed," and "Sheriff's Convention," Austin *Weekly Democratic Statesman,* January 30, 1879; "Col. Rip Ford," *Galveston Daily News,* August 7, 1879, and September 16, 1879. Note: The requests for appointments in the first Roberts administration are in the Roberts Papers, Files 1–25, Oran M. Roberts Papers, Texas State Archives, and would make an interesting study of the demographic profile and background of the applicants.
36. "The Inaugural Ball," *Galveston Daily News,* January 22, 1879. Note: In a letter from Roberts to R. W. Campbell, May 17, 1879, he stated, "My mottos [sic] are 'pay as you go' 'let income equal expenses' 'the first and highest object of government is to make its administration efficient and economical' 'work for the real good of the present, and the future will take care of itself.'"
37. "Hasty and Unnecessary Conclusion," *Galveston Daily News,* July 31, 1878; "Judge Robert on the Bar," ibid., July 30, 1878; Jones, *The Search for Maturity,* p. 40; Roberts, "On the Valuations of the Right of Private Property," in Roberts, *Our Federal Relations From a Southern View of Them,* Austin: Eugene Von Boeckmann Printer, 1892, pp. 149–50.
38. Letter, G. McCormick, AG, to Roberts, February 4, 1879; Letter, J. R. Lubbock to Roberts, February 1879; Letter, Secretary of State to Roberts, February 4, 1879; Letter, W. C. Walsh to Roberts, February 4, 1879; James B. Jones, adjutant general's office to Roberts, February 4, 1879; V. O. King, Department of Insurance, to Roberts, April 9, 1879, all in Robert Papers, Texas State Archives; "The Comptroller's Supplemental Report," *Dallas Daily Herald,* May 13, 1880.
39. "Sensibly Said," Fort Worth *Daily Democrat,* March 5, 1879; "The Charitable Institutions," Executive Order, February 6, 1879, Roberts Papers, Texas State Archives; "Governor Roberts and Tax Payment," Austin *Weekly Democratic Statesman,* January 30, 1879; Patsy M. Spaw, *The Texas Senate,* College Station: Texas A&M University Press, 1999, vol. II, pp. 261–66. Note: The Austin *Weekly Democratic Statesman* applauded, noting, "Evidently the Governor would not weep like David over Absalom if the legislature made the payment of a poll tax a prefix to the code investing people with the privilege of voting."
40. Governor O. M. Roberts, "A Bankrupt Nation," *Galveston Daily News,* April 13, 1880; Letter, Roberts to John T. Morgan, December 9, 1880, Roberts Papers, Texas State Archives; William M. Gouge, *The Fiscal History of Texas: Embracing an Account of Its Revenue, Debts, and Currency,* New York: Burt Franklin, 1852, pp. 133–34. Note: According to Brown, *History of Texas,* vol. II, p. 490, Texas bind debt had reached $5,500,000.
41. "Greenbackers and Greenbackers: What Judge Roberts Set Forth Upon the Financial Question," *Galveston Daily News,* August 25, 1878.

42. Quote from *Brazos Pilot* in *Galveston Daily News,* May 17, 1879; "Starting Out Right," Sherman *Courier,* February 14, 1879; "The Treasury Department," ibid., February 8, 1879; "Saved! Saved! Saved! $55,850 in Interest," Waco *Examiner,* quoted in Brenham *Daily Banner,* March 18, 1880; "Ross as a Statesman," *Waco Daily Examiner,* March 30, 1886; Brown, *History of Texas,* p. 491; Thomas L. Miller, *The Public Lands of Texas, 1519–1970,* Norman; University of Oklahoma Press, 1972, p. 62. Note: Governor Roberts in his personal papers had a published schedule or "Statement of the Public Debt of the United States," dated October 1878, with bond maturities and interest rates compiled by John Sherman, Secretary of the Treasury, Roberts Papers, Texas State Archives.
43. "The Future Governor and Education," unknown newspaper clipping, October 15, 1878, Roberts Papers, Texas State Archives; *Message of Governor Oran M. Roberts of the Special School Fund Loaned to Railroad Companies to the Seventeenth Legislature of Texas,* Regular Session, January 11, 1881, Galveston: News Book and Job Office, 1881; William A. McLeod, "Unequal by Design: School Finance and State Development in Texas, 1821–2026," PhD diss., University of Pennsylvania, 2024, pp. 197–203.
44. "Teacher's Convention," Austin *Weekly Democratic Statesman,* January 30, 1879; Oran M. Roberts, "Proclamation for Special Session of the Legislature, by the Governor of Texas [for June 1879]," Austin: May 12, 1879, Roberts Papers, Texas State Archives; "San Antonio Siftings: Gov. Roberts's Veto Message," *Galveston Daily News,* April 30, 1879; "The Governor's Veto," ibid., May 6, 1879.
45. "Gov. Roberts's Veto," *Galveston Daily News,* April 29, 1879; "An Efficient School System," ibid, May 15, 1879; "The Governor's Veto," ibid., May 6, 1879; "Red River Co., Texas," Clarksville *Standard,* June 4, 1880; Roberts, "Fifty Years," pp. 236–37; Williams, *Beyond Redemption,* pp. 147–49; Edmund T. Miller, *Financial History of Texas,* Bulletin no. 37, Austin: University of Texas, 916, pp. 235–36.
46. John A. Adams, Jr. and Bill Page, "John Nathaniel Johnson: The Great Political Agitator, Educator, Journalist, and Doctor," *East Texas Historical Journal,* Spring 2023, pp. 15–16; Moneyhon, *Texas After the Civil War,* p. 202; "Houston Siftings," *Galveston Daily News,* July 24, 1879; "Interstate Extradition," ibid., June 2, 1881; "The Commutation Commotion," Denison *Daily News,* June 21, 1879; "Cameron Awoke," Brenham *Daily Banner,* February 26, 1881; James T. DeShields, *They Sat in High Places: The Presidents and Governors of Texas,* San Antonio: Naylor Company, 1940, p. 314; "Youth and Good Conduct," Fort Worth, *Democrat-Advance,* January 1, 1882; "Special to Democrat-Advance," ibid., December 31, 1881. See also "Gov. Roberts Refuses to Pardon Toettel," *Brenham Weekly Banner,* November 7, 1879, and Georgia J. Burleson, ed. *The Life and Writings of Rufus C. Burleson,* Waco: Burleson, 1901, pp. 360–70.
47. "A Bad Case," article from the *Galveston Daily News* quoted in Fort Griffin *Echo,* July 17, 1880. See also "The Governor's Last Commutation," *Dallas Daily Herald,* April 27, 1880.
48. "Levee at the Governor's Mansion," *Fort Worth Daily Democrat,* February 29, 1879; Pearl C. Jackson, *Texas Governors' Wives,* Austin: E. L. Steck, 1915, pp. 93–94.
49. U.S. Census, 1880, Austin, Travis County, Texas, June 5, 1880, p. 5; "Born at the Governor's Mansion," *La Grange Journal,* April 28, 1880. Note: Thomas J. Spain was the second child born in the mansion, April 27, 1880; Temple Houston, son of Sam Houston, was the first.

50. "Governor Roberts and His Maligners [sic]," Austin *Weekly Democratic Statesman,* November 20, 1879; C. Vann Woodward, *Origins of the New South 1877–1913,* Baton Rouge: LSU Press, 1951, pp. 60–63.
51. "State Finances and the Governor's Veto," *Galveston Daily News,* May 17, 1879; "Proclamation: Executive Office," ibid., June 11, 1879; "Synopsis of the Message," ibid., April 8, 1882; Roberts, "Fifty Years," p. 237; Williams, *Beyond Redemption,* pp. 149–51; Miller, *Financial History of Texas,* pp. 170–71, 214–18; Haley, *Texas Supreme Court,* pp. 126–27; William R. Childs, *The Texas Railroad Commission,* College Station: Texas A&M University Press, 2005, p. 59; Martin, "The Grange as a Political Factor in Texas," pp. 373–77; Earle B. Young, *Galveston and the Great West,* College Station: Texas A&M University Press, 1997, pp. 75–79.
52. State budget data for 1879–80, seen at "State Finances and the Governor's Veto," *Galveston Daily News,* May 17, 1879. See also "State Finances: Extracts from Comptroller Report," *Galveston Daily News,* June 11, 1879.
53. Governor's Message, *Journal of the House of Representatives of the State of Texas: Being the First Session of the Seventeenth Legislature of Texas, Held at the City of Austin, January 11, 1881,* Galveston: A. H. Belo & Co., 1881, pp. 115–16; Governor Roberts, "Message of the Governor," *Galveston Daily News,* January 13, 1881, and "Over the State," ibid., February 25, 1881. See also "Lunatic Asylum Report," ibid., June 11, 1879.
54. "Lunatic Asylum," *Weekly Democratic Statesman,* April 13, 1882; "Governor's Message," *Galveston Daily News,* May 3, 1882; "Austin: Capital Contractor's," ibid., May 27, 1882; "Ross as a Statesman," *Waco Daily Examiner,* March 30 1886; "Governor and Wife Walk to Concert," Fort Worth *Daily Democrat,* March 4, 1879; Leonidas J. Graham, *Report of Board of Managers and Superintendent of the State Lunatic Asylum of Texas, for Fiscal Year 1881–82,* Austin: E. W. Swindells, 1883, p. 7.
55. Sample of appointment letters, O. M. Roberts to Judge King, Brownsville, May 30, 1879; W. L. Spain to A. L. Teagaiden, May 17, 1879; H. P. Mabry to Roberts, July 18, 1879; L. G. Jackson to Roberts, July 16, 1879; "Extradition Law," *Galveston Daily News,* April 13, 1880; Roberts to John Templeton, January 12, 1880, Roberts Letter Book, Texas State Archives; Randolph B. Campbell, *A Southern Community in Crisis,* Austin: Texas State Historical Association, 2016, pp. 354–55, 360. Note: Roberts also stayed in close contact with Secretary of State John Templeton on all vacancies in the Senate and House. By 1880 the governor requested that county officials provide an annual summary of local data; see "Message of the Governor," *Galveston Daily News,* January 27, 1881.
56. "Operation of the Bell Punch Law," *Galveston Daily News,* October 2, 1879; H. P. N. Gammel, comp., *The Laws of Texas, 1822–1897,* 10 vols. Austin: Gammel Book Company, 1898–1902, vol. 8, pp. 1371–75, 1444–50, and vol. 9, pp. 113–16; Roberts, "Fifty Years," p. 240; Miller, *Financial History of Texas,* p. 216; Barr, *Reconstruction to Reform,* p. 86. Note: One of the few saloons that complied with the bell punch law was noted in the July 22, 1880 Brenham *Weekly Banner:* "'Governor Roberts' Parlor', the name of a saloon [not owned by the governor] in the town of Gonzales and the bell punch in this house has paid $34.24 over and above the first payment of $250 to the state. This is probably the only bell punch in the state that has done $250 worth of ringing." See also Brendan J. Payne, "Defending Black Suffrage: Poll Tax, Preachers, and Anti- Prohibition in Texas, 1887–1916," *Journal of Southern History,* November 2017, pp. 815–52.

57. Oran Roberts, "Authorization to survey and organize three hundred leagues of land —provided in the Act of July 14, 1879 and March 6, 1881," Austin: April 7, 1881, Roberts Papers, Texas State Archives; Seymour V. Connor, "Early Land Speculation in West Texas," *Southwestern Social Science Quarterly,* March 1962, pp. 354–62.
58. "Texas—Now and Ten Year Hence," *Texas Mule Ranger,* April 1879; Roberts, "Fifty Years," pp. 239, 247–48.
59. William C. Walsh, *Special Report of the Commissioner of the General Land Office of Texas from August 31, 1880 to March 1, 1882,* Galveston: A. H. Belo & Company, 1882, pp. 6–10; "The Railroad Boom in Western Texas," *Galveston Daily News,* July 26, 1881; "The Order of Time," Austin *Weekly Democratic Statesman,* May 8, 1882; Barr, *Reconstruction to Reform,* pp. 77–79; Miller, *The Public Lands of Texas,* pp. 145–6, 192–3; Connor, "Early Land Speculation in West Texas," pp. 354–62. See also W. C. Walsh, "Memoirs of a Texas Land Commissioner," *Southwestern Historical Quarterly,* 1941, pp. 481–97.
60. "Governor Coke," Austin *Weekly Democratic Statesman,* August 17, 1876; "Letter from Raided Country: Indians on a Raid Near Ft. Stockton," *Galveston Daily News,* April 27, 1878; "Gen. Ord and Gen. Canales Exchange Sentiments—Indian Raids Near Fort Davis," ibid., June 20, 1878; "State Press: Mexican and Indian Raids," ibid., August 30, 1878; Letter, John H. Furman to Roberts, July 18, 1879, Roberts Papers, Texas State Archives; Letter, John B. Jones, Adjutant General to O. M. Roberts, January 12, 1880, "State Troops," *Galveston Daily News,* January 17, 1880. See also Thomas T. Smith, *The U. S. Army & the Frontier Economy 1845–1900,* College Station: Texas A&M University Press, 1999.
61. "Significance of Gen. Ord's Trip to Washington," *Galveston Daily News,* February 8, 1879; "Frontier Protection," ibid., January 23, 1879; Bvt Major General E. O. C. Ord to Hon. O. M. Roberts, January 14 and 15, 1879, in Dorman H. Winfrey and James M. Day, eds., *The Indian Papers of Texas and the Southwest, 1825–1916,* vol. IV, pp. 407–9, Austin: Texas State Historical Association, 1995 (hereafter cited as *Texas Indian Papers*); "Extirpation of the War Office of Texas—Senator Coke," Austin *Weekly Democratic Statesman,* February 6, 1879; "Gen. Ord's Report on the Conditions and Wants of the Frontier," *Galveston Daily News,* January 28, 1880; Smith, *The U. S. Army and the Frontier Economy,* pp. 11–13; Uglow, *A Military History of Texas,* pp. 283–85.
62. Dennis H. Mahan, *Summary of the Course of Permanent Fortification and of the Attack and Defense of Permanent Works for the Use of the Cadets of the U.S. Military Academy,* West Point: U.S. Military Academy Press, 1850.
63. Letter, Roberts to Wm. M. Evarts, November 29, 1880, Roberts Papers, Texas State Archives; J. B. Jones to O. M. Roberts, January 12, 1880, *Texas Indian Papers; Telegram,* Thomas Mirent, Headquarters Department of Texas, San Antonio, Official statement on handling Indians at Fort Sill, February 15, 1879, Roberts Papers, Texas State Archives; "Reign of Terror in the Pan Handle: Petition to the Governor," *Galveston Daily News,* May 29, 1879; "Disarming the Mescalero Indians," ibid., May 14, 1880; Roberts, "Fifty Years," pp. 39–45; Darren L. Ivey, *Ranger Ideal: 1874–1930, Vol. 2,* Denton: University of North Texas Press, 2019, pp. 225–32. Note: Mr. Munson of Denison was the contractor and Col. N. L. Norton the commissioner for the survey.
64. Letters, Ira B. Sadler to Gov. O. M. Roberts, February 3, 1879; Gen. E. O. C. Ord to Governor Roberts, February 13, 1879; Jno. B. Jones to Gov. O. M. Roberts,

February 15, 1879; Richard Coke to Hon. O. M. Roberts, February 18, 1879; General Jno. Pope to Hon. O. M. Roberts, March 17, 1879, *Texas Indian Papers*, pp. 412, 416, 417, 418, 419; Roberts to General Davidson, Comdy. Fort Elliot, July 31, 1879, and Roberts to Brevet Major General John Pope, July 21, 1879, Roberts Letter Book, Texas State Archives; "An Earnest Desire to Extradite Criminals," *Galveston Daily News*, February 9, 1882. See also William C. Yancey, "Injustice to Our Indian Allies: The Government of Texas and Her Indian Allies, 1836–1867," MA thesis, University of North Texas, August 2008.

65. Letter, Office of the Mayor of Galveston to Roberts, August 21, 1879, Roberts Paper, Texas State Archives; Telegram, Roberts to Dr. E. H. Watte and Dr. A. P. Brown, Board of Health, Galveston, November 3, 1880, Roberts Papers, Texas State Archives; "The Board of Health," Galveston *Daily News*, July 25, 1879. See also "The Law of Galveston Quarantine: Statement of the Board of Health of Galveston of the Reasons for the Establishment of Quarantine Against New Orleans of July 21, 1879," Galveston: News Book and Job Office, 1879; Letter, Roberts to County Judges and Mayors, September 4, 1882, *Greenville Times* (MS), September 9, 1882; O. M. Roberts," Quarantine Proclamation," Austin: May 10, 1880, Roberts Papers.
66. "Washington: Gratifying Reports from the Rio Grande," *Galveston Daily News*, November 9, 1878.
67. "The War With Mexico" Cincinnati *Enquirer*, reprint in the Austin *Weekly Democratic Statesman*, August 1, 1878: "Gen. Sherman's Mission," ibid, August 15, 1878; "Gens. Ord and Trevino—Their Conference," ibid., October 24, 1878; "Mexico and the United States - Ord and Trevino," ibid., January 2, 1879; "The Order to Cross the Rio Grande," *Galveston Daily News*, March 11, 1880; "Fort Davis: Indians Attack an Emigrant Party," ibid., May 16, 1880; Letter Guy M. Bryan to "Rud"—Rutherford B. Hayes, August 24, 1878, in Ernest W. Winkler, ed., "The Bryan-Hayes Correspondence," *Southwestern Historical Quarterly*, July 1923, pp. 317–19. Note: Projections in Washington noted that it was estimated it would take 100,000 troops and two years to occupy northern Mexico fully. General Ord's daughter Lucy Ord married General Trevino in April 1880 and General Ord retired from the army in June 1880. John Mason Hart, *Empire and Revolution: The Americans in Mexico Since the Civil War*, Berkeley: University of California Press, 2002, pp. 218, 329, 349.
68. "Mexican Affairs," *Weekly State Gazette*, February 2, 1878; Letter, Roberts to Secretary William Evarts, U.S. State Department July 18, 1879, and Evarts to Roberts, December 12, 1879, Roberts Papers, Texas State Archives; "The Reported Outrages on Mexican," *Galveston Daily News*, September 11, 1880.
69. Colonel Benavides' 1880 letter seen in "How the Mexicans Love Us," *Galveston Daily News*, April 20, 1886; Letter, Roberts to Wm. M Evarts, Sec. of State, December 9, 1880, Roberts Papers, Texas State Archives; Jerry Thompson, *Tejano Tiger: José de los Santos Benavides and the Texas-Mexican Borderlands, 1823–1891*, Fort Worth: TCU Press, 2017, pp. 266–67, 306–14; John A. Adams, Jr., *Conflict and Commerce on the Rio Grande: Laredo, 1755–1955*, College Station: Texas A&M University Press, 2008, pp. 112–3; "Fiscal Year Border Trade," *Daily News*, July 23, 1881; Robert M. Utley, *Frontier Regulars: The United States Army and the Indian, 1866–1890*, New York: Macmillan, 1973, pp. 359–65; González-Quiroga, *War and Peace on the Rio Grande Frontier*, pp. 352–55. Note: Colonel Benavides served three terms as a representative in the Texas legislature, 1879–1886.

70. Letter from the Secretary of War [Reimbursement to the State of Texas for Expenses Incurred in Repelling Invasions of Indians and Mexicans], Senate, 42nd Cong., 2nd sess., Ex. Doc. No. 19, January 22, 1878, pp. 1–2, 16–20, 29, 45; Richard Coke to O. M. Roberts, December 22, 1879; *Texas Indian Papers*, pp. 432–33, 442–43; "Joint Resolution," House Res. 23,, 46th Cong., 1st sess., [referred to Committee on Military Affairs], April 21, 1879; Letter, Oran Roberts to Senator John Reagan, January 27, 1882, and letter to Senator Richard, January 27, 1882, Roberts Papers, Texas State Archives; William C. Abeyance, "The Old Cavalcade Oran Milo Roberts, Texas's Forgotten Fire-eater," PhD diss., University of North Texas, May 1916, p. 248; "The Texas Claims," *Austin Daily Statesman*, December 18, 1888; Senate, "Payment of State Volunteers, Etc.," 59th Cong, 1st sess., Doc. No. 169, 1905, pp. 32–33; Senate, "Claims of the State of Texas for Defense of the Frontier," 69th Cong., 1st sess., Doc. 67, 1911, pp. 3–5; "Col. Ashbel Smith," *Galveston Daily News*, February 8, 1879. Note: The congressional reports, requests, and data from Texas contain information and amounts submitted and are a confused web of dates, and amounts, that were submitted as many as a dozen times, with the equal number of audits.
71. *New Orleans News*, August 7, 1879, seen in Yancey, "The Old Alcalde," p. 250. Note: Newspapers in Texas were no less opinionated, with the frontier Fort Griffin *Echo*, June 26, 1880, noting: "Personally we have little objection to Governor Roberts, but for the last two years it has been too much governor and too little Texas. The governor was made for the State and not the State for the governor."
72. Message of Gov. O. M. Roberts on Appropriations and Expenditures under the Control of the Governor to the Seventeenth Legislature of the State of Texas, Austin Regular Session, January 11, 1881, Galveston: The News Book and Job Office, 1881, pp. 3–23; "Department of State," *Galveston Daily News*, August 6, 1880; Proclamation of the Governor, "Rewards for the Arrest and Conviction of Persons Charged with the Commission of Crime," Austin: January 1879, Roberts Papers, Texas State Archives. Note: There are over two dozen letters of pardon in the Roberts Papers at the Texas State Archives in Austin, but also a score of letters issued by the governor's office in which pardons were denied. Cash rewards for confirmation of captured fugitives were many; see, for example, Letter, H. L. Spain, Exec Clerk. Governor's office, to Albert Bishop, December 4, 1880, Roberts Papers, confirming reward payment of $250. See also Brown, *History of Texas*, vol. II, p. 491.
73. *Globe-Democrat* quoted in "In Fellowship with Radical," *Austin Weekly Democratic Statesman*, July 22, 1880; "Opinions of the Press," ibid., July 8, 1880; "Hon. J. D. Sayers," Brenham *Weekly Banner*, July 15, 1880; "Governor Roberts and the Newspaper Reporters," *Galveston Daily News*, October 28, 1881; "Governor Roberts Undoubtedly Wants to Go to Senate," ibid., October 16, 1881; "Oran M. Roberts,' San Antonio *Freie Presse fûr Texas*, May 1, 1882.
74. "Gov. Roberts as a Free School Man," and "State Education," *Galveston Daily News*, June 19, 1880; "Circulation Over 150,000 Copies," ibid., June 30, 1882.
75. "Gov. Roberts's Administration," *Galveston Weekly News*, April 1, 20, and 22, 1880; "Burleson County Democratic Meeting," and "Tyler: People Indorse Roberts," *Galveston Daily News*, April 1,1880; "Walker (County): Proceedings of Democratic County Convention," *Galveston Daily News*, July 30, 1880; "Spirit of the Great German Press," translated from the *Freie Presse* by the *Galveston Daily News*, August

17, 1880; "Shaking Up and Shaking Down," ibid., July 30, 1880; Barbara J. Rozek, "Introduction," in L. L. Foster, *The Forgotten Census,* Austin: Texas State Historical Association, 2001, reprint, pp. I–xii to I–xv; "Texas: An English Journal on the Empire State," from the *Hexham Herald,* reprinted in *Galveston Daily News,* October 15, 1881; Cassandre Durso, "Two States with One Goal: Texas and Louisiana Recruit Italians," *Texas Gulf Historical and Biographical Record,* vol. 50, 2015, p. 93.

76. "Gov. Roberts and the Free School Question," *Galveston Daily News,* May 7, 1880; "Ignorant or a Demagogue," Dallas *Daily Herald,* July 15, 1880; "Governor Roberts at Dallas," *Austin Weekly Democratic Statesman,* July 22, 1880; "Canvassing for a Governor," ibid., November 10, 1881; "Governor Roberts Endorsed by the School Teachers," Clarksville *Standard,* July 23, 1880; "Texas State Grange, 1880," in Winkler, ed., *Platforms of Political Parties in Texas,* pp. 192–93; Barr, *Reconstruction to Reform,* pp. 59–62; Robert H. Wiebe, *The Search for Order 1877–1920,* New York: Hill and Wang, 1967, pp. 8–9.
77. "It Should Not Be Done," *Dallas Daily Herald,* March 11, 1880; Roberts, "Fifty Years," p. 244. See also "A Trade Outlook to the South and West," *Galveston Daily News,* February 26, 1880.
78. Roberts, "Fifty Years," pp. 243–45; Gammel, *Laws of Texas,* vol. 9, pp. 113–19; "Governor Roberts," Fort Worth *Democrat,* January 16, 1883.
79. "The Governor and his Critics," Clarksville *Standard,* July 29, 1881. See also Brown, *History of Texas,* vol. II, pp. 490–93; Letter, Governor Roberts to Mr. Blane, Secretary of State, July 26, 1881, at https://history.state.gov/historicaldocuments/frus1881/d470 . Note: Brown, page 493, incorrectly states that Roberts was elected chancellor of the university, a position that did not exist then. See also "Governor Roberts as a Texas Milk-Maid," *Galveston Daily News,* May 31, 1881.
80. "Gov. Roberts' Action," *Wills Point Local,* n.d., seen in Carthage *Panola Watchman,* August 31, 1881; "The Governor and His Critics," Clarksville *Standard,* July 29, 1881; "Can It Be True?" *Panola Watchman,* August 31, 1881.
81. "Gov. Roberts Declines Proclamation," Clarksville *Standard,* July 29, 1881; "The Governor and the Variegated Religious Creeds," *Galveston Daily News,* July 26, 1881; "The Struggle Ended: President Garfield Dead," ibid., September 20, 1881; "The Press and the Governor," Dallas *Daily Herald,* July 26, 1881.
82. "Destruction by Fire of the State Capital," *Galveston Daily News,* November 10, 1881; "Capital Burning," ibid., November 11, 1881; "The Burned Records [of the Texas Supreme Court]," ibid., January 18, 1882; Letter, Gov. O. M. Roberts to Attorney General J. H. McLeary, November 22, 1881, ibid., November 25, 1881; "The Late Big Burn: Getting to Bottoms Facts—Testimony Taken Before the Fire Inquest," Austin *Weekly Democratic Statesman,* November 17, 1881. See also Michael M. Miller, "Cattle Capital: Misrepresented Environments, Nineteenth Century Symbols of Power, and the Construction of the Texas State House, 1879–1888," MA thesis, University of North Texas, May 2011.
83. "Governor Roberts and the Newspaper Reporters," *Galveston Daily News,* October 28, 1881; "The Canvass for Governor," ibid., June 21, 1882.
84. "The Waco T*elephone,*" *Weekly Democratic Statesman,* August 25, 1881.

CHAPTER 5

1. Frederick Eby, "The First Century of Public Education in Texas," in *Texas Public Schools Sesquicentennial Handbook,* Austin: Texas Education Agency, 2004; J. J. Lane, "The Educational System in Texas," in Dudley G. Wooten, ed., *A Comprehensive History of Texas,* Dallas: William G. Scarff, 1898, vol. II, pp. 437, 440–48 (Lane, "Education"); William R. Hogan, *The Texas Republic: A Social and Economic History,* Norman: University of Oklahoma Press, 1846, pp. 136–59; G. L. Crocket, *Two Centuries in East Texas,* Austin: Hart Graphics, 1982, pp. 316–10. See also Kristin D. Morgan, "The Preservation of Historic Schools & Community Identity in Suburban Texas," MA thesis, University of Georgia, 2016, pp. 57–70.
2. Burleson, ed. *Life and Writings of Rufus C. Burleson,* pp. 360–70. "Gov. Roberts and Public Free Schools," *Galveston Daily News,* May 15, 1879; "Teacher's Convention," Austin *Weekly Democratic Statesman,* January 30, 1879; Barr, *Reconstruction to Reform,* p. 63; Note: For an overview of the evolution of public education in Texas see Frederick Eby, *The Development of Education in Texas,* New York: Macmillan Company, 1925; and Carl H. Moneyhon, "Public Education and Texas Reconstruction Politics, 1871–1874," *Southwestern Historical Quarterly,* January 1989, pp. 393–416.
3. Laws Relating to the Agricultural and Mechanical College of Texas from June 1, 1875 to January 23, 1878, Austin: A. J. Peeler, 1878. Note: The term "normal school," according to Ty Cashion (see note vii following), came from the English usage from the French *école normale,* the chief aim of which was to prepare teachers for elementary public schools.
4. Letter, Stephen Dandry to Col. A. J. Peeler, June 27, 1879, George Pfeuffer Papers, Texas A&M University, Cushing Archives; "Population and Manufactures North and South," *Galveston Daily News,* January 30, 1881.
5. Roberts, "Fifty Years," p. 248.
6. Letter, Roberts to Leonard A. Abercrombie, May 30, 1879, and Roberts to B. Sears, July 16, 1879, in Roberts Papers, Texas State Archives.
7. Letter, G. Sears, General Agent to Governor O. M. Roberts, February 1879, seen in Austin *Weekly Democratic Statesman,* February 6, 1879; "Governor's Message," *Galveston Daily News,* June 11, 1879; "Gov. Roberts and Public Free Schools," and "An Efficient School System," ibid., May 15, 1879; "An Eloquent Reference to Mr. Peabody," ibid., July 23, 1881; Ty Cashion, *Sam Houston State University: An Institutional Memory 1879–2004,* Huntsville; Texas Review Press, 2004, pp. xvii–xix, 4–6; Land, Education, p. 462.
8. "The Sam Houston School: Opening Ceremonies," *Galveston Daily News,* October 11, 1879; Lane, "Education," p. 462. Note: Colonel Goree was the aide-de-camp to General James Longstreet during the war.
9. *Governor's Messages, Coke to Ross, 1874–1891,* pp. 752–53; Roberts, "Fifty Years," p. 219. Note: The "classical education" was offered in part because the University of Texas had not yet opened.
10. Letter, Thomas S. Gathright to Louis L. McInnis, July 25, 1878, Thomas Gathright Papers, Texas A&M University, Cushing Archives; *Fourth Annual Report of the President of the Agricultural and Mechanical College of Texas, College Station*: 1880, p. 4;

Henry C. Dethloff, *A Centennial History of Texas A&M University, 1876–1976,* College Station: Texas A&M University Press, 1975, vol. I, pp. 31–35, 51.

11. *Governor's Messages, Coke to Ross, 1874–1891,* pp. 213–15, 221–23, 249–50; Robert L. Hunt, *A History of Farmer Movements in the Southwest,* College Station: Texas A&M Press, 1934, p. 18.
12. "The Agricultural College and the State University," *Austin Weekly Democratic Statesman,* February 6, 1879. Note: Newspapers across the state began to publish articles on the value and trend of universities, often referring to Thomas Jefferson and the creation of the University of Virginia, e.g. "The Two Legislatures—City and State," and "The Sacred School Fund," ibid., February 6, 1879.
13. *Governor's Messages, Coke to Ross,* pp. 249–50; "A Message from the Governor," Austin *Weekly Democratic Statesman,* February 6, 1879; Roberts, "Fifty Years," p. 245, 247–48.
14. "Report of the Outgoing Directors at the January Session of the Board, 1879," *Texas State Journal, 1879,* pp. 205–10; O. M. Roberts, "Governor's Message, June 10, 1879," *Galveston Daily News,* June 11, 1879. Note: The so-called new dormitories were ramshackle wooden buildings that did not reflect well on the college.
15. "Report of the Visitation Committee,'" *Texas Senate Journal, 1879,* pp. 509–11; Dethloff, *A Centennial History,* vol. I, p. 53; "Report of the Outgoing Directors at the January Session of the Board, 1879," *Austin Weekly Democratic Statesman,* February 6, 1879; Letter, O. N. Hollingsworth, Board of Education, to Gov. O. M. Roberts, February 7, 1879, *Weekly Democratic Statesman,* February 6, 1879.
16. "Rev. C. P. B. Martin," *The Presbyterian,* October 22, 1873, and November 1, 1873; "Montgomery County," *Galveston Daily News,"* December 15, 1874, and July 13, 1875; Martin, "An Agricultural College," ibid., July 14, 1883; "The Agricultural and Mechanical College," *Weekly Democratic Statesman,* February 20, 1879; Clarence N. Ousley, *History of the Agricultural and Mechanical College of Texas,* Bulletin no. 8, College Station: December 1, 1935, pp. 45–47.
17. Thomas Gathright to Governor Oran M. Roberts, May 24, 1879, Gathright Papers, Texas A&M University, Cushing Archives; "Governor Roberts and Public Free Schools," Galveston *Daily News,* May 7, 1880; Dethloff, *A Centennial History,* vol. I, p. 56.
18. "Agricultural and Mechanical College: Commencement Exercises," *Galveston Daily News,* June 26, 1879; "Agricultural College Report," ibid., June 11, 1879; Letter Gathright to George Pfeuffer, New Braunfels, July 7, 1879, Gathright Papers; Roberts, "Fifty Years," pp. 237–38.
19. "The Crisp-Hogg Controversy," *Galveston Daily News,* October 29, 1879; Dethloff, *A Centennial History,* vol. I., pp. 57–59.
20. "The A. and M. College," November 9, 15, 1879, and "College Investigation," *Galveston Daily News,* November 21, 1879.
21. Dethloff, *A Centennial History,* vol. I, p. 60; "College Investigation," *Galveston Daily News,* November 20, 21, 22, 1879; "Hamilton Prioleau Bee," Ron Tyler, ed., *The New Handbook of Texas,* Austin: Texas State Historical Association, 1996, vol. I, p. 458. Note: The *Handbook* entry makes no mention of Bee's time at Texas A&M.
22. Letter, Governor Roberts to President Gathright, May 21, 1879, seen in *Galveston Daily News,* November 15, 1879; "College Investigation: Board of Directors Present," ibid., November 19, 1879; Roberts to Gathright, October 21, 1879, and November 15, 1879, ibid; "Minutes of the Board of Directors, November 18–24,

1879," George Pfeuffer Papers, Texas A&M University, Cushing Archives. Note: The Academy of Music was a public meeting hall built ca. 1876 and often referred to as Cavitt's Hall, with a seating capacity of 600, the largest gathering facility between Houston and Waco and in operation until the late 1890s, was located on Main Street where the LaSalle Hotel now stands; see Bill Page, comp., "The Academy of Music," June 2022, Cushing Archives.

23. "College Investigation: Board of Directors Present," *Galveston Daily News,* November 19, 1879.
24. "College Investigation," *Galveston Daily News,* November 20, 1879; "College Investigation: Proceedings Before the Directors," ibid., November 21, 1879.
25. "College Investigation," ibid., November 21, 1879.
26. "Minutes of the Board of Directors, November 18–24, 1879," Pfeuffer Papers, Texas A&M University, Cushing Archives; "College Investigation," *Galveston Daily News,* November 23, 1879; Ousley, *History of the A&M College,* p. 50.
27. Letter, H. P. Bee to Hon. George Pfeuffer, November 14, 1879, and T. M. Scott to George Pfeuffer, November 16, 1885, Pfeuffer Papers; Rufus L. Burleson, Waco, to Governor O. M. Roberts, November 20, 1879, Louis L. McInnis Papers, Cushing Archives.
28. "The Texas Agricultural College," *New York Times,* November 28, 1879.
29. "The *Bryan Pilot," Galveston Daily News,* November 30, 1879, "Columbus," ibid., January 16, 1880; "Ex-President Gathright's Views," *Daily Democratic Statesman,* December 23, 1879; Ousley, *History of the A&M College,* pp. 50–55; Hunt, *A History of Farmer Movements in the Southwest,* pp. 20–24.
30. Ousley, *History of the A&M College,* p. 51.
31. "Statement from Board," November 24, 1879, George Pfeuffer Papers; College Station, *Texas Collegian,* December 1879; "The Investigation," Brenham *The Daily Banner,* November 23 and 25, 1879; "A Plan of Reorganization," in letter Jno. G. James, President, to Governor O. M. Roberts, July 1880, *Fourth Annual Report of the President of the A&M College of Texas,* College Station: 1880, pp. 3–14; Dethloff, *A Centennial History,* vol. I, pp. 66–69. Note: Gathright's final check number 489, from the A&M College, for the period from October 1, 1879 to February 14, 1880, was in the amount of $85.
32. "Agricultural and Mechanical College," *Galveston Daily News,* November 29, 1879. See also John G. James, President, to Gov. O. M. Roberts, "Report of the President of the Board of Directors of the A. & M. College," Clarksville *Standard,* January 19, 1883.
33. "There are 193 Cadets," Austin *Weekly Democratic Statesman,* December 1, 1881.
34. Letter, Roberts to Thomas Gathright, May 30, 1879, Roberts Papers, Texas State Archives; Letter, Thomas Gathright to O. M. Roberts, "Prairie View School Report," *Galveston Daily News,* June 11, 1879; George R. Woolfolk, *Prairie View: A Study in Public Conscience, 1878–1946,* New York: Pageant Press, 1962, p. 67.
35. Constitution of the State of Texas, 1876, Art. VII, Sec. 14, p. 14; H. P. N. Gammel, comp., *The Laws of Texas, 1822–1987,* vol. III, p. 1482; "President Gathright Given Charge of the Colored College," *Galveston Daily News,* January 23, 1878; "A. and M. College and Prairie View Normal School," ibid., April 8, 1882; Woolfolk, *Prairie View,* pp. 29, 36.
36. Dethloff, *A Centennial History,* vol. I, p. 54; John A. Adams Jr., "How Alta Vista Became Prairie View: Lawrence Washburne Minor and the Beginnings of Public

Higher Education for African Americans in Texas," *Southwestern Historical Quarterly,* January 2024, pp. 279–81. See also Frederick Eby, *The Development of Education in Texas,* New York: MacMillan Company, 1925, pp. 274–76.

37. "The Colored College: Can We Afford to Let It Drop!" *Galveston Daily News,* February 8, 1879; "Prairie View School Report," ibid., June 11, 1879; "Fighting Executive Authorities," ibid., April 4, 1882; "A. and M. College and Prairie View Normal School," ibid., April 8, 1882; Woolfolk, *Prairie View,* pp. 68–69.
38. "Educators in Council," *Galveston Daily News,* February 2, 1879; "The Colored College: Can We Afford to Let it Drop," ibid., February 8, 1879; "Prairie View Normal School," ibid., February 27, 1880; "Afternoon Session," ibid., July 5, 1879; "Hempstead Courier," Brenham *The Daily Banner,* September 3, 1879; "The Peabody Fund," ibid., November 30, 1879; Woolfolk, *Prairie View,* pp. 43–47, 81. See also "National Aid for the Education of the Colored Race," and "An Eloquent Reference to Mr. Peabody," *Galveston Daily News,* July 23, 1881.
39. Letter, Roberts to J. P. Cooper, November 3, 1880, Roberts Papers, Texas State Archives; "Governor Roberts to Comptroller Brown," *Weekly Democratic Statesman,* January 26, 1882; Woolfolk, *Prairie View,* pp. 41–44.
40. "Prairie View College," *Galveston Daily News,* June 19, 1880.
41. Memo, Governor O. M. Roberts, Gov. & Presdt. of the Board of Directors of the A&M College, Appointment of Ernest H. Anderson, Principal of Prairie View Normal School, November 13, 1880; Letters, Roberts to E. H. Anderson, December 21, 1880, and Roberts to W. C. Rankin, November 15, 1880, and Roberts to J. D. Sayers, November 16, 1880, Roberts Papers, Texas State Archives; Adams, "How Alta Vista Became Prairie View," pp. 285–86; "Prof. Abernathy," *Galveston Daily News,* November 10, 1880. Note: An indication of Roberts's close attention to events at Prairie View was a protest by an assistant teacher who claimed he should be paid as "principal" for the seven days prior to Anderson's appointment, yet no payment was made; letter, Roberts to J. W. W. Abernathy, December 4, 1880. See also Horace A. Young, "A History and Appraisal of the Colored Teachers' State Association of Texas," MA thesis, University of New Mexico, 1949.
42. "The Roberts-Brown Imbroglio," *Waco Daily Examiner* January 26, 1882.
43. Lawrence D. Rice, *The Negro in Texas 1874–1900,* Baton Rouge: LSU Press, 1971, pp. 227–28.
44. "Governor Roberts to Comptroller Brown," Austin *Democratic Statesman,* January 26, 1882; Letter, Roberts to President John James, January 26, 1882; Roberts to W. W. Brown, January 26, 1882, and Roberts to James H. Raymond, January 26, 1882; Roberts to Anderson, January 27 and 29, 1882; Roberts to Charles Wiggins, January 26 and 28, 1882; Roberts to E. H. Anderson, February 1, 1882; and Roberts to Burroughs, February 6, 1882, Roberts Letter Book, Texas State Archives; Woolfolk, *Prairie View,* pp. 66–75; Lawrence D. Rice, *The Negro in Texas 1874–1900,* Baton Rouge: LSU Press, 1971, pp. 226–29.
45. "Prairie View Normal School," *Galveston Daily News,* November 29, 1879; Adams, "How Alta Vista Became Prairie View," *Southwestern Historical Quarterly,* January 2024, pp. 283–5; Woolfolk, *Prairie View,* p. 72; Adams and Page, "John Nathaniel Johnson," *East Texas Historical Journal,* Spring 2023, pp. 17–19.
46. Alexander Hogg, "University of Texas," and "Location of the University," *Weekly Democratic Statesman,* August 11, 1881; Dethloff, *A Centennial History,* vol. I, p. 32. Note: Hogg noted that "At first we must have lecture rooms temporary, if you

please, afterwards laboratories, libraries, museums, galleries, hall for societies, gymnasiums and other appliances for physical culture and recreation—these will grow with the years."

47. Elizabeth Silverthorne, *Ashbel Smith of Texas: Pioneer, Patriot, Statesman, 1805–1886,* College Station: Texas A&M University Press, 1982, pp. 209–10; "Constitution of the Republic of Texas," *Laws of the Republic of Texas in Two Volumes,* Houston: Printed at the Office of the Telegraph, 1838; "Our State: The Subject of State Education," Austin *State Gazette,* November 3, 1855.
48. "Our State: The Subject of State Education," Austin *State Gazette,* November 3, 1855; "Universities—Law and Fund," Austin *Texas State Gazette,* October 19, 1867; *Journal of the House of Representatives of the Republic of Texas,* 3rd Congress, 1838, pp. 279, 317.
49. Roberts, "Fifty Years," pp. 246–49; C. C. Gillespie, "State Collegiate Education," Austin *State Gazette,* January 23, 1858; "The Governor's Programme," *Galveston Daily News,* January 28, 1881; "The State University and the A. and M. College," *Texas School Journal,* June 1883, pp. 114–15; Dethloff, *A Centennial History,* vol. I, pp. 16–49. Note: Colonel C. C. Gillespie, C.S.A., commanded Twenty-Fifth Texas Cavalry from 1862 to 1865, and after the war worked as a Methodist minister and editor of the *Texas Christian Advocate* until his death in 1876.
50. Roberts, Reminiscences, p. 7.
51. L. C. Anderson, "Prairie View," *Houston Post,* September 21, 1882; "Mass Meeting at Hempstead," *Galveston Daily News,* August 29, 1882; "Prairie View Normal School —Closing Exercises—Governor Roberts Present," ibid., June 20, 1882; T. H. Bowman, Texas Secretary of State, *Report,* Austin: 1882, p. 5. See also Willie A. Tarrow, "A University for Negroes of Texas—A Promise Unfulfilled," MA thesis, Prairie View University, August 1946; "Fighting Executive Authority," *Galveston Daily News,* April 4, 1882. Note: Comptroller W. M. Brown issued an opinion against the governor that funds from the University Fund could not be used for Prairie View Normal School.
52. "Outlook for the State University," *Galveston Daily News,* September 12, 1882; Roberts, "Fifty Years," pp. 246–50; John A. Adams, Jr., "A Promise Unfulfilled—Edward L. Blackshear: Crusader for the 'Colored University' in Texas 1882–1901,'" *East Texas History Journal,* June 2024.
53. William J. Battle, "University of Texas at Austin," *Handbook of Texas,* 1996, vol. 6. pp. 643–44; Lewis B. Cooper, *The Permanent School Fund of Texas,* Fort Worth: Texas State Teachers Association, 1934, pp.107–22; see also H. Y. Benedict, *A Source Book Relating to the History of the University of Texas,* Austin: University of Texas, 1917. Note: For a detailed assessment of public higher education in Texas during its formative years between 1872 and 1885 see letter, Roberts to Thomas D. Wooten, April 18, 1888; and "Message of Gov. O. M. Roberts to the Eighteenth Legislature," *Senate Journal,* January 10, 1883, in Roberts Papers, BCAH.
54. "The Public Land Question," *Galveston Daily News,* October 2, 1879; "Are the People or the Wire Pullers the Source of Power?" Clarksville *Standard,* June 30, 1882; Roberts, "Fifty Years," pp. 252–54; "Railroads and Texas Ports," *Galveston Daily News,* January 29, 1881; "Agricultural and Mechanical College Report," ibid., June 21, 1882.
55. A. W. Spaight, *The Resources, Soil, and Climate of Texas,* Galveston: A. H. Belo & Company, 1882; O. M. Roberts, *A Description of Texas, Its Advantages and Resources,*

St. Louis: Gilbert Book Co., 1881; "Governor Roberts's Texas," *Galveston Daily News,* October 28, 1881; "Governor Roberts' Book," Clarksville *Standard,* October 28, 1881; "The News," *Galveston Daily News,"* October 12, 1881; Barbara J. Rozek, *Come to Texas,* College Station: Texas A&M University Press, 2003, pp. 105–7; Joe C. Truett and Daniel W. Lay, *Land of Bears and Honey,* Austin: University of Texas Press, 1984, pp. 8–9. See also Frederic W. Simonds, "Geographic Influences in the Development of Texas," *Journal of Geography,* May 1912, pp. 272–84.

56. "The Farmers' Alliance," *Galveston Daily News,* January 29, 1881; John S. Spratt, *The Road to Spindletop,* Austin: University of Texas Press, 1970, pp. 51, 63, 91, 113, 157, 211; Roberts, *A Description of Texas,* pp. 126–27; Truett and Lay, *Land of Bears and Honey,* p. 9.

CHAPTER 6

1. O. M. Roberts, "From Gov. Roberts: He Again Defines His Position," in Austin *Statesman,* June 23, 1882, seen in Alvarado *Bulletin,* July 7, 1882; "Governor Roberts," Fort Worth *Democrat,* January 16, 1883; "Governor Roberts," Austin *Weekly Democratic Statesman,* January 25, 1883; Chriss, *Six Constitutions Over Texas,* p. xvii. Note: In advance of the fall 1882 Texas Democratic Convention "uninstructed delegates" from over a dozen counties were instructed to vote for Roberts if his name were placed in nomination; see "The Gubernatorial Problem," *Galveston Daily News,* July 15, 1882.
2. "Gath and Governor Roberts," *Galveston Daily News,* March 31, 1882.
3. Roberts, "Message of Gov. O. M. Roberts to the Eighteenth Legislature," *Senate Journal, January 10, 1883,* Roberts Papers, BCAH; O. M. Roberts, "The Relation of Public Education to the Government of the State of Texas." *Bulletin of the University of Texas,* June 17, 1890, pp. 7–9; Roberts, "A History of the Establishment of the University of the State of Texas," *Southwest Historical Quarterly,* April 1898, p. 236; "Comptroller's Department [surplus balance]," Austin *Weekly Statesman,* December 20, 1883; Hendrickson, *Chief Executives of Texas,* pp. 105–9; "The Roberts and Ireland Administrations Compared," *Galveston Daily News,* July 20, 1884; "The Old Alcalde' Philippic Attack," ibid., June 30, 1882; "Governor Roberts," Brenham *Daily Banner,* June 22, 1882; Barr, *Reconstruction to Reform,* p. 65.
4. J. J. Lane, *History of the University of Texas Based on Facts and Records.* Austin: Henry Hutchings State Printer, 1891, pp. 1–4; Edward King, *Texas: 1874,* Houston: Cordovan Press, 1974, p. 67.
5. "Local Intelligence," and "The State University," *Weekly Democratic Statesman,* January 25, 1883; Lane, *History of the University of Texas,* pp. 6–12; Roger A. Griffin, "To Establish a University of the First Class," *Southwestern Historical Quarterly,* October 1982, p. 136; Frederick Eby, *The Development of Education in Texas,* New York: MacMillan Company, 1925, pp. 285–89; Robert H. Wiebe, *The Search for Order 1877–1920,* New York: Hill and Wang, 1967, pp. 118–21. Note: At some point while he was a law professor Roberts also had a small home at the corner of Nueces and 22nd Street, four blocks west of the campus. See also Brown, *History of Texas,* vol. II, pp. 506–14.
6. O. M. Roberts, "A History of the Establishment of the University of the State of Texas," *Southwest Historical Quarterly,* April 1898, pp. 233, 240, 259–60; Lane,

History of the University of Texas, pp. 12–20, 273; "Non-Resident Students," Austin *Weekly Statesman,* September 20, 1883; Griffin, "To Establish a University of the First Class," p. 146. Note: On Terrell's advocacy and influence, Governor Roberts said he "had a lively interest in the University and was regarded as one of its leading promoters and friends." see also "Texas Diplomat Has Filled Many Posts," San Antonio *Express,* March 26, 1911.

7. Memorial, "Teachers' Association of Texas to His Excellency O. M. Roberts," Governor, seen in Roberts, "A History of the Establishment of the University," pp. 241–42. Note: Committee members were Oscar H. Cooper, chairman, W. C. Crane, S. G. Sneed, R. W. Pitman, Smith Ragsdale, O. N. Hollingsworth, and John G. James, president of the A&M College of Texas.
8. "The Coming Election," Brenham *The Texas Sentinel,* August 17, 1881; "Election Returns," September 9, 1881, and "Austin Declared Victor," October 28, 1881, in Clarksville *Standard*; "The Board of Regents of the University," *Galveston Daily News,* October 28, 1881; Roberts, "Fifty Years," pp. 246–47; Gould, *Alexander Watkins Terrell,* pp. 78–81, 122; Roberts, "A History of the Establishment of the University," p. 251; Alexander W. Terrell, University of Texas Commencement Address, June 15, 1898, Austin: Board of Regents, 1898; "Rangers Once Stationed on Capital Grounds in Anticipation of Bandit Raids," *Brady Standard,* December 25, 1931. Note: Over a dozen Texas communities vied for the university, to include Austin, Waco, Albany, Williams's Ranch, Hempstead, Tyler, Grapevine, Matagorda, Lampasas, Thorp Springs, Houston, Galveston, and Caddo Grove. Roberts noted with regard to his home town: "During the canvas for the location I was personally placed under what might be considered a serious embarrassment by the nomination of Tyler, which was the place of my home, that I had prepared as a residence for the balance of my life, surrounded by many much valued friends, and situated in a section of the state where I had lived for forty years."
9. "Governor Roberts Message to the Seventeenth Texas Legislature," April 6, 1882. See also Lane, *History of the University of Texas,"* pp. 197–99; and Jane K. Worthington, "Picturesque Pioneer Days of University's Existence Recounted by Son of Founder [Oran Milo "Gov" Roberts, Jr.]," Austin *Statesman,* May 6, 1923.
10. Lane, *History of the University of Texas,* pp. 317–21; Elizabeth Silverthorne, *Ashbel Smith of Texas,* College Station: Texas A&M University Press, 1982, pp. 209–16; Griffin, "Establishment a University of the First Class," pp.148–50.
11. "The University," Clarksville *Standard,* July 24, 1882; Roberts, "Fifty Years," pp. 246–47; "Report of the Regents," *Weekly Democratic Statesman,* January 25, 1883; Roberts, "History of the Establishment of the University," p. 256.
12. "What a University Regent [Ashbel Smith] Says," *Galveston Daily News,* August 15, 1882; "Terrell's Card," ibid., March 25, 1892; Hans W. Baade, "Law at Texas: The Roberts-Gould Era (1883–1893)," *Southwestern Historical Quarterly,* October 1982, p. 166. Note: Governor Sul Ross would follow the same course of action, accepting an appointment as president of the A&M College of Texas in the last few weeks of his administration, and then going to the college when his term expired. See Adams, *Sul Ross at Texas A&M.*
13. Eby, *Development of Education in Texas,* p. 286; Roberts, "History of the Establishment of the University," pp. 253–54; Chriss, *Six Constitutions Over Texas,* pp. 141–43; "The Seguin Times Remarks," reprinted in *Galveston Daily News,* December 3, 1882; Baade, "Law at Texas," p. 161.

14. "Are the People or the Wire Pullers the Source of Power?" Clarksville *Standard,* June 30, 1882; Silverthorne, *Ashbel Smith of Texas,* p. 219.
15. "A Letter for Those Interested in the State University," Clarksville *Standard,* June 2, 1882; "The State University [re: Rev. Dr. Dabney]," Fort Worth *Daily Democrat,* May 5, 1883; "Report of the Regents," *Weekly Democratic Statesman,* January 25, 1883; "The University and the Press," *Galveston Daily News,* September 16, 1883; Roberts, "History of the Establishment of the University," p. 263. See also Lane, *History of the University of Texas,* pp. 268–75.
16. "Report of the Regents," January 25, 1883; "The State University [re: Prof. Mallet]," Clarksville *Standard,* July 4, 1884. See also John G. James, President to Gov. O. M. Roberts, "Report of the President of the Board of Directors of the A. & M. College," Clarksville *Standard,* January 19, 1883.
17. Roberts, "History of the Establishment of the University," p. 263; "University Regents," *Galveston Daily News,* July 15, 1882; "Non-resident Students—The 'Others' of the Law," Austin *Weekly Statesman,* September 20, 1883; Lane, *History of the University of Texas,* p. 14.
18. "Educational," and "The Medical College," *Galveston Daily News,* June 27, 1883.
19. "From Austin: Mrs. Roberts Obsequies," *Galveston Daily News,* November 29, 1883; "Mrs. Roberts," Clarksville *Standard,* November 30, 1883; Jackson, *Texas Governors' Wives,* p. 95.
20. Silverthorne, *Ashbel Smith of Texas,* p. 221; site visit by author to the Briscoe Center for American History, Austin, Texas, August 28, 2024.
21. "A Natal Day: Ceremonies of the Opening of the University," *Galveston Daily News,* September 16, 1883; "University of Texas—The Inaugural Exercises," Austin *Weekly Statesman,* September 20, 1883; "The State University," Clarksville *Standard,* September 21, 1883; "The University," Dallas *Daily Herald,* January 15, 1885; Baade, "Law at Texas," pp. 167, 182; Governor Roberts, June 1884 Commencement Address, Roberts Papers, Texas State Archives. See also "Borne Back Ceaselessly into the Past: *FISHER V. UNIVERSITY OF TEXAS,* The Freedmen's Bureau Act, and the 'Originalist' Meaning of Color Blindness," *George Mason Law Review,* vol. 21, 2014, pp. 313–27.
22. "Various University Matters," September 17, 1883, and "The Honest People," Austin *Weekly Statesman,* December 20, 1883; "The Runnels Record," *Galveston Daily News,* March 20, 1884.
23. Baade, "Law at Texas," p. 174.
24. "Galveston's Appeal," *Galveston Daily News,* January 26, 1885; Andrew Morrison, ed. *The Port of Galveston and the State of Texas,* Galveston: G. W. Engelhardt & Co., 1890, pp. 15–32.
25. "Oran. M. Roberts," *Galveston Daily News,* April 14, 1884; "Four Years Ago Texas," El Paso *Daily Times,* December 9, 1883; Baade, "Law at Texas," pp. 169–73,178, 186; Jared Stallones, "Academic Freedom and the Lost Cause: The Short Career of Professor Joseph Baldwin at the University of Texas," *Vitae Scholasitcae,* 2006, pp. 31–45.
26. "Texas Laughs," Sulphur Springs, *Daily News-Telegram,* May 17, 1955.
27. "Where Is the Alcalde?" Austin *Weekly Statesman,* February 7, 1884; "The Farmer," Brenham *Weekly Banner,* December 9, 1886; Barr, *Reconstruction to Reform,* pp. 81–84, 113.

28. "Grangers," Austin *Weekly Statesman*, August 21, 1884; "Texas Farmers," *Galveston Daily News*, August14. 1884; "The Granger Brothers: Education, Agriculture and Practical Work," ibid., August 16, 1884; Hunt, *A History of Farmer Movements in the Southwest*, pp. 23–31.
29. Roberts, "History of the Establishment of the University," pp. 235–39; "Politics and the Grange," *Galveston Daily News*, June 1, 1886; "To Farmers' Alliance and Grange County Business Agents," ibid., July 21, 1888.
30. "The Old Alcalde," *Galveston Daily News*, June 27, 1886; Letter, Roberts to Thomas D. Wooten, President of the Board of Regents, April 18, 1888, Roberts Papers, BCAH.
31. "Is the Old Alcalde on Deck?" *Galveston Daily News*, June 28, 1886.
32. L. S. Ross to O. M. Roberts, February 4, 1886, Roberts Papers, BCAH; "No Longer A Doubt," Austin *Weekly Statesman*, July 1, 1886; "Hon. Oran M. Roberts," *Galveston Daily News*, July 6, 1886.
33. "Close of the Contest," *Galveston Daily News*, February 2, 1887; "Chicago Cattle," ibid., June 27, 1887; Roberts, "Fifty Years," pp. 266–67; "The Farmer," Brenham *Weekly Banner*, December 9, 1886; Judith Ann Benner, *Sul Ross: Soldier, Statesman, Educator*, College Station: Texas A&M University Press, 1983, pp. 156–63.
34. "A Good Man Gone," Austin *Weekly Statesman*, November 19, 1885; "The Capital City Budget," *Galveston Daily News*, December 16, 1887; "The University in Present and Pressing Need," and "University Claims," ibid., May 3, 1888; Baade, "Law at Texas," pp. 176–80; T. U. Taylor, *Fifty Years on Forty Acres*, Austin: Alec Book Company, 1938, p. 86.
35. "Normal Schools," Dallas *Daily Herald*, January 15, 1885; Roberts, "Fifty Years," pp. 269–71; "Lines from Laredo: County Democrats Declare for Ross," Austin *Weekly Statesman*, May 10, 1888; "The State Takes Possession of Its Capitol," ibid., May 17, 1888; "Gov. Ross Renominated," *Galveston Daily News*, August 16, 1888.
36. "A Future for Texas," Austin *Weekly Statesman*, October 18, 1888. See also "The South's Development," *El Paso Times*, January 9, 1889.
37. San Antonio *Express* quotes in *Galveston Daily News*, August 13, 1889.
38. "Programme: First Texas Farmers Institute," Austin *Weekly Statesman*, February 7, 1889; "The Farmers' Institute," and "The Farmers in Earnest," ibid, February 14, 1889; "The A. and M. College and the Hatch Bill," and "The Hatch Bill," *Galveston Daily News*, February 7, 1888; "Farmers' Institutes," ibid., January 18, 1889. Note: Educational farm programs were first held by Germans in the Texas Hill Country by the *Deutschen Farmer Verein* (German Farmers Association) as early as 1882; San Antonio *Light*, June 27, 1882.
39. O. M. Roberts, "On the Valuation of the Right of Private Property," in Roberts, *Our Federal Relations From a Southern View of Them*, Austin: Eugene Von Boeckmann Printer, 1892, pp. 146–59; "The Commission: A Reply to Judge Terrell by Hon. O. M. Roberts," Austin *Weekly Statesman*, March 7, 1889; Gould, *Alexander Watkins Terrell*, pp. 83, 86; Sam H. Acheson, *Joe Bailey: The Last Democrat*, New York: Macmillan, 1932, p. 33.
40. "The Legislature: The Railway Commission Bill," Austin *Weekly Statesman*, February 14, 1889; Roberts, "The Commission," *Weekly Statesman*, March 7, 1889; "Profiles of Railroads," *Galveston Daily News*, February 19, 1893; Roberts, "Fifty Years," p. 275; Childs, *The Texas Railroad Commission*, pp. 58–59; Gould, *Alexander Watkins Terrell*, pp. 114–15.

41. Roberts, "The Commission, March 7, 1889"; Gould, *Terrell*, pp. 110–15, 122; Childs, *The Texas Railroad Commission*, pp. 62–64.
42. "The Railroad Trouble," *Galveston Daily News*, February 17, 1889; "The Legislature," *Austin Weekly Statesman*, March 7, 1889; "Hon. O. M. Roberts: Denial for Nomination for Governor," ibid., October 17, 1889.
43. "Views of Ex-Governor Roberts," *Galveston Daily News*, September 29, 1895.
44. Letter, Minister Richard Hubbard, Tokyo, to O. M. Roberts, Professor of Law, February 10, 1888; and Roberts, "Roberts' Select Cases for Students of Law," Roberts Papers, BCAH.
45. Letter, O. M. Roberts to Gov. James S. Hogg, "The Old Alcalde on Hogg," *Coleman Voice*, May 5, 1892; Campbell, *Gone to Texas*, pp. 322–25; Cantrell, *People's Revolt*, pp. 79–130; Barr, *Reconstruction to Reform*, pp. 209–14.
46. "Modern Political Methods," Dallas *Southern Mercury*, June 25, 1896. See also Roscoe C. Martin, *The People's Party in Texas: A Study in Third Party Politics*, Bulletin no. 3308, Austin: University of Texas, 1939.xlvii Cantrell, *People's Revolt*, pp. 210–19, 401–6; Campbell, *Gone to Texas*, pp. 324–40; Williams, *Beyond Redemption*, pp. 168–73. See also Gregg Cantrell, *Feeding the Wolf: John B. Rayner & the Politics of Race*, Wheeling: Harlan Davidson, 2001, p. 92.
47. Cantrell, *People's Revolt*, pp. 210–19, 401–6; Campbell, *Gone to Texas*, pp. 324–40; Williams, *Beyond Redemption*, pp. 168–73. See also Gregg Cantrell, *Feeding the Wolf: John B. Rayner & the Politics of Race*, Wheeling: Harlan Davidson, 2001, p. 92.
48. "The Education Committee," Austin *American Statesman*, February 12, 1893; "The Alcalde's Speech," *Galveston Daily News*, February 19, 1893; Texas Legislature, House of Representatives, *House Journal*, 23rd Leg., reg. sess., 1893, pp. 526–31; Williams, *Beyond Redemption*, pp. 151–55. See also Roscoe C. Martin, *The People's Party in Texas: A Study in Third Party Politics*, Bulletin no. 3306, Austin: University of Texas, 1933, pp. 26–40; Lawrence D. Rice, *The Negro in Texas, 1877–1900*, Baton Rouge: LSU Press, 1971, pp. 78–82; and Robert C. Cotner, *James Stephen Hogg*, Austin: University of Texas Press, 1959, pp. 255–58.
49. O. M. Roberts, "A Trip from Austin to Marble Falls," *Galveston Daily News*, July 12, 1888; Ex-Governor Roberts Investor in Marble Falls Lots," San Antonio *Daily Light*, May 25, 1889.
50. "The Democratic Party," *Waco Evening News*, August 26, 1893. See also "Texas' Third Party," *Taylor County News*, July 31, 1891; and "Texas Democracy: The Old Alcalde's Plan to Reconcile All Past Differences," *Crockett Weekly Courier*, January 5, 1894.
51. "A New Political Force," Galveston *Tribune*, May 7, 1896; "Their Platform Did It," *Galveston Daily News*, November 2, 1892; "The Old Alcalde," ibid., May 7, 1896; "Alcalde's Letter," ibid., May 7, 1896; "Old Alcalde's Candidacy," ibid., May 13, 1896; "The Old Alcalde Again," Austin *Weekly Statesman*, May 14, 1896; "Alliance Demands," and "Rapid Growth in Populism," *Southern Mercury*, May 28, 1896; Chester Alwyn Barr, "Texas Politics, 1876–1906," PhD diss., University of Texas, August 1966, pp. 295–98; Payne, "Defending Black Suffrage," pp. 815–20.
52. "The Alcalde's Boom," Galveston *Tribune*, May 7, 1896; "The Old Alcalde," *Galveston Daily News*, May 11, 1896; "He Is in the Race," ibid., May 12, 1896; "Lasker on Roberts," ibid., May 14, 1896; Arthur D. H. Smith, *The Real Colonel House*, New York: George H. Doran Company, 1918, pp. 54–57. Note: Other very progressive "demands" of the Farmers' Alliance included a graduated income tax, establishment

of postal savings banks, a national program to protect natural resources, and that the government should own and operate the railroads. Also, the numbers of Populists in Texas noted in the *Southern Mercury were* from an editorial that first appeared in the *New York World.*

53. "An Alcalde Rumor," *Galveston Daily News,* May 25, 1896; "Rallying to the Alcalde's Standard," ibid., May 16, 1896; "With Organization and Proper Support Populists Will Be Defeated," ibid., May 13, 1896; "Ex-Governor Roberts Withdraws from the Canvas for Governor," Austin *Weekly Statesman,* May 28, 1896; "Governor Roberts' Boom," ibid., May 14, 1896; Procter, *Not Without Honor,* p. 229.
54. "A Gentleman," *Galveston Daily News,* May 25, 1896; "The Roberts Letter," ibid., May 28, 1896.
55. "Roberts Withdraws," Galveston *Tribune,* May 26, 1896; Procter, *Not Without Honor,* pp. 292–93, 296–97; Smith, *The Real Colonel House,* pp. 54–57.
56. "Old Alcalde Gone," *Denton Monitor,* May 21, 1898; "A Noted Texan Gone," *Shiner Gazette,* May 25, 1898; "Ex-Gov. Roberts Dead," Wills Point *Chronicle,* May 26, 1898; "Texans Passes Away," Stephenville *Empire,* May 26, 1898; "An Old Texan Gone," San Antonio *Southern Messenger,* May 26, 1898; "Oran M. Roberts," *El Paso Herald,* June 4, 1898.
57. "Reunion of Parson's Brigade," *Galveston Daily News,* July 13, 1881; "The Blue and Gray: Reunion of Ex-Confederate and Ex-Federal Veterans," ibid., August 5, 1894; "Mountain Remnants: U.C.V. Camp Reunion," ibid., July 26, 1895; "The Reunion of Hood's Brigade," San Antonio *Evening Light,* June 27, 1882.
58. "O. M. Roberts Compromise Candidate 50 Years Ago," *Brady Standard,* August 22, 1930.
59. "Dean H. Y. Benedict Recalls History of Varsity Papers," *Daily Texan,* April 3, 1936. Note: Prior to the *Daily Texan,* the campus newspaper was preceded by the *Texan,* the *Ranger,* and the *Calendar.*
60. Roberts, "The Impending Crisis," in Roberts, *Our Federal Relations,* p. 35; "Texas Teachers [the Congressional Blair Bill]," San Marcos *Free Press, J*uly 8, 1886. Note: The Blair Education Bill was spearheaded by Senator Henry Blair (R-NH) during the mid-1880s, and while it passed in the Senate, it was turned down numerous times in the House, and ultimately the bill failed. Local state control of education would go largely unchanged until the 1965 Elementary and Secondary Education Act. See also Allen J. Going, "The South and the Blair Education Bill," *Mississippi Valley Historical Review,* September 1957, pp. 267–90; Daniel W. Crofts, "The Black Response to the Blair Education Bill," *Journal of Southern History,* February 1971, pp. 41–65; Jeffery A. Jenkins and Justin Peck, "The Blair Education Bill: A Lost Opportunity in American public Education," *Studies in American Political Development,* April 2021, pp. 146–70.
61. "The Southern Historical Society," Austin *Weekly Democratic Statesman,* May 3, 1883; "Historical Matter," *Galveston Daily News,* January 30, 1895; "R. Henderson Shuffler at the University of Texas Sent in the following Excerpt from *The Texas Magazine,* III, July, 1897," *Southwestern Historical Quarterly,* July 1965, pp. 240–41; Roberts, "Austin Texas 1874: Historical Association," and "Minutes of the Historical and Statistical Association of Texas," April 14, 1874, Roberts Papers, BCAH; Richard B. McCaslin, *At the Heart of Texas: 100 Years of the Texas State Historical Association, 1897–1997,* Austin: Texas State Historical Association, 2007; Roberts, "The Proper Work of the Association," *Quarterly of the TSHA,* July 1897, pp. 1–4; O. M.

Roberts, "The Shelby War, or the 'Regulators and Moderators,'" *The Texas Magazine,* August 1897, pp. 49–57; David A. Furlow, "Remembering Rip-Roaring Rip Ford and the origins of TSHA Scholarship," *Journal of the Texas Supreme Court Historical Society,* Summer 2017, pp. 9–17.

CHAPTER 7

1. DeShields, *They Sat in High Places,* p. 310.

INDEX

ABOUT THE AUTHOR

John A. Adams, Jr. is the author of twenty books, including biographies of governors Sul Ross of Texas and John Milton of Florida and the forthcoming chronicle on Edward L. Blackshear, renowned principal of Prairie View A&M University. Adams received the prestigious T. R. Fehrenbach Award for *Damming the Colorado*.